WITH
WANDERING
STEPS

Medieval & Renaissance Literary Studies

General Editor

Rebecca Totaro

Editorial Board

Originally titled the *Duquesne Studies: Philological Series* (and later renamed the *Language & Literature Series*), the **Medieval & Renaissance Literary Studies Series** has been published by Duquesne University Press since 1960. This publishing endeavor seeks to promote the study of late medieval, Renaissance, and seventeenth century English literature by presenting scholarly and critical monographs, collections of essays, editions, and compilations. The series encourages a broad range of interpretation, including the relationship of literature and its cultural contexts, close textual analysis, and the use of contemporary critical methodologies.

Foster Provost
EDITOR, 1960–1984

Albert C. Labriola
EDITOR, 1985–2009

Richard J. DuRocher
EDITOR, 2010

WITH
WANDERING
STEPS

GENERATIVE AMBIGUITY
IN
MILTON'S POETICS

Edited by Mary C. Fenton
and Louis Schwartz

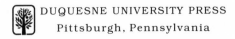
DUQUESNE UNIVERSITY PRESS
Pittsburgh, Pennsylvania

Published in the United States of America by
DUQUESNE UNIVERSITY PRESS
600 Forbes Avenue
Pittsburgh, Pennsylvania 15282

Library of Congress Cataloging-in-Publication Data

Names: Fenton, Mary C., 1959– editor of compilation. | Schwartz, Louis, 1962–
editor of compilation.
Title: With wandering steps : generative ambiguity in Milton's poetics /
edited by Mary C. Fenton and Louis Schwartz.
Description: Pittsburgh, Pennsylvania : Duquesne University Press, [2016] |
Series: Medieval & renaissance literary studies | Includes bibliographical
references and index.
Identifiers: LCCN 2016026122 | ISBN 9780820704883 (cloth : alk. paper)
Subjects: LCSH: Milton, John, 1608–1674 — Criticism and interpretation. |
Ambiguity in literature.
Classification: LCC PR3588 .W545 2016 | DDC 821/.4 — dc23
LC record available at https://lccn.loc.gov/2016026122

∞ Printed on acid-free paper.

CONTENTS

———⟶≫≪⟵———

PART THREE: PLACES

ACKNOWLEDGMENTS

———⁂———

The essays in this collection are all expanded and revised versions of papers originally delivered at the 2011 Conference on John Milton in Murfreesboro, Tennessee. We would like to thank Charles Durham, Kristin Pruitt, Kevin Donovan, and everyone involved in running the conference for once again allowing us the privilege and the pleasure of editing a collection. As those who have attended these conferences over the years know well, Charley, Kris, and Kevin have always given the conference a special warmth and collegiality, and an intellectual generosity from which all participants (including the editors of this volume) have benefited incalculably. Two small, unassuming hotels near the Middle Tennessee State University have been key sites of "generative irresolution" for the lively and productive study of Milton. We are grateful for having had the privilege to edit three conference collections. The editorial task has now moved over to the able hands of Thomas Festa and Kevin Donovan, and we look forward to the volumes that Tom and Kevin will be putting together from the 2013 and 2015 conferences.

We would also like to thank Amy Walker for checking citations for us, Rebecca Totaro and Susan Wadsworth-Booth at Duquesne University Press for their ongoing commitment to these conference-based volumes, as well as the anonymous readers at the press who offered many useful comments and suggestions. Emily Tarchokov offered crucial administrative assistance on the University of Richmond side of this task, and we would also like to thank Heidi Buchanan at Hunter Library of Western Carolina University.

INTRODUCTION

LOUIS SCHWARTZ

The essays in this volume all share an interest in the parts of Milton's work that wander, refusing to move in a straight line or come to a fixed conclusion. They offer a vision of Milton centered on beginnings without clear endings, on figures of cycling or recursion, moments of ambiguity or ambivalence that seem designed never to resolve but instead create a generative tension. As part of his exploration of how each human being can and should align his or her will with God's, Milton concerns himself again and again with how and why a singular and entirely self-sufficient God should have willed a heterogeneous creation into existence, and why therefore in this created universe creaturely forms, ideas, and paths necessarily diverge, why their eventual integration into the divine "all in all" described in book 3 of *Paradise Lost* is always and insistently delayed or projected forward beyond a receding horizon. The poetic and the prose works themselves, moreover, draw readers into aesthetic, rhetorical, and epistemological schemes — plots, tropes, and arguments — that assert the value of differences, assert their own value, while at the same time gesturing offstage to an ultimate but temporally inaccessible source of truth — singular, undifferentiated — that calls all differences into question.

To move through Milton's works, then, is to move through an often uncanny maze of doublings (even triplings and more), a wilderness of both mirrors and sweets that forces us to embrace opposed values, pleasures, and ideas — and to hold them in opposition. These oppositions in turn generate a powerful aesthetic and intellectual energy that impels us toward — creates a desire for — a goal in unity that we are, however, never meant actually to reach (at least not in this world in any final or fixed way). As Milton put it himself, referring figuratively in *Areopagitica* to the building of "the Temple of the Lord": "when every stone is laid artfully together, it cannot be united into a continuity, it can but be contiguous in this world" (YP 2:555). We have in Milton's mind a poising of united "continuity," on the one hand, against a complex of "contiguities," on the other. There are certainties in Milton in regard to that united continuity (premises that, for example, God exists, that he is good, that he must be obeyed), and things bend in his apprehensions to the gravitational pull of these certainties, but despite the firm grasp they had on his mind and faith, he seems to have found them poetically less interesting — at least on their own — than the contingencies that also captured his imagination and sympathy. These are the contingencies of this created world, where things lie next to one another, extending in sensible space and time, where they can be experienced and known in relation to what they touch or touch off, where they fit with or grind against one another, but not as parts of a complete and comprehensible whole. The fixed certainties, therefore, cannot be understood as the key drivers of his discourse. They work in tandem with the resistance created by the certainty of a good but contiguous creation only knowable, apprehensible, in its ongoing and contingent *procreative* energy.

Some readers and critics have followed Stanley Fish in thinking that the differences, tensions, irresolutions, and so on that we encounter in Milton's work are all parts of a test or a trick designed to provoke readers against difference and against themselves each time they are reminded that a deeper truth sponsors everything — a reminder that difference, therefore, makes no difference.[1] Others have gone in the opposite direction, suggesting that Milton was a poet of uncertainties and indeterminations.[2] The authors collected here, however, stand somewhere in the tense middle between these two poles. They follow instead those critics who have tried to come to terms with the creative power of Milton's poetry by exploring how it arises out of conflicting impulses and what William Kerrigan has called the "semantic overspill" of the poetic figure, which in Milton's practice can draw us like the Leviathan in the first epic simile of *Paradise Lost* into interpretive depths that make the meaning of the epic seem "forever beyond us, unsettled and in process."[3] For Gordon Teskey in *Delirious Milton* the poetic power rises from a "rift at the center of [Milton's] consciousness over the question of creation itself, forcing him to oscillate between two incompatible perspectives," affirming, on the one hand, "the absolute authority of God the creator, the principle of absolute order and the ground of our being," and on the other "the poet's need to be a creator (not just a creature) in his own right."[4] Other projects (and there are many) that stand behind the essays in this volume are Gardner Campbell's exploration of provocation in Milton's poetics, his attempt to understand the relational function of difference and hierarchy as they both order and destabilize Milton's universe, as well as important projects by Marshall Grossman, John Rumrich, R. A. Shoaf, William Kolbrener, and others.[5]

Milton's works might be understood as paradigmatic examples of what Coleridge, quoting Petronius Arbiter in the *Biographia literaria*, characterized as the central dynamic of the poetic imagination itself. The paradox of a *free* spirit being *hurled* forward "not merely or chiefly by the mechanical impulse of curiosity, or by a restless desire to arrive at the final solution," but also by "the pleasurable activity of mind excited by the attractions along the way," a motion both forward and retrograde, "like the motion of a serpent, which the Egyptians made the emblem of intellectual power; or like sound through the air."[6] In particular, the ending of *Paradise Lost* (a poem that is really all beginning) offers readers no ending at all but a starting point for wandering. Unhanded by the angel, and ourselves figuratively holding the hands, back through time, of two human beings who are themselves holding hands, we are asked to accept a state of displacement and exile that we already uneasily occupy, comforted only by a promised end we cannot approach in a straight line or at a steady pace, but toward which we must wander slowly. Furthermore, we are told that this end cannot be found by looking outside of ourselves, toward the horizon of what is to come, but only by looking toward a receding, inward horizon toward a "paradise within" (*PL* 12.587) that already exists but is not at all immediately evident. Such an end can guide and even comfort, but we also know that such a guiding remains elusive, turning us back always on our isolated selves in search of what alleviates suffering and contextualizes — gives meaning — to the self as part of a knowable whole. This is another serpent-motion, a recognition of a state of being both at home and in exile, of moving and encircling, both, and it is this state that is at the heart of the poem's dynamic and which it seeks to affirm or "justify." The poem does not and cannot affirm the fixed point out beyond and hidden within the horizon of the existent world nor the separateness of each of its creatures at the expense of the "wandering steps and slow" (12.648) to which those creatures and that world are consigned. It cannot, in other words, assert that either the goal or the wandering is all there is.

This is both the poem's point and its difficulty and why, at its heart, in its description of Eden itself (a figure for the ideal existence we are told we have only outwardly lost and can find again within), Milton placed an emblem that invites us to read the poem a particular way: this is the description of the "mazie error" of the streams of Eden that, drawn up from one river, pour out of one fountain at the head of the garden's central hill, then divide to flow through the garden (*PL* 4.220–35). These streams reunite toward the foot of the hill and rejoin the original flood, only to separate again and "run diverse" out beyond the poem's account. We are never told of their uniting again somewhere out there beyond and below paradise and the horizon of both the earth and the poem's concerns. Instead we digress away from the horizon to the effects that those "crisped brooks" (237) have on the immediate surroundings as they run "nectar, visiting each plant" and flower, allowing nature to pour "forth profuse on hill and dale and plain" (240–43).

Each of the essays collected here responds to aspects of this dynamic, Milton's attention both to unities that lie out there beyond our ken and diversities poured forth before us, seeing them as central to the Miltonic imagination. They explore how Milton's textual irresolutions, tensions, and moments of delicate equilibrium are generative and productive of meaning. The essays suggest, in other words, that perhaps it is best to talk neither about Milton's certainties nor his uncertainties but about his interest in "determinations" (neither indeterminate nor terminating): moments of forking and choice that lead through a series of disciplined fine distinctions on to further forkings and choices — the result of a dynamic design that has the power to make all interpretive choices meaningful. All paths are valid paths, however far they may seem to wander, because they all operate in a field that allows them to wander while also controlling them, giving them a tendency to return, reunite, imply without reaching a completion of themselves as parts of a larger, consistent whole. The poetic design constantly generates the tensions inherent in the discovery of different versions of truth, divergent paths to the assent and obedience Milton's vision of existence requires ultimately of his fit readers. It also presents the tension inherent in the stubborn otherness of creature and creator and between creatures in the ongoing midst of an abundant, multiform creation in which differences proliferate — particularly geographical, historical, and gender differences.

We have divided the volume into three parts, each containing a trio of essays that approach related themes and subject matters: part 1 collects essays that each in their own way explores Milton's representation of theatrical and ritual gestures and rhetoric. The essays in part 2 explore the open-ended nature of human and human/divine relationships in the poetry, and the essays of part 3 all consider the figurative resonances of Eden and of geographical spaces more generally in Milton's imagination.

In chapter 1, "God's Swearing by Himself: Milton's Troubling Coronation Oath," Alex Garganigo carefully examines a primary scene of divine rhetorical performance, the "begetting" of the Son in book 5 of *Paradise Lost*. He offers for the first time an examination of this scene against the backdrop of the long history of English coronation ceremonies and the oaths at their heart, showing how the Father's equivocal oath raises rather than settles questions about the natures of both human and divine monarchy. Garganigo suggests that in creating this ceremonial set piece for his epic and making it "the primal plot-driver" of its narrative and argument, Milton was able to present a rich and historically informed argument about the tense relationship between human and divine monarchy, the way the latter informs the former without necessarily authorizing it. The scene points the reader "forward in history," gesturing "toward the only moment at which the human knee should bend" (34): the moment of Christ's final exaltation at the end of history. For Garganigo, Milton's use of historically vexed ceremonial forms to portray this key moment of divine performance undoes "present tyrannies by imagining, outside the sphere of human politics, the only authority worthy of submission" (34).

Chapter 2, Brendan Prawdzik's "Naked Writhing Flesh: Rhetorical Authority, Theatrical Recursion, and Milton's Poetics of the Viewed Body," is also interested in performance, describing a theatrical poetics at the heart of Miltonic representation. "Milton's stages," Prawdzik argues, whether they are "material platforms in actual theaters" or "centers of ethical agency framed by encompassing eyes in the world at large, are sites of negotiated nakedness where the body, *clothed in gesture*, strains to mediate its difference from other bodies intertwined in the field of vision" (37). Prawdzik explores a wide-ranging set of examples of such "staged" moments in Milton's work, showing how they help create "a feedback loop of theatrically recursive authority" that both leads us to reconstruct the "ethical body of [the] author" and challenges that reconstruction: "When we read Milton with an active mind, alive to the text's ironies and ambiguities, its invitations to interrogation and re-creation, as well as its checks and balances, our truths and desires entangle in a textual pneuma, and neither author nor reader departs unchanged" (60).

What Milton's *The Art of Logic* can tell us about *Paradise Lost*, and in turn what the poem can tell us about the treatise itself, is the focus of chapter 3: James J. Rutherford's "Argument in Heaven: Logic and Action in *Paradise Lost*, Book 3." Rutherford shows how the logical structure of Milton's invocation to light resonates with the theological commentaries of his time, particularly the logical structure of arguments about Trinitarianism. Rutherford ultimately suggests that Milton produced a deliberately bad argument in the invocation, and that *The Art of Logic* illustrates what is wrong with it. Turning next to the dialogue in heaven, Rutherford provides a contrast to the invocation, showing how the dialogue provides logical arguments that meet the Ramist standards, but also demonstrating how even formally valid arguments can be problematic, insofar as Ramist logic itself is problematic. For both Milton's contemporaries and modern scholars, the problem with Ramist logic is that it seems to be rhetorical: one simply plugs preconceived ideas into the logical machine in order to get a more persuasive result, ultimately coercing one's readers or interlocutors, rather than using logic, to help them arrive at new knowledge. Rutherford argues that though Milton himself is aware of this general critique, the dialogue — in addition to presenting Milton's theological principles — defends the Ramist logical method. The logical structure of God's argument is in accordance with the method (his "high decree" [*PL* 3.126] about human freedom corresponding to a special kind of axiom discussed in the handbook). Rutherford then goes on to consider the influence the arguments have on the Son and whether the Son is forced to act in accordance with God's plan. After a careful discussion of a previously overlooked intertext between the treatise and the Son's speech, their shared reference to the Nisus and Euryalus episode from Virgil's *Aeneid*, Rutherford concludes that the Son is not forced, at least not in such a way that contravenes the "high decree" about free will. The purpose of the Father's speech, in other words, is not to force a conclusion but to present the Son with a genuinely free choice.

The essays in part 2 turn to Milton's treatment of relationships. In chapter 4, Maggie Kilgour, like Rutherford, turns to the central place of Virgil in Milton's imagination. She examines Milton's adaptation of a key Virgilian topos, what she identifies as a tense, recursive dynamic that looks back even as it follows its heroes forward: "the story of progress" told by the *Aeneid* is, for Kilgour, "shadowed by the poet's sympathies for those left behind . . . [those] who are not allowed to grow up, or who refuse to become part of the process" (86). If Aeneas's quest "demands self-sacrifice," Kilgour notes, "it also requires the sacrifice of others" (86). For Virgil, "maturation brings an individuation that is equivalent to alienation, including that from the self since, ironically, such individuation depends on the total repression of the individual's personal desires. It seems a particularly lousy deal" (87). Keeping this dynamic in mind, Kilgour presents us with a Milton who uses reference to Virgil to meditate on what it means to grow up. What are the losses entailed in maturation, and how can and should such losses be integrated into an adult self-awareness? After tracing the impact of this aspect of Virgil on Milton's work, she concludes with a discussion of Adam and Eve newly displaced from the garden, their paradisal growth cut short and facing the challenge of what growth will mean outside of Eden with an uncertain future into which they must carry the pain of losses both already endured and foretold.

Chapter 5, Danielle A. St. Hilaire's "Reason, Love, and Regeneration in *Paradise Lost*, Book 10" also contemplates the final state of Adam and Eve as they are poised to leave the garden. She examines a question raised by book 10's regeneration scene: where can we place the responsibility for Adam and Eve's initial repentance, and thus their subsequent wandering steps toward regeneration? St. Hilaire contends that neither Eve nor Adam can be said to be the hero of the epic's regeneration narrative because regeneration is not the work of heroic individuals: it is by its nature a kind of relationship, initiated by God, an undertaking that requires mutual acknowledgment, mutual striving, mutual engagement with the other. The problem with assigning the cause of Adam's and Eve's regenerations to a heroic act of love on Eve's part, as some critics have done, is that doing so occludes both the importance of reason in manifesting love in the world and the extent to which such manifestations of love must be collaborative. Love consists in the use of reason for the benefit of another, and thus choosing between love or reason — or between Adam or Eve — in assigning the source or cause of regeneration in the poem misses the extent to which Milton's theology of regeneration treats right reason as a necessary component of love and of faith, and relationship rather than individual effort as both the means and end of grace.

In chapter 6, "Preferring His Mother's House: Jesus at Home and in Exile in *Paradise Regained*," Margaret Justice Dean, anticipating the central themes of part 3, explores the sanctity of place — or at least the true source for Milton of whatever sanctity a place can be said to have. She considers another valediction: Jesus's leaving the temple, his father's house, at the end of *Paradise Regained* and his choosing to begin his ministry in obscurity by returning to his mother's. Dean argues that the tension between these two houses, the father's and the mother's, and the ideas of sanctity and hierarchy that they each imply is at play throughout the brief epic, and ultimately Jesus's unexpected choice serves to affirm the incarnation, "sanctifying the human condition and the 'house' in which it dwells" (116). At stake is what sanctifies a place, and Milton, according to Dean, comes down firmly on the question, asserting that it is Jesus's presence in a place — including the temple itself — that sanctifies it, not anything inherently holy about it. Jesus can sanctify any place, including his mother's lowly house, and in doing so he elevates the private and the inner, as well as obscurity and submission to "the continuing cycle of humiliation and exaltation" that will characterize his subsequent human experience (until his final incarnate reascension to heaven). This counters the fixed, hierarchical, and inherent theory of holiness presented in the poem by Satan, a form of idolatry that must be smashed by the living, incarnate mode of sanctity that Jesus models and that Adam and Eve are told to practice at the end of *Paradise Lost*.

The seemingly anticlimactic yet powerfully iconoclastic conclusion of *Paradise Regained* functions in a way similar to the subject of the first essay in part 3: Eden's fate as a place of contested holiness and vexed historical resonances in Paradise Lost. Chapter 7, Maura Brady's "'An Island salt and bare': The Fate of the Garden in *Paradise Lost*," examines the destruction of Eden and the "profound ambivalence" (140) at the heart of what she rightly calls one of the epic's most poignant scenes: the image of the whole of Eden swept away in Noah's flood only to end up a desert island, "The haunt of Seals and Orcs, and Sea-mews clang" (*PL* 11.835), in what we now call the Persian Gulf—the actual geographical destination of those rivers that we are told in book 4 originally flowed under, through, down, and out of the garden's mountain. In the presentation of this gigantic and cataclysmic perversion of the very processes that once fed and sustained the garden, Eden, according to Brady, becomes not only a place from which human beings are displaced but also one that is itself displaced and vacated of all its original sanctity. As she puts it, the passage "touches both the sorrow of exile and hope for the future, but it is perhaps most eloquent of all as a figure for the ground in between: the places where humans must dwell for now, and the quiet, poised attentiveness they will need as they watch and work for whatever still matters about place in a fallen world" (155).

Chapter 8, Talya Meyers's "Images of the East in *Paradise Lost*," looks to history for an account of Milton's representation of Eden and its invasion by Satan. Meyers argues that the images of the "East" Milton used in *Paradise Lost* have their origins, in part, in the long tradition of European epic that precedes them, in which encounters with non-Europeans, and particularly Easterners, are frequently central to the plot. Milton's East, unlike that of his predecessors, however, is the product of a later historical moment, one in which Europe had become more familiar with and involved in the Eastern world itself. Milton's East is also figurative, appearing not in the form of actual Eastern characters but as a vast variety of seemingly disconnected images that lend imaginative force to Milton's descriptions of the garden and of Satan. Meyers explores these images both as the reflection of Milton's historical moment and as important components of his interpretation of Eden's Fall. She argues that some of these images make up a unified, recursive narrative, one in which Eden, the cradle of Western Christianity, emerges after the Fall as a symbolic site for the later imagination of Eastern imperial power, one that can be incorporated into the European imagination in new ways but that, in actuality, poses very real challenges to the European world.

Finally, Joshua Lee Wisebaker also addresses the cultural history of European relations with the world beyond Europe, taking a particular interest in colonialism and the representation of the New World. In chapter 9, "Alternative Histories and the New World in *Paradise Lost*," Wisebaker, like Meyers, considers the historical context of Milton's depiction of paradise, noting how early modern depictions of New World lands and peoples tended to emphasize both their temporal and cultural otherness, often conflating these two kinds of difference. The perceived cultural differences of the Native Americans were absorbed into a generalized Eurocentric model of historical process by asserting that they inhabited an earlier stage of human social development, existing in a recognizable European cultural past. Wisebaker argues that Milton's depiction of Satan's encounter with Adam and Eve in the garden registers this concern with New World temporal difference insofar as the Eden that Satan encounters is figured as his own ontological past, a "Heav'n on Earth" (*PL* 4.208), with him, again, as antagonist. Wisebaker argues that the temporal relation between conqueror and conquered spreads itself out across the historical account of the epic's final books as a typological or cyclical recurrence. Temporal difference, Wisebaker argues, partially, but crucially, defines the cyclical nature of fallen time in the epic.

Wisebaker's concluding remarks about Michael's description of spaces in the New World that had yet to be inscribed by the violence of fallen history brings the book to a conclusion on an appropriately open note. The archangel gestures over a historical horizon that readers of the epic have passed beyond. Still, the gesture remains, as Wisebaker asserts, open to history yet to be inscribed and the alternative choices that might make it different from what has already been written with what Milton elsewhere called "so much waste of wealth and loss of blood" (Sonnet 12). Literary criticism has only a modest role to play in that process, but we do at least hope that the essays in this collection represent a few more useful bends in the "mazie" wandering of commentary on Milton's work, running "diverse" out there beyond the horizon of our present understanding and engagement and nurturing a wide variety of what Coleridge called "attractions along the way." The critical and scholarly project of making sense of Milton's work may seem, to quote Kerrigan again, "forever beyond us, unsettled and in process," but that doesn't mean that the maps we create as we make our way along the forking paths of the poem are not getting richer in detail and nuance with each provisional, wandering step.

לֹא עָלֶיךָ הַמְּלָאכָה לִגְמוֹר, וְלֹא אַתָּה בֶּן חוֹרִין לִבָּטֵל מִמֶּנָּה.

"You are not expected to complete the task, but neither are you free to desist from it" — Rabbi Tarfon, Mishnah, *Tractate Avot* 2:16.

PART ONE

SPEECH, GESTURE, AND RITUAL DISPLAY

———— ✻ ————

CHAPTER 1

God's Swearing by Himself

Milton's Troubling Coronation Oath

ALEX GARGANIGO

At a pivotal moment in British history, two visions of the ancient constitution faced off against each other in a courtroom.[1] Charles I had been indicted for something akin to crimes against humanity, which included breaking his coronation oath by trying to "overthrow the rights and liberties of the people" that it had committed him to protect.[2] At the trial before his beheading in January 1649, Charles advocated a view of monarchy as hereditary and divine, in contrast to his accusers' understanding of it as elective and contractual (with subjects reserving an implicit right of refusal). When the president of the High Court of Justice, John Bradshaw, characterized him as an "elected king," Charles vigorously denied it, insisting that "England was never an elective kingdom but an hereditary kingdom for near these thousand years." Charles went on to stress the importance of his coronation oath: "*I am sworn* to keep the peace by that duty I owe God and my country, and I will do it to the last breath of my body.... otherwise, I betray my trust and the liberties of the people."[3]

In response, the prosecution lectured the king that

> your oath [and] the manner of your coronation doth show plainly that the Kings of England — although it's true by the law the next person in blood is designed — yet if there were just cause to refuse him, the people of England might do it. For there is a contract and bargain made between the King and his people, and your oath is taken. And certainly, Sir, the bond is reciprocal: for as you are

the liege lord, so they are the liege subjects.... This we know now — the one tie, the one bond, is the bond of protection that is due from the sovereign; the other is the bond of subjection which is due from the subject. Sir, if this bond be once broken, farewell sovereignty.[4]

In the short term, the elective principle won out, underpinned as it was by the notion of reciprocal oaths making a contract between ruler and ruled. Charles I was executed, and a republic declared, accompanied by a new oath: the Engagement to a commonwealth without a king and House of Lords. This did not last, however, and the republic soon gave way to yet another replacement: an unelected Lord Protector — not elected by the people at any rate, though possibly, in another sense, by God. Then the Restoration of 1660 seemed to provide a well-nigh unquestionable confirmation of the hereditary principle: Charles II was crowned king because his father had been king and because God had brought him back to England. The elective principle would not entirely reassert itself until the Glorious Revolution of 1688, when the English arguably cashiered a Catholic monarch who had encroached too far onto his subjects' liberties: James II. In his place they installed a double monarchy composed of James's Protestant daughter and son-in-law, William and Mary, who took new coronation oaths devised by Parliament. But heredity had not entirely vanished. Far from a Lockean withdrawal of the people from a social contract the monarch had broken, many saw these events as another Restoration, this time of the true blood heir to Charles II — "true" in the sense of Protestant. However, since the center of gravity between king and Parliament had shifted (with the monarch eventually to dwindle into a figurehead), the issue became almost moot. Yes, the monarchy was still hereditary rather than elective, and kings were to be crowned and sworn in, but a process had been set in motion that by the nineteenth century would deprive the monarch of real executive power, ceding it to an elected prime minister.

Succession giving way to election: in this essay I would like to suggest that the unabashed Whiggery of this account, with the significance it grants to the events of both 1649 and 1688, can help us to read *Paradise Lost*, a poem, after all, whose chronologically first event, the speech-act that touches off the revolt in heaven, is a kind of coronation oath.[5] Addressing the assembled angels in book 5, God announces,

> This day I have begot whom I declare
> My only Son, and on this holy hill
> Him have anointed, whom ye now behold
> At my right hand; your head I him appoint;
> And *by myself have sworn to him shall bow*
> *All knees in heaven, and shall confess him Lord.*[6]

Critics have struggled to explain the details of God's dense speech, for example, glossing "begot" as "exalted," rather than as "created" or "given birth to" — a procedure complicated by the various acts of mediation at work in readers' access to it (the narrator of *Paradise Lost* quotes Raphael quoting God quoting an oath he apparently swore previously). It should hardly surprise that the powerful words of the Supreme Being come across as distant and hard to apprehend at first; indeed, the distance and the difficulty in part create that power. But even if the difficulty was not present in the original utterance and simply derives from the multiple acts of transmission, the poem's readers have no choice but to interpret the text they have on the page in front of them. In Raphael's version of God's speech, "begot" seems to mean two things: both that God created or gave birth to the Son *and* that God has promoted him on "this day," whatever span of time that refers to. Attention to the history of the English coronation oath can illuminate such ambiguities, which reflect the conflict between hereditary and elective theories of monarchy that characterizes that history. Before I explain fully how this is so, however, let us look at a few more important aspects of the speech's dense ambiguity and the questions it raises.

In general, the utterance's density stems from its layering of multiple speech-acts on top of one another. In a classic Austinian performative, similar to the christening of a ship or a declaration of war, God *appoints* the Son as head of the angels. Even the apparent constative, "I *declare* / My only son," which purports to describe an existing fact, may function as a performative that brings something new into being as far as the assembled angels are concerned: to declare someone his "only son," thereby excluding other candidates, is already to make him their head — a leader other than God, a leader they apparently didn't know they had, and a leader who may or may not replace God. Thus, if there is ambiguity in the phrase "I declare" functioning as both constative and performative, there is even more in the amphibologies created by "your head I him appoint" and "by myself have sworn to him shall bow." In the first phrase, "your head" could function as an appositive to "I" (essentially, "I, your head, appoint him..."). The phrase could thus mean (1) "I, God, appoint the Son to be your head"; (2) "I, God, who am already your head, now appoint the Son to be your new head, replacing me"; (3) "I, God, appoint the Son, who is currently your immediate head but still subordinate to me, to the higher position of supreme head, supreme to all of us"; (4) "I, God, appoint the Son, who is currently no one's head, to be your immediate head, but still subordinate to me, and I remain the supreme head." None of this would matter if Milton were a Trinitarian and believed God and the Son to be the same entity, but *De doctrina Christiana* makes Milton's anti-Trinitarianism clear. This phrase in *Paradise Lost*, then, seems to raise a question about the exact relationship between God and the Son. Is it one of identity or of difference? Do the "I" and the "him," pronouns placed right next to each other, designate one person or two?

The second phrase might seem less troubling. "I...by myself have sworn to him shall bow..." could mean either that "I, God, *have made a sworn promise to the Son* that all angels shall bow down to him" or that "I, God, have sworn, without any particular audience, that all angels shall *bow down to the Son.*" The difference between the two possibilities is comparatively slight, but the shorter phrase, "by myself have sworn," creates more divergent alternatives. God may have "sworn by himself" in at least three possible senses: first, in being the only one to swear; second, in doing so in the presence of no one else; third, in invoking himself, rather than someone else, as guarantor of his word. The first and third seem most likely.

The speech thus creates many problems, not just the ones outlined here.[7] Among the most important, however, is why God needs to swear at all. The same question had been asked by many students of the biblical texts on which Milton based this passage (Gen. 22; Isa. 45; Ps. 110; Heb. 6; Phil. 2; and Rom. 14); and God's oaths had proved a troubling limit case for thinkers as various as Philo Judaeus and George Lawson.[8] William Ames, for example, had wondered whether God demeans himself in swearing, employing a speech-act made necessary by the unreliability of humans and their commitments.[9] By contrast, many early modern apologists for state oaths (oaths of allegiance, oaths of office, courtroom oaths, coronation oaths)[10] had made the fact of God's swearing in Genesis 22 and elsewhere part of an argument against Christ's apparent prohibition of all oaths in Matthew 5:33–37 ("Swear not at all").[11] Central to their case for the necessity of such public oaths was Hebrews 6:13–17's reminder that God had sworn the Abrahamic covenant "by himself," which implied divine approval for oath swearing that created peace and reconciliation: "an oath…is…an end of all strife."[12] But even this passage was problematic because it implied that oaths are only sworn "by the greater" (Heb. 6:16): by invoking some higher power that guarantees the swearer's promise or assertion. For when God swears, there *is* no higher power, nothing outside God and his creation. Hence, he can only swear "by himself." This and other concerns led Ames to deny that God really swears.[13] Finally, if swearing usually ends strife, why does the oath of Milton's God *create* strife?

I would like to argue that Milton turned the problem of God's swearing to his own advantage in *Paradise Lost*, making it the centerpiece of this key episode, which should be seen as a modified coronation ritual. His God, in other words, swears a coronation oath, but crucially not for himself, and this is what sets the plot of the epic into motion. In the English version of the ceremony, the monarch's coronation oath had provided one of the clearest indications both of the social contract renewed there and thus of the limitations upon royal power. Almost from its inception the English coronation had included reminders not just of the divine right principle of succession (the crowning of the king in Westminster Abbey, the anointing of his body with holy oil) but of the contractualist principle of election and accountability (the king's swearing to rule well and preserve the church in return for his subjects' obedience).

However, even to call the ritual a coronation in the first place was to privilege one element at the expense of many others and play up the principle of divine right. For the coronation involved considerably more than crowning. At Charles II's coronation on April 23, 1661 — "the single most expensive and elaborate ceremony of Charles II's life," but one fairly representative of those during the Stuart era — the king processed in state from Westminster Hall to Westminster Abbey, accompanied by many notables carrying various ritual objects, including the regalia: the crown, orb, scepter, and other royal accessories.[14] Among the four swords of state used in the rite, the blunted one known as the Curtana was borne by the Earl of Oxford. After entering the abbey, Charles was formally "acclaimed" or "recognized" as king when the Bishop of London turned to the four corners of the abbey, each time asking the people if they were willing "to doe [their] Homage, service, & bounden duty"; they "signified their willingness by their loud Acclamations, all with one voice crying, God save King Charles."[15] Charles may even have broken precedent by addressing the people during the recognition.[16] He then took a multipart oath to govern well, consisting of questions and answers and a hand on the Bible at the altar. Later, he was anointed on the hands, arms, breast, shoulders, and head. The formal crowning came next, as one part of the process of "investment": the donning of various garments and objects, including the sword of state and the spurs. When St. Edward's Crown was placed on his head, "the *People*, with *loud* and *repeated Shouts*, cried, GOD SAVE THE KING," and cannons were fired off at the Tower of London.[17] After being formally enthroned, Charles received homage in the form of oaths of fealty from the bishops and nobles, punctuated by further shouts of approval from the audience. He then pardoned all and sundry, took Communion as part of the Mass, and left the abbey for a banquet in Westminster Hall. Interspersed throughout the proceedings were prayers, blessings, anthems, and Bible readings. While Pepys and company were suitably impressed, the republican Edmund Ludlow saw the spectacle as a "superstitious ceremony of anointing their idoll" and complained of "the mocking of the people, in asking in a formall way, when they administered the oath to him, whether they would have this man to reigne over them."[18] The whole ritual could just as easily have been called an anointment, a consecration, an enthronement, an installation, or a swearing-in.

By contrast, the coronation of the Son in *Paradise Lost* consists solely of God's announcement to the assembled angels that he has *already* begotten the Son, *already* anointed him, *already* sworn an oath that they shall obey him. If most or all of these were ritual events, they appear to have taken place in the past, and with no audience. Raphael's description of God's proclamation offers nothing more: no ritual objects, no ritual words other than God's 16 lines (5.600–15), no other ritual officers. Unlike English monarchs, who had for more than seven centuries sworn an elaborate coronation oath, the Son says exactly nothing. God swears the oath *for* him. Both the audience and the person at the center of the ritual participate only insofar as they listen. By comparison, even the absolutist Charles II seems to have allowed a more contractualist coronation ceremony than that of Milton's God. What are we to make of all this?

Book 5's coronation of the Son seems *both* deeply troubling, a possible betrayal of Milton's republican principles, *and* a template for a reformed coronation oath and ceremony, not unlike those that would arrive after the Glorious Revolution. Students of Milton have become used to the notion of the Divine Exception — that republicanism is appropriate for every state *except* that in heaven. But after we compartmentalize and hive off the heavenly monarchy — recalling that monarchy only appears there because Milton's larger principle is that the best should govern and because God and the Son clearly possess more merit than anyone else, whereas no human could possibly be in that position on earth — we remain troubled, and well we should. Milton puts pressure on the Divine Exception, allowing a sense that this is all unfair to bleed over temporarily into our consideration of heaven.

This essay will first examine Milton's pronouncements on the English coronation ritual and oath in order to remind us that he was most interested in its contractual and consensualist aspects and condemned their opposites. Then it will revisit the history of the coronation and coronation oath and discern within it a struggle between contract and succession in which the former gains the upper hand. In light of this Whiggish or perhaps Miltonic history, *Paradise Lost*'s coronation oath and ceremony appear curiously truncated and retrograde, apparently privileging the succession principle. A look at *De doctrina*'s discussion of the intertexts of God's self-oath only deepens the sense that it deliberately raises issues of voice, agency, and mediation that make God's role in the coronation ritual seem problematic because it is coercive and monopolistic. However, Milton's intention throughout is to provoke in the reader troubling thoughts not so much about God as about the system of reciprocal oaths underpinning the restored English monarchy. Such thoughts would only have been magnified by Satan's remarks against swearing obedience to God in book 4 (93–98), which should be seen as

Milton's attack not on God himself, or even the Son, both of whom merit their posts, but on meritless earthly monarchs who style themselves gods and demand cringing loyalty oaths from their subjects.

MILTON AND THE CORONATION OATH

In his prefatory poem to the second edition of *Paradise Lost* (1674), Andrew Marvell was the first to identify book 5, lines 600–15 as a coronation of the Son: "Messiah *crowned*."[19] But Marvell's succinct phrase did not provide a full-blown reading of the exaltation scene. In the 1980s Stevie Davies made a first pass at one, emphasizing the element of feudal fealty but paying insufficient attention to oaths as such and to changes in the coronation rite over its long history.[20] However, no subsequent critic, not even David Norbrook in his brilliant account of Milton's republicanism,[21] has pressed Marvell's insight to its logical conclusion and read Milton's coronation and oath in the immediate context of the Restoration of Charles II and the fierce debate over oaths of allegiance and oaths of all kinds that accompanied and lingered after his coronation. To do so would involve reviewing Milton's pronouncements on the coronation and oaths in the prose, as well as tracing the history of the English coronation rite up to and beyond the Restoration.

In 1660, at a time when he was also writing *Paradise Lost*, Milton's *Brief Notes upon a Late Sermon* emphasized the reciprocity between the monarch's coronation oath and the subject's oath of allegiance.[22] In response to Matthew Griffith's fulsome celebration of absolute monarchy in his sermon on *The Fear of God and the King*, Milton claimed that the only way even to consider monarchs legitimate would be to think of them as obliged by the coronation oath to represent their subjects' interests in return for their consent to be governed, as expressed in oaths of allegiance. But even that is not entirely satisfactory; nor does it make monarchs absolute: "how could that person be absolutely supreme, who reignd, not under Law only, but under oath of his good demeanour given to the people at his coronation, ere the people gave him his Crown? And his principal oath was to maintain those Laws which the people should chuse? If then the Law it self, much more he who was but the keeper and minister of Law, was in thir choice; and both he subordinat to the performance of his duty sworn, and our sworn allegiance in order only to his performance."[23]

Better, in fact, to replace monarchy with the republic outlined in *The Readie and Easie Way to Establish a Free Commonwealth* (also of 1660) alongside its desperate appeal to covenant-swearing Presbyterians added to the second edition, which appeared in the same month as the *Brief Notes* (April). While the first edition of *The Readie and Easie Way* (February 1660) had only glanced at the issue of state oaths in referring to the nation's abjuration of kingship in the Engagement of 1649–50 (a kingship now characterized as an "abjur'd and detested thraldom"), the second edition inserted a ten-page digression reminding Presbyterians and others of the oaths they had sworn, first to restrain an out-of-control king in the Protestation (1641) and Solemn League and Covenant (1643), and then to abolish kingship in the Engagement.[24] England was forced to end king and kingship, he implies, because Charles had broken the social contract to which he had sworn or covenanted at his coronation. The English people "took themselves not bound by the light of nature or religion, to any former covnant, from which the King himself by many forfeitures of a latter date or discoverie, and our own longer consideration thereon had more & more unbound us, both to himself and his posteritie."[25] While the Yale editors gloss "any former covnant" as the Solemn League and Covenant, it clearly has a much wider scope; Charles I was not a party to that covenant and thus could not have "forfeited" it. For the English, and especially English Presbyterians, "any former covnant" must have included the social contract or covenant that, according to one understanding of the laws of nature and nations, preceded but was made visible in the coronation ceremony, with its coronation oath for the king and oaths of fealty from lords spiritual and temporal, followed by subjects' oaths of allegiance and supremacy to the king. If the parliamentary oaths of the 1640s and 1650s constituted elaborations of this original implied contract, Charles, strictly speaking, had only "forfeited" or broken his coronation oath, as Milton had insisted in the regicide tracts.

But Milton had long been interested in the coronation oath and ritual. The *Brief Notes* and *Readie and Easie Way* merely pick up on similar lines of argument in the commonwealth tracts and Commonplace Book, arguments that focus on the oath's contents and position within the ceremony

as a marker of the monarch's accountability to the social contract it instanti-
ated. Even apparent minutiae, such as the name of a ceremonial sword (the
Curtana), who was to carry it in the coronation, and why, matter a great deal
to Milton.[26] The Commonplace Book's sections on laws, the king, and the
subject cull passages from Raphael Holinshed, John Stow, and John Speed
that cast the coronation ceremony as an oath-taking ceremony. The oath
must come *before* the crowning, and it primarily concerns upholding justice
and the laws: "the crowning of K[ing]s in England," says Milton, is "not
admitted till thire oath" is "receav'd of justice to be administerd, according
to the laws" (YP 1:427–29).[27] If monarchs do not uphold the laws, they
are subject to correction. According to Milton, the Curtana is to be carried before the monarch by the Earl of Chester "in token that he" has "the
autority to correct the K[ing] if he should see him swerve from the limits of
Justice."[28] As *The Tenure of Kings and Magistrates* and the *First Defence* put
it, "that sword of St. Edward, called Curtana" is present in order "to mind
them [monarchs] . . . that if they errd, the Sword had power to restraine
them" and they are "liable to punishment."[29] These sentiments are congru-
ent with the proposal in the Parliament's Nineteen Propositions to the king
in 1642 that the medieval office of High Constable be revived so that the
latter might "prosecute the King if he violated his coronation oath."[30]

The commonwealth tracts defend the infant republic by extending the
argument about contract and reciprocity. In a paragraph in the final chapter
of *Eikonoklastes* (1649), Milton responds to Charles's meditations on death
in the final chapter of the *Eikon Basilike* (also 1649) and discusses the contents of the coronation oath:

> Those objected Oaths of Allegiance and Supremacy [to which Charles refers in
> charging that his subjects have broken them by fighting and killing him] we swore,
> not to his Person, but as it was invested with his Autority; and his autority was by
> the People first giv'n him conditionally, in Law and under Law, and under Oath
> also for the Kingdoms good, and not otherwise: *the Oathes then were interchang'd,*
> *and mutual*; stood and fell together; he swore fidelity to his trust (not as a deluding
> ceremony, but as a real condition of thir admitting him for King; and [William] the
> Conqueror himself swore it ofter then at his Crowning) they swore Homage and
> Fealty to his Person in that trust. There was no reason why the Kingdom should be
> furder bound by Oaths to him, then he by his Coronation Oath to us, which

he hath every way brok'n; and having brok'n, the ancient Crown-Oath of Alfred above mention'd, conceales not his penalty.[31]

According to Milton, the last clause of King Alfred's oath states that "the King should be as liable, and obedient to suffer right, as others of his people," for, if the people are accountable to law, "the King should be [equally] accountable" and "answerable" to law, both in his courts and his great court of Parliament.[32] Milton's point is presumably that "right" and "penalty" mean "execution" in Charles's case. The paragraph rehearses Parliament's justification for the civil war — that it was fighting the king's first body to save his second — with its insistence that this did not constitute a breach of subjects' oaths of allegiance to the king since they only applied to his second body, his body politic rather than his body natural.[33] To *Eikon Basilike*'s charge that Parliament had not only broken the oaths of allegiance but, in calling on Charles to consent to its abolition of episcopacy, had tried to force him to break the part of his coronation oath promising to preserve the church, *Eikonoklastes* responds that the coronation oath was not that specific and, in fact, bound him to consent to *any* law made by his people, past, present, or future — in other words, not to veto legislation.[34]

Moreover, in its insistence that power "was first given him," and by extension all kings, "conditionally" by the people, and that the monarch's coronation oath is no "deluding ceremony, but…a real condition of thir admitting him for King" and thus the exact counterpart of subjects' oaths of allegiance in a mutual interchange of oaths, the paragraph suggests the same account of the coronation oath's genesis that had appeared some months earlier in *The Tenure of Kings and Magistrates*.[35] Thus, according to Milton's *First Defence* (1651), the coronation highlights the people's expressed consent. Making a questionable case that ancient British kingship was not hereditary but by implication elective, Milton argues that this elective principle is enshrined in the current rite's *recognitio* or *acclamatio*, in which the people shout their approval of the king: "I positively assert that their [the ancient Britons'] kingship was not hereditary, which is evident both from the succession of their kings, and from their way of creating them; for the approval of the people is asked [*petuntur*] in express words. When the king has taken [*dedit*] the accustomed oath, the archbishop, stepping to the four sides of the platform erected for the purpose, asks [*rogat*] the body of the people four several times in these words, 'Will ye consent [*consentire*] to have this man your king?'"[36]

Once the people have consented, the coronation oath, in Milton's expansive interpretation, binds the king to many things. He cannot dissolve Parliament until all grievances have been considered, nor can he veto laws it makes concerning public safety.[37] He must follow Parliament's advice and use the militia to defend the people.[38] Perhaps most important, he cannot make "a scorn of his regal Oath" by interpreting it selectively, "by his own will," "conscience[,] and reason" — contrary to Parliament's.[39] Milton even resurrects the baseless charge Parliament brought against Charles I that, after 1625, when he was first crowned, Charles had conspired with Archbishop William Laud to alter his coronation oath by leaving out the *quas vulgus elegerit* clause, which we will examine in a moment, thus opening the door to other violations of the people's rights, laws, and customs.[40] For if the king scorns his coronation oath as a merely ceremonial and "brutish formality," he breaks the contract with his subjects, whose obligations under their oaths of allegiance cease.[41]

Milton's insistence on contractual kingship — if there had to be any kingship at all — appears not to have wavered, for in his very last publication before his death in 1674 he emphasized the elective nature of Polish kingship as undergirded by a coronation oath. In his translation of the Polish lords' declaration accepting Jan III as king and describing the coronation ceremony, *A Declaration; or, The Letters Patent of the Election of This Present King of Poland John the Third, Elected on the 22d of May . . . 1674*, forms of the word "elect" appear frequently, and the contractual nature of the kingship is stressed. The king, "the most Serene Elect," must consent to "bind himself by an Oath, to perform the conditions concluded with those persons sent by his Majesty, before the exhibition of this present Decree of Election" and to "provide in best manner for the performance of them by his authentick Letters." And indeed, he did as much when he took his "solemn Oath . . . on the 5th day of the Month of June, in the Palace at Warsaw, after the Letters Patent [were] delivered upon the Covenants, and Agreements, or Capitulations," presumably to the Polish lords' demands.[42] It is significant that the translation's title page downplays the coronation itself by calling attention to the lords' election of Jan "on the 22d of May," rather than to the date of the coronation the next month, June 5. Likewise, the tract's title calls attention to it as an act on the part of the lords rather than the king, *their* "Letters Patent" or articles upon which he had to agree in order to gain their support.

A Whig or Miltonic History
of the Coronation Oath

All these texts suggest a history of the English coronation ritual as part of a march toward the more obvious statement of the social contract after the Glorious Revolution, when a newly revised coronation oath threatened to reduce the monarch to the status of just another subject.[43] As Roy Strong shows, Charles II's coronation in 1661 hewed to the fourth version of the rite since its origins in the Middle Ages; the Glorious Revolution would produce the fifth and final one, used with relatively minor variations up through Elizabeth II's coronation in 1953 (see table 1).[44] By the early modern period, the ceremony had become an amalgam of *conflicting political principles:* succession versus election, royal versus ecclesiastical power, and royal versus parliamentary sovereignty. Did the ceremony mark the king's succession by divine right and patriarchal inheritance to a throne already his, *or* the people's choosing of him as one among a number of candidates? Did the archbishop's anointing him with holy oil and placing the crown on his head signify the king's subordination to the church, *or* his superiority to it? Did the presence of his subjects in a body at Westminster Abbey, along with their shouted "acclamation" of "God save the King!" and the oaths of fealty presented by the lords spiritual and temporal, indicate their subordination *or* their superiority to the king? The answer was a little bit of both, or, more precisely, an oscillation between these principles at various points in the rite's history.[45] The coronation oath acted as a barometer of the balance of power within the English constitution — at the very least of the monarch's perception of that balance.

The oath's form and position relative to other parts of the ceremony, particularly the acclamation, oaths of fealty, anointing, and crowning, reflected which principles had apparently gained ascendancy at a given time. We

Table 1. Essential Elements of English Coronations, 901–1953

1st Recension (901–956)	Anointing	Crowning	(Acclamation)	(Cor. Oath)		
2nd Recension (973–1154)	(Acclamation)	(Cor. Oath)	Anointing	Crowning		
3rd Recension (1189–1274)	(Cor. Oath)	Acclamation	Anointing	Crowning		
4th Recension (1308–1684)	Acclamation	Cor. Oath	Anointing	Crowning	Fealty Oaths	
Interregnum (1649–1660)						
Charles II (1651) Pre-Acclam Pre-Cor. Oath Cor. Oath 1/Covs	Acclamation	Cor. Oaths 2–3	Crowning	Fealty Oaths 1	People's Oaths	Fealty Oaths 2
O. Cromwell (1653)	Sp. HC Oration	Instr. Gov. Read	Prot. Oath			
O. Cromwell (1657)		Prot. Oath	Prot. Oath	(Acclamation 1)	(Acclamation 2)	
R. Cromwell (1658)		Prot. Oath				
5th Recension (1689–1953)	Acclamation	Cor. Oath	Anointing	Crowning	Fealty Oaths	

Cor. Oath: Coronation Oath
Prot. Oath: Protectoral Oath
Covs.: Covenants (Scottish National Covenant, Solemn League and Covenant)
Pre-Acclam.: Pre-Acclamation
Instr. Gov. Read: The Instrument of Government Read Out
Sp. HC Oration: Oration by the Speaker of the House of Commons
Parentheses indicate that the speech-act is the equivalent of a later one with that title, of what will be called an acclamation or coronation oath.

begin with the issue of the oath's placement, assuming that priority indicates priorities. In the first coronation order in the tenth century, the royal oath came at the very end — after anointing, crowning, and a form of popular acclamation (the prompted "God save the King!" from the abbey's four corners) — and it was less an oath than a set of promises to rule well.[46] It came almost as an afterthought: the king had already become or been recognized as king via those three subrituals; the oath did not constitute a condition for becoming king. But from the Second Recension (973) onward, as Milton noted in the Commonplace Book and *Brief Notes*, the royal oath *preceded* the anointing and crowning, as if the latter two were contingent upon the royal oath and subjects reserved (at least nominally) the right to refuse this person as monarch.[47] This relative subordination of the crowning and anointing to the royal oath suggests a further wrinkle. With the brief exception of the Third Recension (1189–1274), the acclamation has always preceded the coronation oath, making the latter seem contingent upon the former. Moreover, the coronation oath and acclamation have always stuck together as a block relative to that formed by the anointing and crowning, thus stressing their reciprocal nature. By contrast, the new oaths of fealty sworn by the lords spiritual and temporal after the coronation oath and crowning from the Fourth Recension on (1308–1953) seem even more of an afterthought, a gloss on the general acclamation given by all the people earlier in the service, as well as a kind of oath of office by which these lords hold their titles and lands. Even so, the appearance of these oaths of fealty in 1308 strengthened the contractual element.

Compared with the seventeenth century's other coronations, the unusual coronations or installations of the 1650s emphasized words more than objects, contract more than kinesthetics. In the absence of the anointment on all four occasions, and of the crowning on the last three, oaths loomed large. They were more swearings-in than coronations. Charles II's coronation by the Scots at Scone in 1651 trumped all others with its multitude of explicitly contractual and reciprocal oaths: not one but two sets of coronation oaths for the king, including his approval of the Scottish National Covenant and the Solemn League and Covenant; at least two acclamations and an oath for the people as a whole; two sets of oaths for the lords temporal; and pointedly none for churchmen.[48] Cromwell's first installation in 1653 stripped the rite down to little more than the protector's oath of office preceded by an explanatory text: the Instrument of Government.[49] Addressing his first protectoral Parliament almost a year later (September 12, 1654), Cromwell would revealingly characterize his installation as a "Solemnity" at which "I took the Oath to this Government." In that speech he repeatedly stressed that in everything he spoke, "I do not bear witness to myself" and his own legitimacy as protector because so many other people had already done so at the installation and afterward. He ended by commanding members of Parliament to express their consent to the constitution's "Fundamentals" by swearing an oath to "the Government, as it is settled in a Single Person and a Parliament."[50] I will return to these comments shortly.

Cromwell's more kingly second installation in 1657 still lacked a crowning and anointing but placed an investiture of robes, scepter, sword, and Bible just before the oath and the two sets of pseudo-popular acclamations.[51] Once again, he would later refer to this ceremony as a swearing-in: "my Oath…to govern 'according to the Laws' that are now made" — the new constitution known as the Humble Petition and Advice.[52] When Cromwell died in 1658, his son Richard was proclaimed Lord Protector by the Privy Council throughout London by heralds and a procession and then sworn in at Whitehall with little ceremony other than acknowledgment of his new status by the Lord Mayor and aldermen of London. One of the council's justifications for the transfer of power was that Oliver had "declared, and appointed" his son to "succeed him in the Government of these Nations." The official proclamation of Richard's succession, repeated four times in the streets of London, was accompanied by shouted acclamations and contained the words "We…do now hereby, with *one full voice,* and *consent of tongue and heart,* publish and declare the said Noble, and Illustrious Lord Richard to be rightfully protector of this Commonwealth."[53] In its omission of the crowning and its absence of the anointing (announced as having already taken place), as well as in its focus on issues of consent by tongue and heart, Milton's coronation of the Son in *Paradise Lost* is thus closest to those of the 1650s, particularly Cromwell's — and in certain respects even more to the swearing-in of his son Richard at the command of his father. While Gordon Campbell and Thomas Corns read the exaltation scene as a test of the angels' loyalty and a reflection on Richard's coronation as a "dreadful example of how not to transfer power,"[54] I will concentrate on its reduction of the coronation rite to little more than God's oath, without meaningful interaction among the participants and thus without an opportunity to express genuine consent.

The contents of the coronation oath had also changed over time, reflecting different conceptions of the monarch's status relative to his subjects and church. In its first three recensions (901–1274), the oath consisted of three promises: (1) "that the Church of God and all Christian people preserve the peace at all times"; (2) "that [the king] forbid rapacity and all iniquities to all degrees" of people; (3) "that in all judgments [the king] enjoin equity and mercy."[55] With the Fourth Recension of 1308 (from Edward II to James II), the oath settled into a question-and-answer format:

> The archbishop (or bishop) goes to the king and in a moderate and distinct voice asks (*interroget*):
>
> ARCHBISHOP: Sir, will you grant, keep, and by your oath confirm to the people of England the laws and customs granted to them by the Kings of England, your lawful and religious predecessors, and namely the laws, customs, and liberties granted to the clergy and to the people by the glorious king, St. Edward, your predecessor?
>
> KING: I grant and promise to keep them.
>
> Then the archbishop explains to him what he shall swear:
>
> ARCHBISHOP: Sir, will you keep peace and godly concord entirely (according to your powers), both to God, the holy Church, the clergy, and the people?
>
> KING: I will keep it.
>
> ARCHBISHOP: Sir, will you to your power cause law, justice, and discretion in mercy and truth to be executed in all your judgments?
>
> KING: I will.
>
> ARCHBISHOP: Sir, will you grant to hold and keep the just laws and customs [*iustas leges et consuetudines*] that the people shall have chosen [*quas vulgus elegerit*], and to defend and uphold them to the honor of God, so much as in you lies?
>
> KING: I grant and promise so to do.
>
> [*The king grants a pardon to the clergy.*]
>
> With an oath or with the Eucharist [*sacramento*] upon the altar in front of everyone, the king confirms that he shall keep all these promises.

We see here that the archbishop first asked the monarch whether he wished to take an oath to preserve "the laws, customs, and liberties granted to the clergy and to the people by the glorious king, St. Edward [the Confessor]."[56] After agreeing, he was asked to swear three promises. When he had assented to each promise separately, he went to the altar to swear formally to keep them all, hand on Bible, and, in the early coronations, on or near the Eucharist. Two of the sworn promises were essentially the first and third provisions of the previous coronation oath: to preserve the peace and the church; to see that justice and mercy were done throughout the realm. The provision against rapacity and iniquity, however, disappeared, to be replaced by what Roy Strong calls a "revolutionary" new one. Under great pressure from the barons, Edward II now swore to uphold the "just laws and customs...that the people shall have chosen" (*iustas leges et consuetudines...quas vulgus elegerit*).[57]

Until 1689 almost every subsequent oath, in Latin, French, or English, including those of Charles I and II, retained this wording and offered some kind of footnote to its fundamental ambiguity. The core issue was whether the future perfect *elegerit* (shall have chosen) in *quas vulgus elegerit* should be construed as *has chosen* (perfect tense, referring to laws the people have already chosen by the time of the coronation) or *shall choose* (future tense, laws the people shall choose after the coronation) — both meanings available in the Latin.[58] The former ("has chosen") implies a balance of power in favor of the monarch, who is obliged only to respect existing laws at the time of the coronation, but not later ones. The latter ("shall choose") suggests a balance in favor of Parliament, which reserves the option of making new laws that the monarch must not veto — an interpretation of the word that Milton broadcast in *Eikonoklastes* and the *First Defence*.[59]

After 1308, the meaning of *quas vulgus elegerit* tacked back and forth between these two poles. All that can be said here about the Tudors and early Stuarts is that they tried to imprint the expanding power of the monarchy upon their coronation oaths, subordinating church to state and Parliament to sovereign (the "shall choose" to the "has chosen").[60] In the run-up to the civil war, Parliament accused Charles I of breaking his coronation oath by allegedly tyrannical innovations in taxation and church government, and it specifically cited the *quas vulgus* clause. There was even false speculation that

Charles and Archbishop Laud had conspired to omit the clause altogether, a charge Milton repeated in the *First Defence*.[61]

Not surprisingly, in his son Charles II's first coronation at Scone in 1651, the Scots did their best to remove all ambiguity and to subordinate king to people. They replaced the ambiguous *quas vulgus elegerit* with very precise language amounting to the "shall choose" reading on steroids. Charles promised to obey and enforce all preexisting covenants and *any* law, civil or religious, that the Scottish Parliament should in future pass.[62] In Cromwell's first protectoral oath, multiple preambles stressed that he was accepting the reins of power offered by Parliament and people in the Instrument of Government (in effect, a written constitution), and he swore not to "violate, or infringe the matters and things contained therein, but, to my power, observe the same...And...in al other things, to the best of my understanding, govern these Nations according to the Laws, Statutes and Customs, seeking their Peace, and causing Justice and Law to be equally administred."[63] If the phrase "Laws, Statutes and Customs" failed to specify past or future, the rest of the text did appear to tie his hands in ways previous oaths had not. His second protectoral oath, repeated by his son the following year, likewise equivocated on the *quas vulgus* question. Despite identifying him as "chief Magistrate of these three nations," his oath returned to more monarchical language, promising to protect reformed Protestantism, govern "according to Law," and preserve the peace, safety, and "just Rights and Privileges of the people."[64]

In 1661, Charles II's orthodox second coronation returned to the language his father had used. The *elegerit* in the final question remained "have" without the "chosen"; and the introduction retained the references to the prerogative and established church.[65] However, the decisive break in the restored monarchical tradition came with William and Mary at the Glorious Revolution. Complaining of the "doubtfull Words and Expressions" in the former coronation oath, Parliament decided on new, more precise wording and fixed it in a special law prescribing it for all future monarchs.[66] Both monarchs were read the Declaration of Rights and offered the crowns by Parliament, which both revised the oath and attended the ceremony en masse. William accepted the Declaration and the crown, acknowledging the monarchs' subordination to parliamentary law.[67] Swearing the oath in unison, both William and Mary agreed to "Governe the People of this Kingdome of England and the Dominions thereto belonging according to the Statues in Parlyament Agreed on and the Laws and Customs of the same" — that is, all parliamentary laws, both before and after the coronation.[68] Queen Anne's coronation oath in 1702 made the shift even clearer, adding language taken from loyalty oaths that subjects had sworn to various regimes in the seventeenth century, which bound her not to evade the oath through "equivocation, or mental reservation."[69] Never before had the coronation oath, even in Charles II's humiliating Scottish coronation, questioned the monarch's integrity and in effect reduced her to the status of subject in quite this way.

One might object that a Miltonic, contractualist understanding of the coronation oath and ceremony does not necessarily imply republican antimonarchism, perhaps just support for an elective monarchy of the kind mentioned by John Bradshaw and others at Charles I's trial.[70] Yet even Bradshaw was not defending monarchy per se at the trial, and *Paradise Lost*'s heaven and heavenly coronation are clearly not elective. As some historians of political thought have pointed out in an effort to deradicalize the politics in *Paradise Lost*, this contractualist understanding is also consistent with limited monarchy and mixed government.[71] However, Milton's poetry, with all its intricacies, is not prose. It does not always present ideas straightforwardly, and apparent contradictions can arise between, say, the celebration of monarchy in heaven and its denigration on earth. Those contradictions are not to be resolved by assuming that Milton wants the same form of government in both places, thereby contorting his entire career by pegging him as a secret monarchist or mixed monarchist in *Paradise Lost*. Heaven is the exception that proves the rule that republics are the best governments. In any case, many clearly antimonarchist republicans, such as Algernon Sidney, Henry Vane, Henry Neville, Marchamont Nedham in his republican phases, and very likely Bradshaw and many others on the High Court of Justice, held views similar to Milton's about the reciprocal nature of the oaths of allegiance and coronation, and of the latter as a safeguard against absolutism and a temporary expedient on the road toward nonmonarchical government.[72]

Even if one sticks to the prose and compares Milton's pronouncements on monarchy from 1649 onward, one must place most emphasis on the latest works in the sequence, those closest in time to *Paradise Lost*. *The Readie and Easie Way* (1660) makes it unambiguously clear that God wants earthly polities to be republics in one way or another — republics in which the only king is God, not any single human.[73] While Milton's defenses of republicanism from *Tenure* to the *Second Defence* have been shown to allow some small room for righteous kings,[74] monarchy is clearly a second best, an anomaly, an expedient on the way to republicanism. This is the gesture of the *First Defence*, Milton's most forceful apologia for republican government and citizenship — republic first, king second and only if absolutely necessary — and it is certainly the gesture of his writings in 1660 and 1674. *The Readie and Easie Way* makes an increasingly desperate and dangerous case against the return of any kind of monarchy; and as monarchy's return becomes inevitable in April 1660, *Brief Notes upon a Late Sermon* only grudgingly concedes a limited, elective monarchy as the lesser of many evils — and unlikely to last.[75] There, as in the *First Defence*, he insists that while the occasional king can muster enough merit to rule well, most can't.[76] *Letters Patent* (1674), published under the restored monarchy, in effect repeats that grudging admission in its implied support for elective monarchy in Poland and thus, by implication, for electing a non-Catholic king in England. And to return to 1660, most of Milton's writings in the months before the Restoration, including *A Letter to a Friend*, *Proposalls of Certaine Expedients*, *The Present Means and Brief Delineation of A Free Commonwealth*, and *The Readie and Easie Way*, entertain the idea of a loyalty oath of some kind that restates the Engagement's unconditional refusal of monarchy.[77] Focusing on oaths, then, demonstrates that Milton's heart was antimonarchist and that *Paradise Lost* best expresses this brand of republicanism.

Intertexts of God's Oath

In order to appreciate God's oath as part of an unsatisfactory coronation ritual that robs participants of autonomy, we must scrutinize its intertextuality. While the self-referential oath of Milton's God appears to have no classical precedents, it has a few early modern ones and a host of biblical ones. God's self-oath resembles its Renaissance forebears (the oaths urged on Shakespeare's Romeo and Bassanio on the one hand and Donne's God on the other) in that it involves pressing *someone else* to make a commitment to action. Shakespeare's heroines ask their lovers to swear undying fidelity to them "by thy self." In "A Hymn to God the Father," the anxious Donne recklessly and punningly orders God to grant him life after death: "Swear by thyself that at my death thy Sun / Shall shine as it shines now, and heretofore."[78] For a Trinitarian like Donne, these lines only ask God to commit another part of himself (the Son) to save the poet (another of God's sons). But a non-Trinitarian might hear the lines differently: as committing God to commit a third party (the Son) to future action. In any case, of the three-plus people adjured (or urged to swear an oath) here, only one (Bassanio) clearly goes through with it.

More immediately, though, God's swearing for others in *Paradise Lost* resembles a set of statutory rather than literary oaths: the mandatory state-oaths enacted by the Cavalier Parliament after the Restoration. As the centerpiece of the suite of laws known as the Clarendon Code (1661–65), the Corporation, Uniformity, and Vestryman's Oaths required numerous officeholders to swear that *other people* were not bound by the Solemn League and Covenant of 1643 to change or reform the government: "I do declare that I do hold there lies *no Obligation* upon me *or any other person* from the Oath commonly called the Solemn League and Covenant *to endeavour any Change or Alteration of Government,* either in Church, or State."[79] They were thus forced not only to take an oath before entering office but also to take one that imposed commitments on other people without their permission. All these intertexts highlight the apparent arbitrariness and coercion involved in Milton's God committing others to do things without giving them a chance to object.

Attention to the scriptural models for God's self-oath in *Paradise Lost* reveals something more complex: its status as a coherent tissue of biblical quotations about exaltation and, crucially, *mediation* (Gen. 22:16, Isa. 45:23, Ps. 110:4, Phil. 2:9–11, and Rom. 14:10–11).[80] A survey of Milton's comments on these texts throughout *De doctrina* in a number of different contexts demonstrates that, cumulatively, they problematize notions of voice and agency with respect to God's words and those of his representatives. These passages and comments are central to an understanding of Milton's at-times equivocal treatment of Arianism in book 5 of *Paradise Lost*.[81] God's oath combines biblical quotations that make several points about the Son, his relationship to God, and both God and Son's relations to humankind. *De doctrina* describes these relationships by outlining at least three roles or *offices* for the Son: prophet, priest, and king. Only the last two concern us here, but all can be subsumed into Milton's scheme under the rubric of mediator.[82]

The Abrahamic covenant is the main background for many of these offices and transactions. In Genesis 22:16, God swears for the first time by his own name, solidifying his earlier covenant to multiply Abraham's seed (Gen. 13:13–17). It's a curious moment because, like *Paradise Lost*, it involves an oath in the past tense now announced to one of God's creatures. In order to prevent Abraham from killing Isaac at the last minute, an angel announces that God has already sworn a promise that "in blessing will I bless thee, and in multiplying I will multiply thy seed as the stars of heaven." The oath is doubly distanced from Abraham by being announced by someone other than God (the angel) and by being phrased in the past tense: "By myself *have I sworn, saith the Lord*, for because thou hast done this thing, and hast not withheld thy son, thine only son."

In addition to being an oath moment, and a self-referential oath moment at that, it's also a father-son moment for Abraham and Isaac that anticipates God's relationship to his only begotten Son. If Isaac (the type) is a near-sacrifice, the Son (the antitype) will become an actual sacrifice on the cross. The difference is not only one of near death versus real death. In a sense the situations resemble each other in that neither son ultimately dies: Isaac is reprieved; Christ resurrected. Yet the two sons diverge in their knowledge of and agency in the sacrifice. Isaac remains ignorant of the sacrifice until the last moment; Abraham chooses it for him. As for Christ, this Son will later choose to sacrifice himself for humanity (*PL* 3.236–41). In *Paradise Lost*'s exaltation scene, the dynamic, like the wording ("by myself have sworn"), approaches that of Genesis 22:16 rather than Christ's Crucifixion because God the Father chooses the Son's exaltation for him — and, I argue, swears his coronation oath for him. The Son seems to have no choice in the matter: his wishes are not discussed and seem irrelevant at this point. This would hardly figure as an issue in a Trinitarian understanding of the Son's relationship to God, but it looms large in Milton's Arian thinking. God has simply made him his successor, just as Abraham has paradoxically ensured by the attempted sacrifice that Isaac will be his successor to the status of covenanter with God, bearer of the promise.

Both Isaiah 45:23 and Hebrews 6:16 rehearse the Abrahamic covenant and divine self-oath. Hebrews 6 offers the Son as a second guarantor of God's promise, yet another agent of his voice: "For when God made promise to Abraham, because he could swear by no greater, he sware by himself....Wherein God, willing more abundantly to shew unto the heirs of promise the immutability of his counsel, confirmed it by an oath. That by two immutable things...we might have a strong consolation [hope]...as an anchor of the soul...the forerunner is...Jesus, made an high priest for ever after the order of Melchizedek" (13, 17–20). The Son will continue to implement God's part of the covenant (that is, to help Christians implement it) by mediating as a priest-king between them and God (Heb. 6:20, 10–12).

A related passage from Psalm 110 raises the issues of agency and voice by featuring God's speaking through the psalmist David — it is, after all, prefaced by the title "A Psalm of David" — and apparently through a third party who speaks its opening line about the Israelite king: "The Lord said unto my lord: 'Sit thou at my right hand, until I make thine enemies thy footstool'" (Ps. 110.1). When this speaker describes God crowning David in the coronation ceremony ("The Lord hath sworn, and will not repent, Thou art a priest for ever after the order of Melchizedek'" [110.4]), it involves another quotation of a quotation (David quoting the speaker quoting God). Hebrews adds yet another chain to the link when it quotes this verse throughout chapters 5–7; and Hebrews 6:13 it turns God's mere oath in Psalm 110:4 ("The Lord hath sworn") into the self-oath of the Abrahamic covenant: "For when God made promise to Abraham, because he could swear by no greater, he sware by himself." Hebrews thus explicitly connects God's two oaths: the first and self-referential one that seals the Abrahamic covenant (Gen. 22:16); the second and non-self-referential one that makes Christ the eternal mediator (Ps. 110:4; Heb. 5–7). We can now see that the sources for *Paradise Lost* 5.607–08 relate the Abrahamic covenant and the father-son relationship to the Son's succession, sacrifice, mediation, and coronation — all the while asking questions such as, who is speaking, and for whom?; who is taking action, and for whom?

For Milton, Christ's resurrection from the dead and creation of the universe are both species of mediation, of doing tasks for God; and mediation is an instance of divided agency. *De doctrina* sees Christ's exaltation, referred to in *Paradise Lost* 5.602–15 and described by William Hunter in *Bright Essence*, as prefiguring his Resurrection, and thus that of all believers, via Christ's sacrifice, at the end of time.[83] More important for our purposes, Christ mediates for God when, according to Milton, he creates the visible universe. *Paradise Lost*'s various narrators provide further echoes and even more mediation. In *De doctrina*, Milton cites the coronationlike passages in Isaiah 45:23 and Philippians 2:9–11 — both sources of *Paradise Lost* 5.607–08 — as examples of Christ's roles as Creator, as the Word that emanates from God to create the universe and that is therefore an entity distinct from God.[84] In *De doctrina*'s chapter on the Creation, Milton makes his anti-Trinitarian point that the Father and Son are separate beings by arguing that God created the world "per" or via his Son, who is the "less principal cause."[85] He refuses interpretations of Isaiah 45:23 that insist on the Son's doing the creating. Instead, Milton argues, God does it, not the Son — or only the Son as representative of but not part of God. Milton confronts Trinitarian arguments that the Son is part of God by contesting their use of Isaiah 45:23, one of our self-oath passages, as a proof-text:

> Another argument [Trinitarians offer] is brought from Isa. xlv. 12, 23. "I have made the earth…unto me every knee shall bow." It is contended that this is spoken of Christ, on the authority of St. Paul, Rom. xiv. 10, 11. "we shall all stand before the judgment seat of Christ: for it is written, As I live, saith the Lord, every knee shall bow to me." But it is evident from the parallel passage Philipp. ii. 9–11. that this is said of God the Father, by whose gift the Son has received that judgment seat, and all judgment, "that at the name of Jesus every knee should bow…to the glory of God the Father"; or, which means the same thing, "every tongue shall confess to God."[86]

Milton's invocation of Isaiah's self-oath and the passages from Romans and Philippians encourage us to see *Paradise Lost*'s exaltation scene as an instance of creation by speech-act, a moment that looks forward and backward to the epic's other acts of creation. A speech-act, the Father's "decree" (*PL* 5.602), creates the Son as king. It also informs the assembled angels that the Son was the Word by which God created them, and by which he will create humans and their universe, as well as the hell necessary to punish the soon-to-be rebel angels, and, eventually, unregenerate humans. Hence, it also creates obedience and disobedience in God's creatures, if indirectly. Following the lead of Isaiah 45:23, Milton's God turns the event into a creation of loyalty and obedience in an imagined answering speech-act. *Paradise Lost* 5.607–08 sharpens this notion of an answering act of loyalty, but turns it into primarily a non-speech-act, a corporal gesture. Only the knees will bow and confess Christ Lord: "by myself have sworn to him shall bow / All knees in heaven, and shall confess him Lord." In a moment comparable to God's "den[ying]" "language of man…To beasts, whom God on their creation-day / Created mute to all articulate sound" (*PL* 9.553–57), God virtually removes all opportunity for a verbal response; instead, that response will be physical. Only God performs the speech-act in this coronation ceremony.

By having God in this moment create bodily obedience and basically silence all voices, Milton once again raises the whole issue of who's speaking, and for whom. In *De doctrina*'s chapter on the Son of God, Milton returns to Genesis 22:16, the scene of God's first self-oath sealing the Abrahamic covenant. There he confronts both this issue and the anti-Trinitarian view that the Son is not God, in spite of the fact that some Scriptures refer to angels (and, by extension, Christ, as another representative of God) by his name:

> The name of God seems [at times] to be attributed to angels, because as heavenly messengers they bear the appearance of the divine glory and person, and even speak in the very words of the Deity. *Gen. xxi. 17, 18. xxii. 11, 12, 15, 16. "by myself have I sworn, saith Jehovah."* For the expression so frequently in the mouth of the prophets, and which is elsewhere often omitted, is here inserted, for the purpose of showing that angels and messengers do not declare their own words, but the commands of God who sends them, even though the speaker seem[s] to bear the name and character of the Deity himself.[87]

Genesis 22:16 is thus one of several passages where "God said" really means "a representative of God said."[88] In another place, Milton amplifies the argument by making it a matter not just of words but also of promises: "the name of Jehovah [sometimes] signifies two things, either the nature of God, or the completion of his words and promises."[89] This returns us to the issues of who is speaking in *Paradise Lost* 5.607–08 and who is an agent. For once, God seems to speak for himself—and yet he doesn't: he really speaks for the Son in the exaltation scene. *De doctrina*'s caution that sometimes the phrase "God speaks" means "an agent of God speaks" allows us to see the flicker of Trinitarianism that the exaltation scene creates — a flicker quickly extinguished, but from Milton's point of view troubling all the same.[90] At a moment when an apparent transfer of power from Father to Son has taken place or is taking place, the urgent question arises of who's in charge.

The passage's notoriously slippery temporal markers ("This day," "I have begot," "I declare," "I have anointed," "I appoint," "I have sworn") simply underscore the problem of agency and mediation. When exactly did God do these things, or is he doing them as he speaks? And do the problems arise only because we hear his speech as mediated by Raphael for Adam and Eve, and thus by Milton for us? Did God in fact say something different? The tense of "I...by myself have sworn" has a hitherto unnoticed origin that solves one problem while creating others. The "I have sworn" of Milton's God does several things: (1) it honors the fact that in the Torah God is more frequently reported by an underling as *having sworn* in the past than as actually appearing to swear for himself in the present; (2) it constitutes a deliberate archaism, mimicking biblical Hebrew's propensity to use a past-tense verb, usually the perfect ("I have sworn"), to indicate actual swearing in the present; (3) it hints at the problem of pinning down origins, such as exactly when in the Torah God swears a covenant about land and a chosen status for the Jews; and, most important, (4) it creates a problem for Milton's English readers, who emphatically did and do *not* swear ceremonial oaths in the past tense.

First, we can conclude our discussion of *De doctrina*'s treatment of God's indirect speech by noting that in the Torah he is always reported by someone else as swearing; it is always some version of "the Lord swore" or "'I have sworn,' saith the Lord." And in this indirect, quoted discourse, God sometimes does refer to his own swearing, but still in the past tense.[91] Second and more important, ancient Hebrew had what might be called a promissory perfect tense. For whatever reason, the way one swore official oaths at official oath ceremonies was to depart from the normal present tense and speak the past tense: literally, "I *swore* to do X" or "I *have sworn* to do X," but understood as "I *hereby swear* to do X" and thus as a present-tense performative speech-act with binding force.[92] In effect, the perfect tense marks the utterance as a powerful performative that binds the swearer, making her accountable for nonperformance.[93] Hence, the form biblical speakers, human or divine, used to swear an oath in their own voice is always *nishbati* ("I have sworn") — in actuality meaning "I have *been* sworn."[94] For example, God's oath to Abraham in Genesis 22:16–17, as reported to him by the angel in the previous verse, is "By myself I have sworn, saith the Lord" (*b-i nishbati, nam Ieue*); and this is how everyone else swears for themselves in the Torah.[95] There are, as far as I can tell, no instances of the verb *shaba* (to swear) in the literal present tense, first-person active indicative. Hence, what the Authorized Version and most other translations, including the Septuagint and Vulgate, render as "I have sworn" may equally well be translated as "I swear." The angel may thus be saying to Abraham in Genesis 22:16, "The Lord says, *I swear* by myself that...."

Therefore, the perfect tense in *Paradise Lost*'s "I...by myself have sworn" plays the dual role of adhering to Hebrew practice in a Hebraic situation of oath swearing — a studied archaism not all that different from the poem's epic Latinisms and Hellenisms — and of hinting at God's complete otherness with respect to time, when compared with humans: his oaths are simultaneously past and present, if not future. This is all well and good, especially for readers with a good knowledge of Hebrew. But the rest of us have little choice but to assume that "I...have sworn" straightforwardly indicates an action in the past — at the very least an action that *began* in the past. And if God indeed swore the oath in the past, why didn't he do so in front of witnesses, and why does he only tell the angels now? Moreover, why does he swear an oath for other people, who will do the bowing and scraping he mentions? These problems create confusion and encourage us to ask whether we are actually reading God's original words, or even a halfway decent translation or approximation of them, especially of the sequence of events implied by the different tenses: past, present, and future. Milton does this to place us in the same position as the angels listening to God's announcement in book 5, especially Satan: that of being overwhelmed by the dizzying alternatives. And it muddies the whole question of what exactly God says in this pivotal speech. For us the tense of God's oath compounds our sense of distance from him, a distance created not just by ontology (God and humans are different orders of being) but by transmission as well.

God's self-oath thus crystallizes the many problems of mediation created by his speaking to us through (a series of) his creatures. What things and, crucially, what *sequence* of things, made it through undistorted? But if, according to Milton, the word "God" in various Scriptures can denote angels speaking for God, the passage in book 5 also raises the opposite question: for whom is *God* speaking here? Why should he speak for the angels, whom he requires to "speak" through their bodily gestures of submission to the Son, comparable to Adam and Eve's showing obedience by abstaining from the bodily act of eating the fruit? Or for that matter, should God speak for the Son himself, who, like a king in an earthly coronation ceremony, should do the swearing on his own?

Republican Unease over the Son's Coronation

To help answer such questions, let us consider how the coronation ceremony in *Paradise Lost*, book 5, responds both to the intertexts of God's self-oath and to the contractualist evolution of the English coronation oath's form and placement. One thing would have stood out for Milton: the coronation of the Son is everything but a mutual contract. Succession beats out election as the animating principle, and Milton intends this absolutism to be seen as a problem. Without subscribing to the neo-Romantic argument that Satan is hero and God villain, I only contend that God's oath and speech are designed to raise a question like the one Satan asks later in book 5: has God "by decree... to himself engrossed / All power, and us eclipsed under the name / Of king anointed" (774–77)? There are in a sense two main questions here. Has God monopolized all roles in the coronation? And if so, what are we to think of it?

The exaltation of the Son could be seen as either a reformed rite or a maimed rite. If reformed, it constitutes an attempt to imitate the installations of the 1650s by chucking out all the usual mummery and ceremony: the actual crowning, the oblations, the communion service, the Trinitarian hymns, the processions, most of the regalia, the proliferation of state apparatchiks performing menial duties with menial objects — possibly even the anointing (which God announces rather than displays).[96] By privileging the verbal over the visual and material, Milton strips away much of the ritual dimension of the ritual. Perhaps, he suggests, earthly transfers of executive power should be as sober and barebones as this, little more than the swearings-in of the Protectors. Preferably the leader will be not a monarch but an elected leader, sworn in.

However, it is much easier to see a rite maimed by its absolutism, even as it re-presents a maimed version of the English coronation. It thus offers no pattern for earthly ritual. How exactly is the Son's coronation so despotically monarchical, despite its excisions? First, it hardly counts as a participatory ceremony at all, more as an announcement or "decree" of a fait accompli: the *earlier* exaltation and anointment of the Son, which may be two actions or two descriptions of the same action (*PL* 5.602, 605). Within this announcement lies the only classic speech-act in the present tense, the performative "your head I him appoint," which, in any case, seems merely to describe the previous closed-door activity (606). Hence, the oath, which usually preceded the anointing in the earthly rite, now trails it as an afterthought in a ceremony that seems an afterthought. Nor is it sworn in English's present tense, but rather announced in the problematic past tense as what appears to be another fait accompli, presumably one that happened after the exalting and anointing and before God's present announcement: "This day I have begot…have anointed…have sworn" (603–07). It is neither a sine qua non for the exalting or anointing to take place, nor part of a set of reciprocal oaths. Second, it conspicuously recalls Cromwell's speech to Parliament in September 1654, in which he recalled his first installation, promised that "I do not bear witness to myself," and then required members of Parliament to swear an oath of obedience to him.[97] Oaths were understood to be acts of calling on God as witness, and Milton's God *does* bear witness to himself ("by myself have sworn"), even as he requires obedience from the angels.

Third, the self-oath replaces dialogue with monologue, God depriving almost everyone of a voice.[98] God plays the roles of all officiants in the English coronation ritual, including the archbishop who anoints and crowns the king; he even steals the role of king himself in swearing the oath for the Son, ostensibly the one proclaimed king.[99] The interactive call-and-response format, in which the archbishop asked the monarch to swear the oath item by item, has gone missing. Moreover, whereas the coronation oath usually applied, like most oaths, only to its swearer, spelling out a commitment on the monarch's part about his or her own future behavior, God's oath commits himself and the Son to almost nothing, amounting to little more than a command that *others* do something. There is no pretense of reciprocity, contract, popular election. Into a single speech he collapses the coronation oath, the oaths of fealty, and the archbishop's call for the people's acclamation, putting the latter in the wrong place: after the oath.

The audience of angels presumably remains silent as God intones the decree, and his oath is worded in such a way as to command them to bow: "to him shall bow / All knees in heaven, and shall confess him Lord" (*PL* 5.607–08); there is no indication that they disobey. Despite Stevie Davies's characterization of these actions as an oath of allegiance or obedience, the angels make no verbal oath at all.[100] Moreover, God's oath departs in a crucial way from its immediate sources. Isaiah 45:23 reads, "By myself I have sworn, from my mouth has gone forth in righteousness a word that shall not return: '*To me* every knee shall bow, every tongue shall swear.'"[101] Philippians 2:9–11 says of Christ, "God also hath highly exalted him, and given him the name which is above every name: That at the name of *Jesus* every knee should bow, of things in heaven, and things on earth, and things under the earth; and that every tongue should confess that Jesus Christ is Lord." Romans 14:11 proclaims, "For it is written, *As I live*, saith the Lord, every knee shall bow *to me*, and every tongue shall confess to God." Where are the tongues in Milton's oath? "By myself [I] have sworn to him shall bow / All knees in heaven, and shall confess him Lord" (*PL* 5.607–08): in *Paradise Lost* only the knees do the confessing, as emphasized by Satan's and Abdiel's later remarks about "knee tribute" rather than "tongue tribute" (5.782, 817). The assembled angels have no chance before the ceremony ends to consent verbally, and if their consent or acclamation appears in the bodily form of bowed knees, it departs from the English coronation ritual in coming conspicuously *after* God's oath, as do their later dancing and singing of unspecified hymns. Absent is the genuine verbal reciprocity of mutual oaths.[102]

I am not making an Empsonian argument that Milton encourages readers to reject God as tyrant and side with a victimized Satan — only a Norbrookian one that this passage provokes in readers a temporary republican dismay over a noncontractualist, nonrepublican ceremony in which

God hogs all the roles. Even by the standards of the English monarchy, this truncated coronation and coronation oath conspicuously lack reciprocity and consent.[103] That dismay dissipates when readers recall that God and the Son *deserve* their offices because of their merit, their obvious superiority to all other candidates for them, as books 3 and 6 make especially clear in the Son's case (*PL* 3.236–38, 290; 6.806–92, esp. 814–22, 853, 887–88). But it lingers when applied to earthly candidates for rule, who do not so clearly excel all others in the capacity to rule well and thus should be elected by some form of popular consent rather than succeed to supreme power by mere accident of birth. And this is what the open-ended dismay the episode should create in republican and other readers is designed to do. The troubling aspects of the episode sharpen rather than blunt the edge of Milton's earthly republicanism, which some historians of political thought have tried to downplay by ignoring the antimonarchical force of texts such as *The Tenure of Kings and Magistrates* and *The Readie and Easie Way to a Free Commonwealth* while playing up Milton's grudging concession in the *First* and *Second Defences* (themselves clear arguments against kingship) that the occasional king can rule well and in the best interests of the people.[104]

In England, Milton wishes an elected/selected grand council to rule "to perpetuitie," as *The Readie and Easie Way* puts it, until the Second Coming of Christ, the only man who really deserves to be king: "our true and rightfull and only to be expected King, only worthie as he is our only Saviour, the Messiah, the Christ, the only heir of his eternal father, the only by him anointed and ordain."[105] Written at roughly the same time as *The Readie and Easie Way*, *Paradise Lost*'s account of God's troubling coronation oath "by himself," as well as its depiction of Adam and Eve essentially breaking an oath of allegiance to God by eating the fruit, are part and parcel of his opposition to coronations and the oaths of office and allegiance required by the Restoration church-state in the Clarendon Code. In making this moment the primal plot driver of the epic's narrative and argument, Milton points his readers forward in history toward the only moment at which the human knee should bend to monarchy, undoing present tyrannies by imagining, outside the sphere of human politics, the only authority worthy of submission. William Blake had it right when he depicted *his* Milton as rising up "from the heavens of Albion ardorous," taking off "the robe of the promise," and ungirding himself "from the oath of God."[106]

CHAPTER 2

—➤✦⬅—

Naked Writhing Flesh:

Rhetorical Authority, Theatrical Recursion, and Milton's Poetics of the Viewed Body

BRENDAN PRAWDZIK

"Clothes make the man. Naked people have little or no influence on society."
— *Mark Twain*

Rhetoric has typically been seen as the art of using language to produce a desired effect in an audience. This sense suggests an essential dislocation between orator and auditor, author and reader, and privileges words as the medium of disembodied truth over the body as language's situated vehicle. Aristotle's definition of rhetoric as the power of determining what is persuasive in any given situation of course suggests more of a negotiation. Even Plato's Socrates, who in *Phaedrus* champions the intellectual rarefaction of dialectic over the performed truth of rhetoric, develops the sensuous metaphor of the chariot soul precisely to win his young auditor toward truth. The dialogue frames this persuasion in terms of sexual seduction as it employs carnal rhetoric to define philosophy's true goal as the mind's transcendence of the body through discourse, aesthetic contemplation, and the aggressive curbing of sense and desire. Socrates knows that so long as he aims to persuade this young philologist, he cannot escape rhetoric: the co-constitutive, fleshy, erotically charged negotiation of a truth through embodied, socially situated language.[1]

Suggesting an antipathy to the body internal to rhetoric and its training, Milton scholars have often presupposed a Cartesian structure of authority in tension with the animist materialism of Milton's late poetry.[2] The logic of the cogito, which posits a consciousness preceding materiality as definitive of Being, led René Descartes in *Les passions de l'âme* (1649) to systematize a rational faculty able with relative ease to master passions. Stanley Fish's model of authority essentially reconstructs the architecture of the Cartesian subject: for Milton, "the only arena in which a free agent can act effectively...is the internal arena of the will."[3] The poet within the arena enforces doctrine upon readers outside its walls, while the world and its delusions must not gain entry. I will counter that the representation of bending bodies in Milton demonstrates that the "internal arena of the will" opens to the social arena of theater, and that in *Paradise Lost* it is precisely the denial of bilateral connectivity in the actor-spectator, orator-auditor, author-reader relationship that distinguishes Satan's authority from that of the poet he so resembles.

Truth's corporeality and alliance with the passions, a focus that provides the core theme of *Areopagitica*, merges with Milton's interest in drama as an ethical vehicle. This convergence develops by 1667 into a theatrical poetics in which negotiations between self and society play out through viewed bodies as the poet seeks to locate a material agency neither based on the logic of the Cartesian cogito nor accepting of the ethics-annihilating materialism of Thomas Hobbes. As opposed to "drama" and "dramatic," I choose "theatricality" and "theatrical" in part to free the representation of human action from the generic category of drama, thus enabling insight into how the social energies of drama play out meaningfully in the poetry and prose. Theatricality also taps into the architecture, properties, modes of acting, and spectatorship of theater as a cultural institution. As a means of representing not only virtuous action and spiritual expression, but also inauthenticity and indecorousness, theatricality offers vivid linguistic resources for cultural critique and intervention.

Milton's stages, whether material platforms in actual theaters or centers of ethical agency framed by encompassing eyes in the world at large, are sites of negotiated nakedness where the body, *clothed in gesture*, strains to mediate its difference from other bodies intertwined in the field of vision. Scholarship linking Milton to drama and theater has tended to swerve around the body. On the one hand, drama appears as a mode of literary production for the literary author. Considered as a dramatist, Milton belongs alongside other *authors* of drama, such as Thomas Randolph, Ben Jonson, and especially Shakespeare.[4] Drama, the scholarship implies, is an arrow in the poet's quiver of genres. As literature, it helps to monumentalize the author while allowing him to escape theater's transformative interactivity and flux. Timothy J. Burbery's *Milton the Dramatist* (2007) directly pursues the revision proclaimed in its title, but does so without accounting for the political and religious contexts that evolved in tandem with theater; for Milton's repeated use of theater forms to pursue ethical, political, and religious critique according to seemingly antitheatrical values; or for the rich evidence of theatricality (as opposed to dramatic intent) in *Paradise Lost*.[5]

The scholarship on Milton and the theater has often considered drama to be a rhetorical mode for Milton, one that suggests a didactic relationship between an elite, intellectual author and a faceless public in need of instruction. Barbara Lewalski's *"Paradise Lost" and the Rhetoric of Literary Forms*, for example, considers drama as part of a generic toolkit enabling the poet to reach and to shape a reading audience.[6] Thus, "drama" has tended to circle us back to Milton the Cartesian subject despite the social dynamism that, for historians and literary scholars, characterizes the early modern stage that helped to inform Milton's view of embodied rhetoric.[7] Theatricality is not about how Milton *uses* drama but about how both the author and his literary representations are caught up in theater's social energies.

Milton repeatedly looks to the theater as a vehicle for exploring emotion as a function of bodies in the visual field. Theater's critics regularly insisted that staged drama works through the senses to rouse passions and inspire debased action. In the words of Stephen Gosson, "these outward spectacles effeminate and soften the hearts of men; vice is learned with beholding, sense is tickled, desire pricked."[8] Vicious passions embodied on stage conduct through the eyes into the heart, softening its fortitude, enflaming desire, and prompting spectators, in the words of Philip Stubbes, to return to "their secret conclaves" and "play the sodomites, or worse."[9] In terms of the effect of staged drama on spectators, Milton's sketches for biblical and British historical tragedies in the Trinity manuscript, his response to Tertullian and

Lactantius in the Commonplace Book, and his proposal for state-sponsored literary performances in *Reason of Church-Government* show more sympathy with the likes of Philip Sidney and Thomas Heywood, who defend the stage in principle as a vehicle of moral education.[10] Where Sidney tends to intellectualize drama's didactic power, however, Milton repeatedly grounds it in the body's senses and passions. Thus, he shares the antitheatricalists' emphasis on sense and emotion but credits playgoers properly to apprehend the exempla presented by a play and thereby to shun vice and emulate virtue. He also builds on a model of counterinfluence derived less from debates about the stage than from rhetorical manuals and the literature of religious controversy. Here, the gesture of the socially encompassed rhetor responds to a counterinfluence flowing into the heart and stimulating the passions. Whether actor, orator, priest, prophet, or worshipper, the rhetor bends his body in accordance with the demands and constraints of an ever-evolving rhetorical situation.

The Hercules Gallicus ("Anglicus") in the frontispiece of the 1699 second edition of Marius D'Assigny's *The Art of Memory* (fig. 1) depicts the standard model of rhetorical authority, which sees the rhetor as moving and shaping the audience as from a separate ontological plane.[11] Chains issuing from the tongue of Hercules link to the heads of his hearers. The slackening of the chains implies a taming by rhetorical force that compensates for the aged hero's diminished strength.[12] His emphatically gesturing right hand appears to reach toward the spear of Minerva; thus, the image works to transcend the embodiment of rhetorical authority by defining the connectivity of the chains as a unilateral relationship of power grounded not in physical strength but in wisdom. Another icon of rhetorical authority (fig. 2), from the frontispiece of John Bulwer's 1644 *Chironomia*, the second of two volumes on the rhetorical use of hand and finger gestures, appears similarly to show the Roman orator Hortensius declaiming from a pedestal to a throng below. Visible lines of influence link his gesturing hands to the heads of his hearers. In part because Hortensius stands on a pedestal alone above the blurred throng, we readily assume that like Hercules he exerts unilateral authority over audience passions and behavior. But his hearers are not tame; they are visibly roused. Once we question whether these lines of influence may also work in the other direction, we find no way to extricate the

Fig. 1. Anonymous, frontispiece of Marius D'Assigny's *The Art of Memory* (1699).
Used by permission of the William Andrews Clark Memorial Library, University of
California, Los Angeles.

Fig. 2. William Marshall, frontispiece (detail) of John Bulwer's *Chironomia; or, The Art of Manuall Rhetoricke* (1644). Used by permission of the William Andrews Clark Memorial Library, University of California, Los Angeles.

orator's authority from the roused bodies that now seem to pull on his hands. As Bulwer notes, Hortensius's expressive gesture was both a strength and a liability, earning him a reputation as an effeminate populist. "Otherwise a man excellent," he "was taxed with this genuine or contracted affectation of the *Hand*...and called Stage-player."[13]

Mid-seventeenth-century religious polemic abundantly deploys theatrical rhetoric to expose the indecorum and to undermine the authenticity of preachers, polemicists, and worshippers. The "gestures" of indecorous preaching or worship were understood as a privileging of the seen body over the devoutly expressive soul. For instance, Richard Bernard, in his sacred rhetorical manual *The Faithfull Shepherd* (1607), bemoans the "thrasonicall" gesturing of preachers who, "by acting [as though] upon a stage, cannot but shew their vaine and phantasticall motions ridiculously in a pulpit, which they have used in prophane pastimes." William Prynne's notorious antitheatricality appears in his critique of Anglican worship. He decries "the Gesture of rising and standing up during any part of Divine Service" and deems such gestures "fitter for the Stage than the Church or Gospel, and to provoke laughter than Devotion." The antitheatrical tenor of religious polemic and satire reached a peak in attacks on enthusiasts, such as the Ranters and early Quakers. For instance, George Emmot declares that within his *Northern Blast* "are shewed the manner of [Quaker] Meetings... their Quaking, Shreekings, and ridiculous actions." Playlets like Samuel Sheppard's anti-Ranter *Joviall Crew* (1651) and tracts, such as Richard Blome's 1668 *Fanatick History*, advertising "antick" gestures on their title pages — "Mad mimick Pranks... and ridiculous actions and gestures" — make clear that what emerged in the 1640s as lancing critique had become a means not only of undermining spiritual authenticity but also of entertaining.[14] The language of the "ridiculous" further delegitimated gestural worship by framing it as characteristic of physical comedy.

Milton was drawn to theater's interplay of influence and counterinfluence because it offered ways to explore the challenges of materially and socially situated agency and authority. Specifically, the theater offered a social microcosm where sinews of identification — connective threads of vision and passion — would entangle and, disentangling, leave participants altered. This corporealization of the visual field approaches what Maurice Merleau-Ponty, in *Le visible et l'invisible* (1964), would describe as "the coiling over [*l'enroulement*] of the visible upon the seeing body, of the tangible upon the touching body." Theater figures with optimal economy how vision and authority emerge from *within* the field of what is visible, "as though it were... in a preestablished harmony" with a visible context of seeing flesh.[15]

The use of antitheatrical rhetoric to underscore the fetishizing of the external or visible to the neglect of ethos and spirit thoroughly informs Milton's representation of Satan in *Paradise Lost*. Milton repeatedly complicates satanic authority by suggesting through the represented body a counterinfluence of passion flowing in from fleshy fields of the visible.[16] For instance, as Satan first rises from the fiery lake he is described as throwing "round... his baleful eyes / That witness'd huge affliction and dismay / Mixt with obdurate pride and stedfast hate." "Witness" seems to be what the eyes are *doing*, that is, ranging over the terrain of bodies below. Yet the enjambment of 57–58 ("dismay / Mixt"), which reveals "affliction and dismay" to be "mixt" with "pride" and "hate," suggests, rather, that "witness" should be glossed as "show."[17] Thus, as Satan presents a commanding form of "obdurate pride and stedfast hate" and expresses authority through a gaze sweeping over miserable anonymous bodies, his eyes, conduits of passion and windows to the soul, betray to onlookers profound loss and faintness of heart that place him emotionally on par with his "followers" (*PL* 1.56–58, 606). The form of his face cannot be extricated from the eyes of the spectators for whom it was rhetorically produced. Nor can it fully dissemble Satan's own loss and fear.

From the dialectic of influence and counterinfluence emerges a form of authority built on loss and constantly menaced by threat of exposure. Milton repeatedly sounds audience response as hissing or as "exploding" to manifest this menace that works upon the form of authority. From *explaudere*, "to explode" means to clap, to stamp, or to heckle an actor in scorn from the stage.[18] It also suggests the modern sense of "to burst forth upon," a menacing version of what Merleau-Ponty calls a "dehiscence of Being" to describe the bursting out of phenomena upon vision, the flesh of the visible upon the flesh of the seeing.[19] In the book 7 invocation, a "barbarous dissonance" explodes upon the Orphic bard in this way, threatening dismemberment. When Satan debates Abdiel, a reluctant applause reveals the fragility of his power: "as the sound of waters deep / Hoarce murmur echo'd to his words applause / Through the infinite Host" (*PL* 7.30–39, 5.872–74). The applauding body churns like an ocean under lunar influence, "waters deep" coaxed from the pull of Abdiel's zeal-imped reason toward the emotive appeal of Satan's illogic.[20] It moves by its own inertia, gaining momentum as though by hearing itself. "Murmur" recalls the discontented Israelites under Moses and Aaron in Exodus 14, registering audibly a tenuous authority that, in Satan's case, must constantly shift to meet a middle ground of desire.

———— ✳ ————

The gestures of the body work at once to mediate and to maintain the distance between the bodies of the actor and of the audience that ever threatens to collapse upon him. As that threat persists in the field of vision, clothing, like gesture, works like a protective second skin. It mitigates a hostile gaze felt to issue from a social body, a panoptic God, or the conscience or superego. Fallen Adam uses fig leaves "to hide / The Parts of each [from] other, that seem most / To shame obnoxious, and unseemliest seen" (*PL* 9.1092–94). Yet in attenuating this "guiltie shame" by veiling the naked body, this second flesh works also to expose what it veils: "hee cover'd, but his Robe / Uncover'd more" (1058–59). The antiprelatical tracts assail the "troublesome disguises" of "Church-maskers" who "cover and hide" the "righteous verity" of a "naked" Gospel "with the polluted cloathing of…ceremonies" (YP 1:828). Anti-Episcopal readers appear as spectators menacing exposed prelatical bodies: "O what a death it is to the Prelates to be thus unvisarded, thus uncas'd, to have the Periwigs pluk't off that cover your baldnesse, your inside nakednesse thrown open to publick view" (YP 1:668).

This view of authority as menaced by "opposite spectators" (*Animadversions*, YP 1:726)[21] anticipates aspects of Jacques Lacan's gaze theory. Where Merleau-Ponty posits all phenomena as bound by the connective tissue of a reflexive optics, Lacan theorizes a sadism implicit in the gaze. The subject gazing on the object is menaced from the periphery by a generalized gaze inhabiting the field of the Other. This menace bespeaks the subject's limited control over a social and material context that, encompassing him, belies the illusion of a stable, independent self. This sense of menace lends urgency to the objectifying gaze and intensifies its need to express a relation of dominance.[22]

Much of Lacan's theory is predicated on a simple geometrical tension between center and circumference: the gaze of a centered body focusing on a focal point in the circumference is menaced by an answering gaze spilling in from the periphery. Milton regularly places authority figures at the center of environing spectators. The "opposite spectators" menacing Hall constitute "the inevitable net of God, that now," Milton jeers, "begins to inviron you round" (YP 1:726). Samson tears down a Philistine temple turned "spacious Theatre" that, "half round," is completed as circle by the gazing "throng" placed behind him: "The other side was op'n," the Messenger tells us, "where the throng / On banks and scaffolds under Skie might stand" (*Sam.*, 1605–10).

Whereas Descartes's tracts on optics and the passions develop a model of instrumental rationality by which the agent can directly encounter menaces and overcome them, the geometrical tension between centered agent and environing spectators significantly constrains the agency of the Cartesian subject. This constraint owes to the fact that Descartes's understanding of agency is premised upon the assumed structure of the eye as a focusing lens. But once we acknowledge the blurred presence of a periphery, the hard round of the lens becomes pervious. The agent becomes menaced by the periphery since the activity of instrumental reason can only confront one stimulus of passion at a time and cannot adequately deal with the stimuli accosting from all sides. Consider how Descartes depicts the soul's response to fear. First, a phenomenon must stimulate a passion understood *as fear*. The will cannot directly quell bad passions but can "indirectly by the representation of things which have been customarily joined with the passions we will to have, and which are contrary to those we will to reject."[23] The mind must, as it were, take a snapshot of the passion and, viewing it, determine the fittest response. Experiencing fear when to flee is deemed cowardly, the mind recalls an image of valor. This internal mimesis inspires a passion of boldness that flows from the pineal gland through channels where the inflowing passion is met and conquered. Valorous action is willed and performed.[24] In addition to producing emotions through internal mimesis, the soul can employ rational deliberation, a staging of internal debate: "to excite boldness in oneself and displace fear . . . one must apply oneself to consider the reasons, objects, or precedents that convince one that the peril is not great, that there is always more security in defense than in flight, that one will have glory and joy from having vanquished, whereas one can expect only regret and shame from having fled."[25] For either response to work, the passion must be clearly demarcated, slow, and single. Both require conditions simple enough for reason or imagination to rouse countering passions as quickly as the moving body confronts them. Only by assuming a sparse reality conforming to experimental conditions and by denying the complexity, multiplicity, and ambiguity of the passions can Descartes assert so confidently that "there is no soul so weak that it cannot be well guided to acquire an absolute power over its passions."[26]

In his representation of Satan, Milton succinctly dismantles Descartes's account of instrumental reason's "easy" and "absolute" power over the passions. Toward the close of book 3, Satan demonstrates a skill of theatrical self-presentation expert enough to deceive Uriel, "though Regent of the Sun, and held / The sharpest sighted Spirit of all in Heav'n" (*PL* 3.690–91). Satan first sees the form of Uriel "within kenn" among "all Sun-Shine," which "sharp'nd his visual ray / To objects distant farr" (622, 616, 620–21). Satan also has the advantage of approaching Uriel while the archangel's "back was turn'd but not his brightness hid" (624). Satan thus has time to "change his proper shape" (634) into a guise that he expects will best suit his purposes. He appears in what Milton's description suggests is masque attire: "Under a coronet," wearing "wings / Of many a colour'd plume sprinkl'd with Gold," "his habit fit for speed succinct," and carrying before him a "silver wand" (640–44). Although the disguise succeeds in gaining Uriel's trust, we are nonetheless witnessing satanic theatricality at its utmost advantage. Uriel's exceptional perspicuity, caught "fixt in cogitation deep" (629), reveals him at this moment to be blinder than the reader, who foreknowing can easily see the artificiality of the disguise and the fraudulence it conceals. So far, we remain within the Cartesian paradigm, wherein the eye can see, can focus, and, through instrumental, can reason rouse the appropriate response to conquer the menace — only here Satan's motive is not to exercise courage so as to conquer fear, but to disguise and play-act so as to deceive an angel of God.

Milton quickly demonstrates the vulnerability of Satan's theatricality to shifting contexts, oblique perspectives, and the depth and complexity of the passions when he shows Satan slacken bodily while soliloquizing on Mt. Niphates at the start of book 4. Despite possessing a "prospect" (argument to book 4) unto Eden expressing a relationship of command, he remains vulnerable from other perspectives, including that from which "Uriel once warned" now views a bodily form mastered by passions from within. Satan reveals through countenance and gesture an affective excess that belies the grace-infused form that he was able to manage when confronting Uriel directly. Now the sharp-sighted archangel

> Saw him disfigur'd, more then could befall
> Spirit of happie sort: his gestures fierce
> He markd and mad demeanour, then alone,
> As he suppos'd, all unobserv'd, unseen.   (*PL* 4.125–30)

Here "gestures fierce" ("furious gestures" [argument to book 4]) or sharp movements of the body suggest affective intensity exceeding now neglected formal control. The defining mark of such theatrical hypocrisy is the effect of "disfigur[ement]," the disharmonious mixing of bodily signifiers caused by dynamic, multifaceted passions expressing *through* the simpler form managed rhetorically to show a specific state of being to a single spectator.

Particularly revealing is Satan's face, which instead of resembling one of the distinct passions catalogued by Descartes passes through a range:

> Each passion dimm'd his face
> Thrice chang'd with pale, ire, envie and despair,
> Which marrd his borrow'd visage, and betraid
> Him counterfet, if any eye beheld.   (*PL* 4.114–17)

Passions of "ire, envie and despair," easy enough to distinguish conceptually, manifest subtly as mere shades of a single color, "pale."[27] This disparity reveals inauthenticity or hypocrisy to beholding eyes (especially those "unobserv'd, unseen"). Likewise, Adam easily divines the hypocrisy of Eve's first fallen speech, which Milton depicts as inept theater. Eve fashions her countenance so as preemptively to excuse her sin: "in her face excuse / Came Prologue, and Apologie to prompt." Milton thus depicts in Eve's face a veritable theater of exculpation that begins like any number of early modern plays: the Prologue enters and works to win over the audience by excusing elements of the play that may be distasteful to some and by emphasizing what other virtues are to be expected. Adam instantly reads the embodied contradiction of "distemper flushing" that "glow[s]" in the "Cheek" of a "Countnance blithe" as clear evidence of fallenness (*PL* 9.853–55, 886–87).

Theatricality in Milton is not confined to hypocrisy but extends to his own authorial self-representation. Figures of theatricality appear as early as the 1628 "Vacation Exercise," a multigenre, bilingual speech and ceremony that Milton performed before his Cambridge peers.[28] In the surviving verse known as "At a Vacation Exercise in the College," the young Milton aspires to write a poetry by which "the deep transported mind may soare / Above the wheeling poles, and at Heav'ns dore / Look in" (33–35). The verse, a performance of poetic flight, seems to register the pull of environing spectators on the poetic will, as the wings of the soaring bard become those of a falcon controlled by a falconer audience:

> But fie my wandring Muse how dost thou stray!
> Expectance calls thee now another way,
> Thou know'st it must be now thy only bent
> To keep in compass of thy Predicament.   (53–56)

Custom and audience desire ("expectance") determine his "bent," his flight, his inclination and will, to remain within the "compass," that is, the boundary of decorum figured as a perfect circle. Specifically, the "Predicament" at hand is to stage a dramatic farce distinguished by its clever governing conceit or *inventio*. Preparing to introduce his theme — his underclassmen will play Aristotle's predicaments or accidents of substance, he Ens or Absolute Being, their father — he imagines the *inventio*, that aspect of classical rhetoric most readily associated with the poet's genius, as a naked body requiring rhetorical clothing: "I have some naked thoughts that rove about / And loudly knock to have their passage out," he explains to his mother tongue, "And wearie of their place do only stay / Till thou hast deck't them in thy best aray" (23–26). By describing the invention as "naked thoughts" he emphasizes its outer flesh; the thought of exposure *gives it body*. These "naked thoughts" require the garments of language not merely to become visible but also to be protected from visibility. He requests English's "best aray" so that they "may without suspect or fears / Fly swiftly to this fair Assembly's ears" (27–28).

For Milton, too, the dialectic of influence informs a charged ambivalence (we might call it normative stage anxiety) toward readers often viewed as spectators. Throughout the "Exercise" he oscillates between the type of opposition apparent in the passage of English verse and a desire to tickle and placate, which is characteristic of the comedic actor. Both anxiety and the desire to please stem in part from the salting occasion, a raucous Oxbridge tradition with elements of hazing.[29] After delivering a delightfully obscene (and ostentatiously erudite) flatulence joke relying on Latinate puns, Milton first reveals what will be in his corpus a recurrent form of stage anxiety, the body of hissing snakes: "There must be absent from this assembly that dreadful, hellish sound of hissing. If it were to be heard here today, I would think that the Furies and Eumenides were hiding amongst you, letting loose their snakes and serpents into your hearts."[30] Hissing seems to signal a release of liquid emotion that travels across space, enters bodies, and transforms them into hissing snakes in turn.[31] The hiss generates a hydra.

The hiss works upon the staged body. Milton's depiction in the *Apology against a Pamphlet* of overacting Anglicans hissed off a Cambridge stage shows the body's bending to be a function of the spectator gaze: "In the Colleges so many of the young Divines...have bin seene so oft upon the Stage writhing and unboning their Clergie limmes to all the antick and dishonest gestures of Trinculo's, Buffons, and Bawds; prostituting the shame of that ministery...to the eyes of Courtiers and Court-Ladies, with their Groomes and *Madamoisellaes*" (YP 1:887). In describing the divines as wild gesturers who ape fools and vice figures, Milton pursues an ethical critique based on the bending of bodies. "Writhing," they twist and curl. "Unboning," they remove internal structure, becoming pliant to spectator desire. The divines give over flesh as though sexually to the eyes, "prostituting" their vocation "*to the eyes* of Courtiers and Court-Ladies." This mise-en-scène captures the crucial irony that the attempt to exalt oneself in the field of vision entails a forfeiture of body and authority. The fool, icon of vulgar posturing, embodies this paradox: "They thought themselves gallant men," writes Milton, "I thought them fools." We can see Milton intensely invested in the performance and caught up within the flesh of theater. He responds with hostility to the bad acting—in particular to the Anglicans' poor pronunciation and indecorous gesture—while impelled by the social energy, the sounds and movement, of a critical audience. His own hiss sounds what this abdication deserves: "they were out"—exploded—"and I hist" (*Apology*, YP 1:887–88).[32] Where the body's prostitution "to the eyes" bespeaks the implicit sexuality of the actor-spectator relationship, the hiss of the discerning manifests the latent violence that threatens to "explode" upon a desire exposed. The hiss exposes the writhing and boneless snake.

Like the actors whom Hamlet accuses of "mouth[ing]" lines, "saw[ing] the air too much with [their] hand[s]," and "tear[ing] a passion to tatters" "to split the ear of the groundlings," the Cambridge divines seeking to stand out and gain favor expose themselves as authored.[33] This paradox, by which the authority that would stand out as separate and self-made reveals itself to be controlled by fear and desire, is constitutive of Milton's Satan. During his debate with Abdiel, Satan's need to show himself as radically free and supremely potent, and to convince the rebel angels of their right, requires a myth of self-creation: they "know no time when we were not as now," were not "formd" by "secondarie hands" but "self-begot, self-rais'd / By our own quick'ning power" (*PL* 5.853–61).

Sprung full-formed from Satan's head, Sin herself embodies the ruse of autogenesis:

> All on a sudden miserable pain
> Surpris'd thee, dim thine eyes, and dizzie swumm
> In darkness, while thy head flames thick and fast
> Threw forth, till on the left side op'ning wide,
> Likest to thee in shape and count'nance bright,
> Then shining heav'nly fair, a Goddess arm'd
> Out of thy head I sprung: amazement seis'd
> All th' Host of Heav'n.   (2.752–59)

As a parody of *inventio* emerging full-formed in Satan's likeness, Sin is a product of the "mind" that "is its own place" (1.254), that denies its own situatedness. Yet as an involuntary birth that "surpris[es]" Satan with "miserable pain," leaving his eyes "dim" and dizzily swimming "in darkness," she seems produced less by than upon her parent, more brain tumor than authorial offspring. The syntax models the insentience of this act of generation. The momentary loss of control is experienced by the reader in the difficulty of "dizzie swumm," which can be read as a past participle that takes "thee" as its subject, but may also extend, as a past participial adjective, the appositive phrase "dim thine eyes" further to modify "eyes." In other words, the eyes have been "swumm"; they, "dizzie," are for a moment submersed in darkness. Regardless, we must suspend the essential logic of the syntax across the enjambment until "in darkness" completes it.

Even during this birth of Sin, dynamic corporeal form emerges from within a surrounding field of vision, "at th' Assembly...in sight / Of all the Seraphim" (2.749–50). Here the spectator context emphasizes that the birth is a consequence of Satan's narcissism, as though an involuntary and empty gesture, a movement that surprises the would-be author with his own textuality. After the rebellion's defeat, Sin's Satan-like body becomes not only serpentine — "end[ing] foul in many a scaly fould / Voluminous and vast, a Serpent arm'd / With mortal sting" — but also a ruptured form of involuntary reproduction subject to repeated incestuous rape that produces "yelling Monsters that with ceaseless cry / Surround me" (651–53, 795–96). The sudden springing forth of Sin from Satan's head elicits a response appropriate to the spectator's witnessing of monstrous spectacle: "amazement seis'd / All th' Host of Heav'n; back they recoild afraid / At first, and call'd me *Sin*" (758–60). Satan's surprise of "miserable pain" is answered by the sudden amazement of the surrounding host, an amazement described as a passion that seizes, rather than as a passion expressed by, the audience.[34] The momentary unconsciousness that coincides with Sin's birth is similarly manifested in the arbitrary naming, with no cause or explanation given, of "*Sin.*" The vanity of Satan's paradoxically generative narcissism manifests corporeally, both as a birth and in the passionate response to this birth; furthermore, the naming of Sin generates the echo of a corporeal nothingness. She will be the source of endless involuntary birth and the center of a recurring echo, "With terrors and with clamors compast round" (862).

Unacknowledged and undisciplined, the dialectic of influence and counterinfluence would organize into insentient mechanism, pulling actor and spectators into a closed-circuit loop, a rigid reflexivity of the debased and debased, authored and authored. Such theatrical recursion would yield a zero-level of authority, an entropic ethical state distributed evenly through the system; at the same time, the system's materiality would become uncontrollably dynamic, passing through stages of naked writhing flesh due to unacknowledged and unmanaged internal oscillations.[35] What is ultimately a divestiture of authority comes about precisely through a commitment to a model of absolute authority that denies the dynamic connectivity of passion, vision, and flesh. For Satan's relationship to the rebel throng Milton might have looked to the spectacle of Restoration monarchy and its enabling social climate of "zealous backsliders," of a "misguided and abus'd multitude" (*Readie and Easie Way*, YP 7:452, 463), of an "inconstant, irrational, and Image-doting rabble" (*Eikonoklastes*, YP 3:601), or to the drama and theater culture that modeled and justified Restoration ideology. We might recognize such entropic recursiveness in the successive emergence of hack politicians during any major campaign. Through the lack of critical engagement in the consumption of mass media, the public generates forms of authority in response to its desires; the forms as fragile as these desires are capricious, they are undermined or subsumed by the dialectic that produced them. Such remains the hope, at least.

Milton brings to life such a nightmarish organization of embodied authority during the scene of Satan's return and address to the infernal throng in book 10 of *Paradise Lost*. Before boasting his success in seducing the human beings, Satan first passes through hell "unmarkt, / In shew Plebeian Angel militant / Of lowest order": "invisible [he] / Ascended his high Throne"; "Down a while / He sate, and round about him saw unseen" (10.441–48). Prior to emerging into view, he "unseen" enjoys a "round about" gaze unmenaced (compare *PL* 4.137–45 and *PR* 2.284–97). He then seems to materialize ex nihilo as a "shape Starr bright" emerging "from a Cloud." It is a cheap theatrical illusion performed "with what permissive glory since his fall / Was left him, or false glitter."[36] The "throng" responds like a mass of groundlings: "All amaz'd," they "bent thir aspect, and whom they wish'd beheld" [(10.449–52, 452–54)]. Collapsing the desiring to see into the seeing of what is desired, "wish'd beheld" suggests that the throng collaborates in the field of vision to coproduce the debased theater of Satan's oratory and monarchy.

After euphorically recounting the seduction, Satan stands in his hearers' grip, "expecting" the "universal shout and high applause" (*PL* 10.505) earned by Abdiel when, "unmov'd, / Unshak'n, unseduc'd, unterrifi'd," he "st[oo]d approv'd in sight of God, though Worlds / Judg'd [him] perverse" (5.898–99, 6.36–37). The display of power counters real precariousness. Satan must declare the seduction an unequivocal triumph, hence his facile misreading of the Son's curse. As he waits hoping for unanimous applause, however, divine authority supervenes to transform the scene into an allegory of symbiotic ethical abdication:

> contrary he hears
> On all sides, from innumerable tongues
> A dismal universal hiss, the sound
> Of public scorn. (10.506–09)

Explosion and hissing, "the sound / Of public scorn," pour in from "all sides." Satan becomes the "shape" in which "he sin'd," the serpentine body that, "fawning, [had] lick'd the ground" under Eve's feet (10.516, 9.526). He becomes the "writhing and unboning" fool:

> His Visage drawn he felt to sharp and spare,
> His Armes clung to his Ribs, his Leggs entwining
> Each other, till supplanted down he fell
> A monstrous Serpent on his Belly prone,
> Reluctant, but in vaine, a greater power
> Now rul'd him.   (10.511–16)

Though the hissing tongues encompass Satan, the syntax, rhythm, and enjambments also suggest that actor and audience oppose each other as mirroring reflections: "hiss for hiss returnd with forked tongue / To forked tongue, for now were all transform'd / Alike" (518–20). The phrase "hiss for hiss returnd" plots the effect of an echo on the spatial-temporal poetic line; the enjambed "forked tongue / To forked tongue" and "all transform'd / Alike" further translate the circular depth of the theater to a plane where opposing forms reflect each other.[37]

Rhetor and audience here constitute each other, not in a negotiation of truth but rather in a codependent confirmation of self-serving desires. The monarchal Satan confirms in the rebels a sense of mission and hope, a sense of purpose that matters only as such, though not for its bitterly empty end. Satan becomes the form of that desire, a writhing form of flesh that shifts and bends, that oscillates within the fluctuations of hope and fear, deluded euphoria and desperation at the emotional center of Milton's infernal fallen: "Thus was th' applause they meant, / Turn'd to exploding hiss, triumph to shame" (*PL* 10.545–46). This abdication of embodied authority is through its psycho-affective structure endlessly recursive and degenerate. It infects lesser devils who wait

> Sublime with expectation ... to see
>   ... thir glorious Chief;
> They saw, but other sight instead, a crowd
> Of ugly Serpents; horror on them fell,
> And horrid sympathie; for what they saw

> They felt themselves now changing…
> And the dire hiss renew'd, and the dire form
> Catcht by Contagion.   (10.536–41, 543–44)

This "renew[al]" of "dire hiss" and "dire form" continues to unfold in the serpents' repeated attempts to eat the deluding apples from a newly arisen "multitude" of "forbidden Tree[s]" (554): "oft they assayd," "oft they fell / Into that same illusion" (567, 570–71). "Some say," Milton tells us, that these self-abdicated forms are "Yearly enjoyned…to undergo / This annual humbling…/ To dash their pride, and joy for Man seduc't" (575–77). Thus, the ethically abdicating staged author and audience organize into a system of theatrical recursion that brings only emptiness and a "long and ceaseless hiss": echoing the "clamors…and terrors" of the serpentine forms endlessly encircling the involuntarily, reiteratively birthing serpentine Sin.

Theatricality in Milton is not merely a mode of hypocrisy but is more generally one of negotiated embodied authority: not a choice but a precondition of action. What Michael Schoenfeldt aptly describes as "the invisible lines of force that bond one human with another, for better and for worse," are lively sinews of the poem's ethics, connecting agential bodies in the field of vision.[38] During the separation colloquy Adam's testimony to the power of Eve's eyes upon him suggests a theatrical dimension to marriage and its cultivating labor: "I from the influence of thy looks receave / Access in every Vertue, in thy sight / More wise, more watchful, stronger." By raising the specter of "shame," Eve's gaze ("thou looking on") would "utmost vigor raise," inspiring heroic action in her defense (*PL* 9.309–14).[39] Virtue appears cooperative, premised not only on sociality but also on literally feeling the eyes of another upon oneself.

Sometimes encompassing eyes and their effect upon the passions help to catalyze virtuous action. At the start of *Areopagitica*, a simulated speech to Parliament, Milton identifies with those "alter'd and mov'd inwardly in their mindes" at the thought of addressing governors of a commonwealth. Where it is conventional for such pious patriots to detail "which [passion] sway'd

[them] most" to speak or write, he claims simply that this thought of his audience "hath got the power within me to a passion" (YP 2:486–87). He cares not to specify *which* passion moved him but rather emphasizes that the freedom to speak to his audience inspires a more generalized passion that is, in fact, the tract's animating principle.[40] The phrase "mov'd inwardly in their mindes" directly applies the language of passion, often seen as moving the subject from within, to describe a dynamic rationality; the productive integration of passion and reason (in *Areopagitica* these often appear as one and the same) grounds his argument that prepublication censorship will stagnate the vital force that moves writers to advance the cause of Truth. Even vicious books promote learning *because* they generate passion, regardless of quality: "Wherefore did [God] creat passions within us, pleasures round about us, but that these rightly temper'd are the very ingredients of vertu?" (YP 2:527). The note on tragedy prefacing *Samson Agonistes*, written with a far more guarded view of the relationship between passion and reason in the public sphere, suggests that drama can work medicinally to "purge," "temper," or "reduce...to just measure" unhealthy passions (in part by "stirr[ing] up" "a kind of delight") (CM 1.2:331). Milton's view of literature's effect on the passions and their effect on rationality corresponds with his appraisal of the public sphere: when the culture is healthy, tempered passion leads to greater health; when diseased, unchecked passion hastens decline by promoting self-deluding rationalization.

Across the span of his career, Milton's relationship to his reading public appears to be theatrical in that it inspires visions of the cooperation of the incorporate in the cause of God and Truth — the "house of God...can but be contiguous in this world," built of "many schisms and many dissections," "many moderat varieties and brotherly dissimilitudes that are not vastly disproportionall" (*Areopagitica*, YP 2:555) — while often suggesting an essential antagonism between author and an encompassing, viewing public. Perhaps the most striking idiosyncrasy of Milton's theatricality is the regularity by which figures of the actor and orator appear to occupy the stage alone. Even when decrying player divines in the *Apology*, Milton disregards the content performed and the manner of staged interaction while focusing on the ethical nexus of vision, desire, and action: several may be on stage but essentially one body, one character, is described. The centrality of the individual makes the theatrical scene at times indistinguishable from the scene of oratory. The fluid relationship between oratory and theater owes in part to the central but dubious place of theatricality in the early modern sacred and classical rhetorical traditions, where it usually marks a limit of rhetorical legitimacy. Milton directly references this connection in *Of Education*, where he reworks accounts of how Demosthenes and Cicero became superior orators through the training of the actors Andronicus and Roscius, respectively (YP 2:400–01).[41] He develops this interest further in the seduction scene of *Paradise Lost*, where Satan appears an "all impassiond" classical orator, dangerously skilled in delivery, whose "each part, / Motion, each act won audience ere the tongue" (9.678, 673–74).

Miltonic theatricality shows the self's individual and corporate identities under negotiation. Though Lewalski and also Daniel Shore are right to emphasize Milton's interest in fashioning a fit readership[42] — he saw himself as called to serve "God's glory by the honour and instruction of my country" as an "interpreter & relater of the best and sagest things" (YP 1:810–11) — his bending bodies also suggest limitations of the author's control over textual reception. Are books snapshots of past actions situated within particular cultures at particular times or are they, as in *Areopagitica*, "not absolutely dead things" but rather things that "doe contain a potencie of life in them," that are "as vigorously productive" as the dragon's teeth of Cadmus (YP 2:492)? Does this "potencie of life" work unilaterally or is an ongoing responsiveness part of its vitality? In other words, does a long-dead author's book continue to writhe in nakedness? And if the book is an embodiment of authorial ethos, does it reveal a writhing author?

I want to focus briefly on two representative moments where significant ambiguities at the center of ongoing critical controversy mark limitations of authorial intention while also suggesting Milton's effort to organize and delimit textual renegotiation. The poetic line, in its material dimensions of time and space, can behave theatrically in its manipulation of reader response. Consider the close of Eve's creation narrative:

> thy gentle hand
> Seisd mine, I yielded, and from that time see
> How beauty is excelld by manly grace
> And wisdom, which alone is truly fair.　　　(PL 4.488–91)

The spatial-temporal gap of lines 488–89 at once separates and brings together senses of gentle and violently coercive touch. "Seisd" epitomizes Adam's legalistic language of property throughout the passage and further suggests Eve's status as *feme covert*. Its Latin corollary *rapere*, the "Seisd" can evoke "rape." These meanings directly conflict with "gentle" and what elsewhere appears to be the genuinely loving nature of paradisal marriage. Fish, eliding the enjambment from his quoted text, reads Eve's "yield[ing]" as "obviously" pointing to the episode's primary "moral," namely, the right choosing between vain narcissism and the doctrinally appropriate embrace of marriage.[43] Yet the ironies surrounding the enjambment have also been read as further evincing the poem's challenge to a misogynistic exegetical tradition by foregrounding the tension between its seemingly authoritative affirmations of gendered hierarchy and its reiterations of the language of mirroring equality found in Genesis.[44] The disturbing senses of "seisd" invite a critique of gendered hierarchy in the garden that seems in tension with Eve's pronouncement of the conventionally patriarchal affiliation of femininity with outer "beauty" and the inferiority of this beauty to "manly grace / And wisdom, which alone is truly fair." Even the seemingly obvious sense of "wisdom" as an exclusively "manly" virtue is called into question by the second enjambment between lines 490 and 491. While the superficial "beauty" of woman may be "excelled" by a "grace" that is gendered masculine, the enjambment dislodges "wisdom" from "manly," leaving it potentially ungendered, a capacity shared by either sex. There indeed seems to be a peculiar "wisdom" working through Eve's narrative, a "wisdom" that unsettles the patriarchal truisms it evidently affirms.

As Adam's hand extends across the enjambment to touch Eve at once lovingly and coercively, the poetic line, undulating ironically, plays upon the understanding and desire of readers: "gentle hand" pulls us toward the ideally loving union of first man and helpmeet; "seisd" repulses, leaving us to reflect at a distance — if we are ready to accept the invitation. It is as though this entirely extrascriptural episode were extending *its* hand, beckoning readers at once to uphold the hackneyed antifeminism of exegetical tradition and to cooperate with the poet in its "renovating and re-ingendring" (YP 1:703). Milton uses this phrase, "renovating and re-ingendring," in *Animadversions* to capture the ability of the Logos to rewrite itself through the Spirit working actively in the community of believers. He emphasizes in *De doctrina Christiana* the doubleness of Scripture as both codified law and spiritual law "inscribed upon the hearts of believers" (CM 16:272; my translation).[45] Scholars have often misunderstood the relationship between the "two scriptures," reading Milton's exaltation of the internal Scripture as confirming his antinomianism, that is, a radically individualistic disregard of written law in the light of the Spirit.[46] Yet as both Dayton Haskin and Phillip J. Donnelly show, these senses of Scripture remain largely interdependent: for Milton, the internal law of the Spirit does not simply dispense with written Scripture but, rather, guides the renegotiation of its polysemy, irony, and darkness.[47] As Mary Nyquist demonstrates, the irony opened by "gentle hand / Seisd" rearticulates a tension between senses of the Genesis narrative traceable to conflicting scribal source texts.[48] Such disjunctions seem less intended to enforce doctrine than to lubricate, as it were, the continuing spiritual and passionate re-engendering of scriptural meaning. They allow Milton's own poem to behave like Scripture as he receives it.

The apparent aggression of Adam's seizing hand results from the desire intensified by Eve's departure. Yet the rhetoric by which this scene unfolds shows Eve reaching out in turn to beckon her auditor to negotiate this semiotic instability, so that the more disturbing and more immediate senses of "seisd" might be reconciled to its potentially more loving sense, an eager clutching intended to settle the destined beloved in place. Moreover, the apparently self-contradicting phrase provides Adam opportunity to recognize and to reform his underdeveloped, inadequately responsive sense of what it means to receive a "meet help." Certainly by the time that Adam revises the story of Eve's creation in book 8, what first appeared as a potential claim of proprietorship has softened into a more conventional narrative of budding romance, albeit one that revises Eve's alarmed turning away not only into a coy reticence informed by "Innocence and Virgin Modestie," but also into the subtle invitation of one "that would be woo'd, and not unsought be won" (*PL* 8.501–03). For the poem's reader, the meaning of "seisd" will remain under negotiation, its senses and Adam's very body, as we see it, bending in accordance with each reappraisal of the relationship.

A more entrenched controversy has centered upon the phrase "rouzing motions" in *Samson Agonistes*.[49] The extraordinary ambiguity of "motions" continues to pull readers into exploring the unstable nexus of evidence, intentionality, desire, and meaning at the core of the closet drama and of

Milton's hermeneutics. "Motions" invites wide-ranging senses operative during the middle seventeenth century in debates related to physics, astronomy, biology/anatomy, emotion, theater, politics, and religion. In *Paradise Lost* 11.91 "motions" refers to the regenerative workings of the Spirit within. In *Areopagitica* it designates puppet shows featuring a wooden, nonagential Adam (YP 2:527).

While most scholars have read in "motions" the rousing inner workings of the Spirit, the only mention of "motions" in the KJV Bible refers to the sensual stirrings of arousal in the penis that lead to emission and reproduction. Paul uses this figure of carnality to contrast bondage under the Mosaic law against liberation from the law in the Spirit: "For when we were in the flesh, the motions of sins, which were by the law, did work in our members to bring forth fruit unto death. But now we are delivered from the law, that being dead wherein we were held; that we should serve in newness of spirit, and not *in* the oldness of the letter" (Rom. 7:5). The Greek original reads *pathemata*, or "passions," a word divided between connotations of the immediate presence of the Spirit, on one hand, and of physiological arousal on the other. Thus, the word immediately erects two poles of meaning, an ambivalence that anticipates the uncertainty about Samson's internal state at the moment he determines to pull down the theater's roof. If like Derek N. C. Wood we choose to read Samson as confined within the spiritual darkness of the Old Testament, then it becomes easy to read the allusion to Romans 7:5 as indicative of Samson's inescapable carnality.[50] If we adopt the approach of Joan S. Bennett, who reads Samson's destruction of the theater as a willed breaking from bondage in the Old Law and as typologically linked with Christ's abrogation of that Law, then Romans 7:5 invites a reinterpretation of "motions" that plays out this dispensation as willed liberation.

In contemporary literatures of religious controversy, "motions" could variously evoke spiritual presence, theatrical gesture, demonic possession, and sexual desire. The word "motions" takes on carnal and spiritual meanings in the polemical literature, meanings that depend on whether spiritual authority is intended to be bolstered or discredited.[51] Enthusiasts like the early Quakers used "motions" to refer to the unmediated workings of the Spirit within, while for their attackers in print "motions" was a signifier of the Quakers' carnal theatricality. Bulwer, in his 1649 *Pathomyotamia*, attempts to demonstrate precisely how the "voluntarie or impetuous motions of the mind" lead to specific contractions in the muscles of the face and head, also referred to as "motions."[52] The word can thus signify both the body's gestures and the passions (good or bad, spiritual or carnal) animating them. As such, it points directly to the correspondence between the inner and outer man that Miltonic theatricality insistently explores. The majority view maintaining Samson's heroism continues to stand confidently on the assumption that "motions" signifies straightforwardly as "Spirit."[53] Yet the extraordinary overdetermination of "motions" has proven relentlessly productive, rousing scholars to generate new means of understanding Samson, his God, and interpretation itself.

As with the enjambed "gentle hand / Seisd," the ambiguity of "motions" has catalyzed debate while nonetheless leaving the *essential* poles of that debate mostly stable: Milton firmly stakes out the outer limits of scriptural meaning even as these poles form a gate of life through which new possibilities are birthed. The inevitable tension between scriptural "renovation" and exegetical constraint places Milton's scholars in league with a potentially resistant author they are continually reshaping. Bulwer's subtitle refers to the "*Significative Muscles of the Affections of the Minde.*" What are "muscles" of "affections" and what does it mean that these are "significative"? We enter the irreducible but crucial ambivalence of flesh where inside and outside merge on the very axis of ethics. And as this flesh stimulates more questions — Is Eve born Adam's equal? Is there inequality in Paradise? Is it our responsibility to rectify the contradictions of Genesis by delving into Scripture's deeper truths? Is Samson a terrorist? Is his very skin a matrix of skepticism? — it facilitates historical transformation.

The Miltonic corpus has a strange capacity to make readers visualize — that is, to reconstruct — the ethical body of its author. Reading *Paradise Lost*, Andrew Marvell first saw Milton as a Samson between the pillars threatening to "ruin...sacred truths."[54] It is impossible not to hear something of Milton's defeat in Samson's lamentations. Or in Satan's. It is hard not to see the young "Lady" of Christ's College in the young Lady of the *Maske*. At the same time, the ways we envision Milton guide how we negotiate the polysemy, irony, and darkness of his texts; what we make of their challenges continues to reshape our vision of the poet. Thus, author and reader remain caught within the feedback loop of theatrically recursive authority. Yet reading with strenuous liberty, curious perspicacity, and responsible creativity helps us to avoid being pulled into the negative feedback loop of satanic authority, which leads to uncontrolled writhing leagued with agential entropy. When we read Milton with an active mind, alive to the text's ironies and ambiguities, its invitations to interrogation and re-creation, as well as its checks and balances, our truths and desires entangle in a textual pneuma, and neither author nor reader departs unchanged.

At the core of *Samson Agonistes* is a doubleness that seems characteristic of Milton's living corpus: physical and immaterial, visible and invisible, concrete and elusive, a torsional texture of semiotic sinews. What this volume calls "generative irresolution" seems characteristic of the Miltonic text as a theatrical body that in exerting authority through the negotiations of a contingent relationship ensures its own transformation while struggling to manage and delimit the resedimenting work of reception. The corpus reiteratively exfoliates the very skin of this crossing over that is a given of rhetorical, and thus of poetic, production. The most remarkable characteristic of this corpus is the degree to which it actively encourages textual renegotiations, not merely on the surface but also much more deeply in the poetic and exegetical traditions from which this flesh derives. We are not dealing with radical indeterminacy but rather systems of signification that return us to polarities through which we might continue to work out — both in Milton's texts and beyond — key questions answered only with difficulty and time. The systemic nature of this process saves Milton's poetics from disintegrating into the forces of cultural desire, and makes it, rather, a means toward the indefinite, piecemeal reintegration of Truth (YP 2:549–50).

CHAPTER 3

———————— ⟶⟞⟝⟶ ————————

Argument in Heaven

Logic and Action in *"Paradise Lost," Book 3*

JAMES J. RUTHERFORD

John Milton's *Paradise Lost* is at once a "great argument" and a religious history, a work concerned with the exercise of human reason and with the claims of faith.[1] Much of its power comes from the way the two tasks complement each other, but if the two can align they can also conflict, and it is indeed precisely when interpreters try to determine the limits of understanding Milton's theodicy rationally that they reveal their most fundamental disagreements. As John Leonard observes in his recent reception history of *Paradise Lost*, the relative priority of faith and reason is an issue that "haunt[s] Milton criticism down the centuries."[2] Determining the limitations and functions of human reason within the poem has proved particularly challenging in those scenes where Milton presents sustained arguments conveying his political and theological commitments since there were and are numerous competing standards for judging their validity. Yet there was one discourse in particular in the seventeenth century that was devoted to precisely this problem. That discourse was logic, a subject Milton not only studied but taught, not only read but also wrote about. In what follows, then, I will investigate anew the question of rationalism in *Paradise Lost* through the lens of a book that is seldom studied despite being centrally concerned with the exercise of human reason, Milton's *Artis logicae plenior institutio, ad Petri Rami methodum concinnata* (*A Fuller Institution of the Art of Logic, Arranged after the Method of Peter Ramus*), the textbook he composed as a schoolteacher following the completion of his master's degree and eventually published in 1672.[3]

At first glance Milton's *Art of Logic* may seem like an unlikely candidate for investigating a complex work like an epic poem. Logic, after all, has long been associated with dry pedantry and pointless quibbling rather than with vital debate. Indeed, the Romantics tried to redeem Milton from criticisms such as Alexander Pope's remark that Milton's God "reasons like a school divine" precisely by suggesting that his didactic purpose collapsed before the power of his verse. Whatever his pretensions to a clear, logical theodicy, Milton's poetic instinct led him, Shelley and Blake suggested, to join the devil's party. Reacting against this view, more recent scholars have made a case for the coherence and unity of Milton's theological argument, drawing on his logic textbook to show that Satan's arguments are fallacious while God's are valid, and to show where and how Adam and Eve went wrong. Championing Milton's logic, they open his poetry, again, to Pope's critique. But insisting on the importance of logical method to Milton's verse need not strip it of the dramatic and poetic content the Romantics were so keen to see within it. In what follows, I will present a version of logic that is far more passionately engaged in the dangerous and violent debates of early modern society than a correct but arid method of deduction might seem to allow. In so doing, I will demonstrate both that Milton's poetry is more logical and his logic more poetic than has traditionally been understood.[4]

The Romantic — and, indeed, modern — view that logical discourse is peculiarly dry and unpoetic reflects an ahistorical view of what logic is. The nature and reception of logic in seventeenth century England is in many respects anomalous in the history of the discipline in keeping with its unusual origins, its functions, and its popularity in public discussion. The logic of Milton, "arranged after the method of Peter Ramus," was not so much associated with academic pedantry as with dangerous religious enthusiasms; indeed, in the English-speaking world Ramist logic was associated with a particular religious creed owing to its widespread and nearly exclusive adoption by English and American Puritans.[5] The connection between Ramist logical method and religious persuasion was established early on as a result of its founder's conversion to Protestantism shortly before his death — as a martyr, according to his followers — during the St. Bartholomew's Day Massacre. In his logic textbook, Milton foregrounds the historical origin of his logical method by including a life of Ramus at the end of it; Milton's Ramus is not just a logician but also a hero, first defending his ideas about logic against entrenched Aristotelian authority and then dying in the service of his religious convictions. It is probable that when he composed the textbook, and perhaps even more so when he finally published it, Milton identified personally with a man about whom "all Europe talked from side to side" despite being dishonored in his native country, and who suffered for the cause of religious freedom.[6] There was a danger in having a logical system, which by its nature has a pretense to rational authority, being so closely tied to the moral authority of its founder and with a religio-political movement. Although Ramist logicians touted their objectivity, their opponents, who included both rival logicians and even poets and playwrights, suggested that they had traduced the authority of logic by their interested application of it in doctrinal and political disputes.[7] In the course of the seventeenth century, Ramist dialectic slipped seamlessly toward metadialectic as people both used it and debated its significance in highly charged polemical contexts.

The idea that Ramist logic was a political and not just a rational instrument is reflected in its very structure. Aside from the publicity gained by the controversial life and writing of its founder, Ramist logic achieved popularity as a result of its relative simplicity. After a short course in logic, which required only a partial introduction to complex subjects such as definition and the syllogism (which, in any case, Ramists tended to disparage), a student was equipped to enter the ring of university disputation and eventually public debate. Milton's tactical use of formal logic in prose pamphlets about divorce and regicide, and in his systematic employment of Ramist methods of organization in *De doctrina Christiana*, is emblematic of a logical system oriented toward animadversion and organization as opposed to valid demonstration.[8] In a sense, one could argue that what students learned was not how to use logic but rather how to seem to be logical. On this critical reading, Ramist logic is a "rhetorical" logic; indeed, part of what made Ramist and other humanist logics so distinctive was their appropriation of what had traditionally been rhetorical ideas and methods.[9] This is evident in "invention," the first part of Ramist logic, where practitioners used the rhetorical "topics" to prove a given conclusion or question. Invention comprised a kind of storehouse of conventional arguments establishing relations on the basis of abstract concepts such as quantity, quality, relation, and so on, which could be extracted for the purpose of proving a given argument. In deciding whether or not God is a father, for example, one could make use of a topic such as "relation" to answer in the affirmative: relation teaches that a father necessarily has a son; God has a son, who became Jesus Christ; therefore, God is a father. Once one has thus found the arguments proving one's conclusions, the second part of logic, "disposition," demonstrates how to arrange them as maxims and syllogisms descending from the most general to the most particular. In effect, then, the Ramist logician merely uses logic to support existing arguments rather than to arrive at new ones. As one of Ramus's most hostile modern critics puts it, Ramist logic is "ordered to achieving preconceived aims rather than to descriptively dispassionate theory."[10]

Milton's reliance on logical argument is evident from the outset of *Paradise Lost*. As Richard Strier observes, "the desire to *assert* 'Eternal Providence' is not necessarily rationalistic — something can be asserted, after all, in the face of evidence and common sense — but the intention 'to justify the ways of God to men' is indeed a rationalistic project."[11] But Milton is not merely using logic in his opening paragraph, however: he is also using Ramist logic. In the first paragraph of *Paradise Lost*, the two-part process of Ramist logic is put into figural form. The process of invention helps to account for Milton's anomalous hypothesizing about the possible different origins of his muse, which include "the secret top of Oreb," "or of Sinai," or "Sion hill," and "Siloa's brook" (*PL* 1.6–11). It is a poetic representation of the logical process of *finding* arguments, appropriately enough in various literal topoi or places. Following these geographically diverse solicitations of the muse, Milton describes the form that his argument will take: he will both "assert" eternal providence and "justify" the ways of God to men. These two procedures reflect the two parts of disposition: "axiomatic" reasoning, the use of maxims or simple statements of fact "by which something is shown to be or not to be" (*Art of Logic*, 299), and "dianoetic" reasoning, where "one axiom is deduced from another" (365), resulting in more extended forms such as syllogisms and the methodical arrangement of ideas from the most general to the most particular. The whole opening paragraph of *Paradise Lost* thus represents the general outline of the Ramist system.[12] The first paragraph is indicative of what follows. Throughout the entire poem, Milton continues to make use of Ramist concepts and formal procedures in order to structure his ideas, sometimes in figurative form and sometimes in ways that more precisely reflect typical textbook demonstrations. Ramist logic, I will ultimately argue, is a powerful guide to the artistry as well as the argument of *Paradise Lost*.

Yet Milton, like his contemporaries, realized that Ramist logic, while an efficient instrument, could also be a fallible one. In what follows, I will argue that Milton does not simply naïvely reflect the principles of logic in his poem: he tests their viability in a range of contexts, including those where critics generally assume that he is communicating his deepest held convictions. My focus will be on the invocation and heavenly council in book 3 of *Paradise Lost*, in which God and the Son debate many of the fundamental principles of Milton's religion in conspicuously schematic form — a kind of theodicy within the theodicy. In book 3, Milton not only presents arguments but also illustrates the various capacities and limits of argument. I will claim that the book gradually reveals its precise methods of arguing, starting out by confronting the reader with irresolvable paradoxes (in the invocation) before untangling them by employing increasingly clear logical forms (in the course of discussion between God and the Son). Even in the heavenly conversation nothing is taken for granted. If in the beginning Milton shows the incoherence resulting from carelessly disposing one's arguments, he thereafter embeds a subtle critique of even the best methods of logical reasoning, facing head-on the issue of the notorious circularity of Ramist logic and the willed origins of argumentative premises. Accordingly, my analysis of Milton's Ramism will proceed sequentially through book 3, touching on speeches — including the invocation, God's first speech in defense of his justice, and the Son's offer of self-sacrifice — that illuminate key pressure points, if not breaking points, of Milton's poetic representation of logical reasoning.

LIGHT

At the opening of book 3, Milton alludes to theologically significant issues under the cover of an invocation to light. The first lines of the book are as difficult as anything else he wrote, which led Samuel Butler to ridicule them as the words of a blind man "groping for a beam of light."[13] With its halting rhythm, questioning tone, difficult diction, and unwieldy syntax, the first sentence of the invocation is indeed hard to parse:

> Hail, holy light, offspring of heaven first-born,
> Or of the eternal co-eternal beam
> May I express thee unblamed? since God is light,
> And never but in unapproachèd light
> Dwelt from eternity, dwelt then in thee,
> Bright effluence of bright essence increate.   (PL 3.1–6)

It might seem that logical analysis would help unravel its difficulties. The narrator appears to define his terms, to ask a question that seems to be in need of a response, and might even appear to offer one in the clause beginning with the word "since." Nevertheless, there are significant difficulties that would frustrate attempts to analyze the argument. This difficulty is deliberate on Milton's part. In the invocation Milton has created an argument that invites logical analysis but thoroughly resists it.

Milton's contemporaries were highly susceptible to invitations to make logical sense of opaque theological expressions. Scholars often underestimate the importance of logic within theological commentaries of the early modern period in part, perhaps, as a result of disproportionate attention to rhetoric. However, exegetical texts were often conspicuous in their use of logic, in many cases offering formal syllogistic presentations of biblical arguments. The goal of many writers was to show that the Bible, particularly in the Gospels, is itself logical and only requires the slightest formal transformation to make its ideas clear to the least sophisticated reader. Thus, the indefatigable theologian Johannes Piscator produced large books with titles such as *Analysis logica Evangelii Secundum Matthaeum* (Logical analysis of the Gospel of Matthew [1606]) and *Analysis logica Epistolae Pauli ad Romanos* (Logical analysis of Paul's Epistle to the Romans [1608]) in which the reader is presented with hundreds of pages thick with simplified, syllogistic versions of Scripture in which every difficult metaphor or implied premise is patiently expounded. William Temple, a popularizer of Ramist logic who debated its merits with Piscator and other opponents, performed a similar task for readers of English in *A Logicall Analysis of Twentye Select Psalmes* (1605), thereby showing that even sacred poetry has a logical basis. Using simple syllogisms, even lay readers could gain an understanding of the Bible. Indeed, the Danish pedagogue Niels Hemmingsen (a student of Melanchthon's) was determined to drill students in basic logic so thoroughly that its rules would "come into theyr mindes, euen as it were vppon a sodaine" any time they read the Bible or heard a sermon.[14]

Milton's arrangement of his first tentative statements concerning the nature of the relationship between the Father and the Son in a quasi syllogism about light resonates particularly with a prominent tradition in which theologians and exegetes who wanted to establish the truth of Trinitarian theology put biblical texts like "God is light" (1 John 1:5) into syllogistic form. For example, Roger Hutchinson explains the logical principles underlying "harde textes, and suche as have bene abused for evill purposes" with syllogisms such as the following: "God is light...Christ is the true *lyght*...Ergo Christ is the true God."[15] Milton was almost certainly familiar with the works of his former schoolmaster Alexander Gill, who attempted to express Christian mysteries with rational clarity.[16] In the *Treatise concerning the Trinity*, for example, Gill argues in simple, if contestable, syllogisms: "Whatsoeuer is without beginning, is also without ending; because it hath no Superiour which might bring it to nothing: therefore *God is eternall.* Againe, whatsoeuer comes to nothing, is corrupted by his contrary; but nothing can be opposite to *God*, therefore hee is Eternall." He occasionally risks an analogy, albeit a conventional one, but the formulation usually has the appearance of sound logic: "If you take in a myrrour, the light of the Sunne, and reflect it directly thereon againe, in the Sunne it is one, in the glasse another, and yet the reflection of the beames, is also a third, but for all this, there is but one nature and worde of light, which comprehends al three: so is it in this *Tri-Vnitie* of which I speake."[17]

The reason pedagogues such as Alexander Gill provided logical expositions of the Trinity, of course, is because there were people who disbelieved in it. There were always writers who were willing, at great personal risk, to attack central tenets of Christian theology. In order to argue a minority position, such radicals often relied on the appearance of logical cogency even more than the theologians they attacked. For example, the anti-Trinitarian Socinian John Biddle, whose work Milton knew, was notorious for subjecting Scripture to syllogistic analysis without any recognition of the postbiblical interpretive tradition.[18] For some opponents, the ominous conclusions of writers like Biddle, ostensibly so logical in their methods, threw logic itself into disrepute; others, such as Thomas White, tried to show that anti-Trinitarian logic was simply false or deceptive — what White calls "controversy-logic" — and patiently enumerate their fallacies.[19] In particular, White complains about how "the Arguments which are drawne from reason, for the proofe or disproofe of particular points, are chiefly about Mysteries difficult in nature; against which, Heretikes use to frame the ordinary obvious objections. As, against the blessed Trinity, how the same thing, can be one and three?" One frequently encounters impatience in orthodox writers' reflections on anti-Trinitarian arguments, which are predictably repeated without much modification. Nevertheless, one may assume that the greatest source of White's frustration is not the consequence of repetition but because "such kind of arguments, Universally, are hard to be answered."[20]

Milton's invocation should be read against this tradition of logical exposition and controversy, a tradition that he complains about at the outset of *The Art of Logic*: "the theologians fetch out as though from the heart of logic canons about God and about divine hypostases and sacraments as if these had been furnished for their use; yet nothing is more alien from logic or in fact from reason itself than the ground of these canons, as prepared by the theologians" (7). Given the invocation's obvious implications for Trinitarian theology, one might expect Milton to follow contemporaries such as Biddle — as well as his practice in his own prose works — in making logical arguments for the separate existence of God, the Son, and the Spirit in contradiction of the mystical paradoxes of his opponents. The invocation is not simply a versification of parts of *De doctrina Christiana*, however. At the opening of book 3 of *Paradise Lost* Milton is less interested in conveying his opinions than in interrogating the fundamental terms of the debate, in the process revealing something about the nature of argument itself. Rather than presenting a clear statement of his views, he gives the reader an argument that does not work in accordance with his own logical principles. In giving his invocation the appearance of logic without its content, Milton provides a trap for the unwary, an illustration of what *not* to do.

As tantalizing as it may be as a site for logical interpretation, the invocation withholds the kinds of certainty on which syllogistic arguments must be based. There are too many choices to make. The Miltonic "or," as Peter Herman remarks, presents "unresolved choices leading to aporias."[21] If in the first line Milton addresses light and gives a definition of it (offspring of heaven's firstborn), in the second he offers another one (offspring of the eternal coeternal beam), and then in the third he questions the legitimacy of addressing light at all despite already having done so. "May I express thee unblamed?" the narrator asks. It may be a rhetorical question, but nevertheless the answer to it is not obvious — even if, in having addressed light before asking permission, the poet seems to have decided the issue in the affirmative. The answer to the question may be no, and thus one could intuit a note of hesitation even in the triumphalist gesture of "hailing" light. This seems, indeed, to be the point of a clever metrical effect. In order to pronounce the line as ten syllables one must create an elision between "thee" and "unblamed" (which may be represented typographically as "th'unblamed"), thus making it impermissible to express the word "thee" audibly. The Miltonic narrator seems indecisive about the "mystery" he has adumbrated, giving us reason to pause in our reading, to mull over meanings and consider alternatives, and perhaps even to doubt the legitimacy of going forward.

The main thing that makes Milton's argument so hard to follow is that he does not give consistent definitions of his terms. It is not clear after six lines what "light" is, and it will not be clearer when in the next sentence the narrator gives what amounts to another definition for it ("pure ethereal stream," in line 7). There are simply too many possible denotations. Indeed, scholars have identified numerous sources for Milton's varied use of the term — from Augustine, Tertullian, Ficino, Dante, Vida, Tasso, and Bacon, among others.[22] Many additional meanings of "light" could be adduced from less intellectually impressive sources. In a work such as Thomas Wilson's *A Christian dictionarie Opening the signification of the chiefe words dispersed generally through Holy Scriptures of the Old and New Testament, tending to increase Christian knowledge*, for example, one is confronted with no less than 14 definitions of the word. As Andrew Mattison suggests, "when we first read the line, 'Hail Holy light, Offspring of Heaven first-born,' we are expecting an antidote to the obscurity of the first two books…light is direct, and light is the first of all things, and those two attributes ought to dispel the complexity and temporal and spatial remove of the beginning of the poem."[23] Difficulties immediately emerge, however, as Milton repeats his terms without settling on stable definitions: "but as the invocation goes on, and light divides into different things addressed at different moments by the same word and the same second-person pronoun, the antidote gives way to still more confusion."[24] In the invocation, then, Milton conspicuously muddles the terms of his own argument.

If Milton were a Trinitarian theologian, the polyvalence of his terminology would not be a problem. Such theologians could simply assert that God = light, his Son = light, and so God = his Son. They were able to show to their own satisfaction that ostensibly different terms were in fact the same: in their reasoning, the terms "God," "Son of God," and "light" simply yield tautologies. Milton had discussed such arguments in *The Art of Logic* under the name of "reciprocal axioms." For Milton, reciprocal axioms are "the truest and first knowledge," principles that "though indemonstrable through themselves, are completely manifest by their own light, and do not need the light of the syllogism or any plainer argument for producing knowledge" (322–23). Yet precisely because reciprocal axioms do not need to be demonstrated they need to be used cautiously. In the textbook, Milton is especially concerned that arguments depending on the convertibility of terms might be blindly accepted, and accordingly describes the ways that they can go wrong, enumerating examples — such as "Bread is the body of Christ" — that would result in the interpreter being "deceived by [the] conversion" (339). Ultimately he suggests one should never assume that such terms are convertible if there is any doubt: "omitting all cautions, it is a more expeditious way to reject every conversion, if there is any doubt, as a sophism of the *petitio principii*, as something that attempts to prove a doubtful thing without a middle term" (339). While Milton's logic is often treated as a merely mechanical exercise, it is important to understand that it is also designed to inculcate a critical and indeed skeptical orientation toward arguments. Accordingly, it would be a mistake to assume that the repetitions and redefinitions of "light" in the invocation of book 3 in *Paradise Lost* could be reduced to a logical consistency.

Within the invocation, after the equivocal meditations on light and the description of the travails of the blind narrator, light reemerges: now "Celestial light" will "purge and disperse" all confusion (*Art of Logic*, 51, 54). This has seemed to many to be an unequivocal triumph, intellectually and aesthetically. As Lee Johnson notes, "the invocation is...ringed with a circle of rhyme based on the key word 'light,' a circle which thereby encompasses the scale of creation in its extraterrestrial aspects in the first twenty-five lines and its terrestrial images in the next twenty-five."[25] However, one may wonder once again how well Milton "encompasses" his matter. Does the specter of circular reasoning haunt this aesthetically impressive formal circularity in the invocation? On the one hand, the reader might be illuminated by a celestial light that "Shine[s] inward, and the mind through all her powers / Irradiate[s]" (*PL* 3.52–53), but there is also the darker possibility that one will merely "roll [one's eyes] in vain" (3.23). This skeptical possibility should be held in mind as Milton, following the invocation, more plainly addresses the theological underpinning of his defense of God in the counsel in heaven.

HEAVEN

Just as the appearance of light at the outset of book 3 seems to promise a reprieve from the darkness and confusion of what came before, the transition from a flawed narrator to the discourse of perfect deities renews expectations of Milton's long-awaited "great argument" in defense of God. From the outset of the council in heaven, Milton does indeed make ample use of figures contained in *The Art of Logic*, including various structures and ideas that are by no means inevitable in the course of dialectical debate. In contrast with the invocation, the dialogue in heaven smoothly integrates Ramist principles, but I will suggest that the very ease of that application raises questions about the method. Insofar as Ramist logic is open to the charge of being simply rhetoric in disguise, so are the ostensibly logical arguments of Milton's divine characters. One of the most remarkable things about Milton's representation of their discourse is the way in which he shows his awareness of possible critiques along these lines, such as how logical arguments may be used simply to confirm one's prejudices or to coerce one's interlocutors, in effect robbing them of their will. In book 3, Milton offers a logical expression of his theological principles, in the course of which logic itself is under debate.

After the invocation of book 3 of *Paradise Lost,* God makes a speech describing the imminent fall of human beings and justifying his own actions. His speech has very little in the way of poetic adornment; except for the fact that it is in iambic pentameter rhythm, his language resembles the bare reasoning of *De doctrina Christiana.* As Stuart Curran writes, "God is a logician, not a rhetorician." God's logical style of speaking has been criticized for various reasons. The most common is that God's use of logic makes him unsympathetic and that his highly elaborate logical self-defense betrays what William Empson calls God's "uneasy conscience." As Victoria Silver observes, "the almost algorithmic intricacy of the Father's exposition on creatural free will and divine foreknowledge does little to recommend him or his speech, which sounds mechanical, casuistical in the pejorative sense, and forced." Stanley Fish thought that God's logic, though immaculately correct, was bound to irritate readers because they are fallen.[26] The more damning criticism, however, is that God is not simply an unfeeling logician but a bad one. There have, of course, been many suggestions that God's arguments simply do not prove his case; Empson famously argued that there was indeed no way for him to prove his case, Christianity being inherently irrational. In a recent essay, Thomas Festa goes so far as to suggest that God's arguments are not merely insufficient to prove his case but not proper arguments at all, which he illustrates by turning "Milton's logic back on his God and [observing] the circularity of his reasoning, how his explanations are classic...examples of begging the question."[27] In what follows, I will suggest that both sets of critics are correct. God's speech is at once relentlessly logical and ultimately circular. Yet as I will show, that circularity in no way vitiates its argumentative force.

God's speech unfolds over the course of 55 lines, introducing a number of considerations leading to his ultimate conclusion. Yet his argument is susceptible of concision — indeed, of the sort of drastic concision that was the hallmark of Ramist analyses of speeches and even books. The Ramist's goal is to condense a complex text into a simple — often single-sentence — argument, after which one could use "method" to show the bifurcations

of thought as one descends into details.[28] This technique of simplifica-
tion seems to be used in book 2, for example, when the narrator, following
Belial's highly ornate and rhetorically insidious speech during the council
in hell, provides this comically brief gloss: "Thus Belial with words clothed
in reason's garb / Counselled ignoble ease, and peaceful sloth, / Not peace"
(*PL* 3.226–28). Milton provides a similarly pat summary of the essential
point of God's speech, appropriately enough in book 3's "Argument": "God
sitting on his throne sees Satan flying towards the world, then newly created; shows him to the Son who sat at his right hand; foretells the success
of Satan in perverting mankind; clears his own justice and wisdom from all
imputation, having created man free and able enough to have withstood his
tempter; yet declares his purpose of grace towards him, in regard he fell not
of his own malice, as did Satan, but by him seduced." In this "Argument,"
God is shown to have justified his "ways to men" simply by having "created
man free and able enough to have withstood his tempter." Nothing further
is necessary to establish that fact. In fact, nothing further could be said: it is
a "high decree" (3.126) with no room for justification underneath. In addition, it is a "reciprocal axiom" of the kind described in my previous section,
but this time it is clear that Milton really does think that it represents "the
first and truest knowledge" (*Art of Logic*, 323). His first example of such an
axiom in *The Art of Logic*, appropriately in this context, is "Man is a rational
animal," which because it is reciprocal implies that a rational animal is necessarily a man (320–21). If this is circular reasoning, it is circular in a sense
that *The Art of Logic* suggests should be accepted as reasonable.

The form of the heavenly dialogue reinforces the idea that the circularity
of the reasoning contained within it is significant. The council in heaven is
literally circular: it is 360 lines, the number of degrees in a circle. Immediately
after the invocation, in line 56, the scene shifts to heaven, where we remain
until the narrator "disjoin[s]" (*PL* 3.415) himself from the angels' hymn of
praise and turns his narrative toward Satan's travels. That this is not an accident is apparent in Milton's positioning of circular images before and after
the scene in heaven: for example, this numerological fact in effect answers
Satan's confusion, as he views heaven from the cusp of hell, about whether
heaven is "square or round" (2.1048), and there is irony in the way he can
only see physically apprehensible cosmic circles after the dialogue concludes,
including the "starry sphere" (416), "the firm opacous globe / Of this round

world, whose first convex divides / The luminous inferior orbs" (418–20), and "a globe far off" (422). Milton thus creates in the council in heaven what Francis Bacon had referred to as "a small Globe of the Intellectual World."[29] God's use of an inarguable first principle — amounting to the idea that humans must be allowed to choose without interference because that is what makes them human — is reflected in the circular formal pattern of the dialogue as a whole. More difficult problems emerge, however, as God enters into dialogue with the Son. God's perfect rationality raises no problem in the world that he, after all, created and rules. But is it possible for the Son, in adopting God's inarguable premises and helping to instantiate their conclusions, to retain his freedom?

God's speech appears in a dramatic context. It is not only spoken to clear himself of blame but also to motivate action. The most important thing he says with respect to the subsequent progress of the dialogue in heaven is that human beings will be redeemed. This is the sole part of the speech that his interlocutor seizes upon: "O Father, gracious was that word which closed / Thy sovereign sentence, that man should find grace" (*PL* 3.144–45), the Son replies. There is, however, a catch, though the Son may not yet know it. As the argument for book 3 has it, "The Son of God renders praises to his Father for the manifestation of his gracious purpose towards Man; *but* God again declares, that Grace cannot be extended towards Man without the satisfaction of divine justice" (italics mine). There is, of course, no mention of "satisfaction" in God's first speech, despite its apparent candor. Ramist logic, I have suggested, can be used to defend God against the accusation of unfairness to human beings; however, could Ramist logic also be used to explain God's conduct toward his own son?

At the precise center of the 360-line circular conversation, the Son of God offers himself as a sacrifice: "Behold me then, me for him, life for life / I offer" (*PL* 3.236–37). The offer is philosophically problematic because it would seem to have been determined by God beforehand. After God states that "man therefore shall find grace" (131), he adds the qualification that there must be satisfaction for human sin which humans are not capable of expiating themselves. Humans shall find grace, but grace must find "means" (228). In book 2, Beelzebub asks if any of the fallen angels are willing to travel to earth to corrupt the newly made human beings, but of course it is not really a question: he and Satan have decided that Satan will perform this mission in advance of the gathering in Pandaemonium. There is not this kind of collusion behind God's analogous question to the host of angels, but there is a similar problem regarding the premeditated nature of its result:

> Say heavenly powers, where shall we find such love,
> Which of ye will be mortal to redeem
> Man's mortal crime, and just the unjust to save,
> Dwells in all heaven charity so dear? (*PL* 2.213–16)

The drama of this moment seems almost staged. The problem, as Dennis Burden points out, is that "God promises that Man will find grace...before he has apparently found the volunteer upon whom the provision of grace depends."[30] One could therefore ask: If the Son were not willing to make himself mortal, just how long was God willing to wait for an answer? Could this have been the end of the poem? *Could* the Son have chosen otherwise?

At the opening of the dialogue, God affirms that his foreknowledge of Adam and Eve's fall had no influence on their decisions to eat the forbidden fruit. However, the structure of the dialogue in heaven raises the question of whether the Son of God is free to act in the same way that humans purportedly are. Dennis Danielson registers this possibility when he states that, insofar as God's ultimate purpose involves the Son's mediation, "Milton accepts a *compatibilist* model of divine choice even though he rejects compatibilism as a view of human choice."[31] To be a compatibilist is to believe that one may have free will even though one's actions are causally determined. According to Danielson, then, Milton's theory of free will, as he defines it in God's first speech, does not extend to the Son, who is effectively forced — by the logic of his position — to sacrifice himself, even though he experiences his choice as a free action (he says his glory is "freely put off" [*PL* 3.240]). This is one interpretation of the Son's acknowledgment that the word of his Father — an omnipotent, omniscient, and arguably omnibenevolent being whose predictions and dictums cannot be wrong — is "past" (3.227), which is to say that only the means of instantiating his will are lacking. One could say that the Son, then, almost could be trapped in a syllogism as a hidden premise: the "mediator" (*PL* 10.60) is also the middle term.[32]

Milton's *The Art of Logic*, however, provides alternative perspectives for thinking about the Son's participation in the council in heaven and his status as a free agent. First of all, the influence of Milton's logic is apparent in the formal organization of his language. The speech in which the Son offers to sacrifice himself has a clear argument: "Thy word is past, man shall find grace; / And shall Grace not find means.../ Behold me then, me for him, life for life / I offer" (*PL* 3.227–28, 236–37). He states the facts as he understands them and affirms what seems to be the necessary inference from them. Expressed formally as the kind of connected, compound syllogism discussed in chapter 13 of *The Art of Logic*, the Son states that human beings shall have grace; if they shall have grace, then they shall have the means of achieving it; therefore, human beings shall have means. The influence of *The Art of Logic* is more than formal, however. It is also significant that the Son seems to allude to a passage of poetry that is contained in it:

> Me, me: adsum, qui feci, in me convertite ferrum
> O Rutuli, mea fraus omnis: nihil iste nec ausus,
> nec potuit.
>
> [On me — on me — here am I who did the deed — on me turn your steel,
> Rutulians! Mine is all the guilt; he neither dared nor could have done it.][33]

Critics have described parallels between the Son's speech and Nisus's offer to accept all of the blame for his and Euryalus's slaughter of the Rutulians in book 9 of the *Aeneid*, but they have not noted its presence in the handbook. The two passages share a number of similarities in diction and theme, but the full significance of the allusion can only be appreciated if we consider the presence of the Virgilian quote in the context of Milton's own previous discussion of it.[34]

Milton considers Nisus's speech twice in *The Art of Logic*. The speech is quoted at the end of the textbook in the "Analytic Praxis," in which Milton illustrates how to transform enthymemes (arguments lacking a premise that would make them complete syllogisms) into formal syllogisms. The fact that Milton elaborately discusses the logical form of Nisus's speech provides further reason for performing a similar analysis of the Son's. A more important point is that Milton's other discussion of Nisus's speech in *The Art of Logic* occurs in the midst of a philosophical discussion about causation. In chapter 4 of book 1 of *The Art of Logic*, "Of the efficient cause singly and with others," Milton provides a framework for thinking about the causal and volitional aspects of behavior. In this chapter, Milton observes that "the one having greatest force is often called the sole cause," and that Nisus acts "as though he were the single author, since he was the chief one" (35). His situation clearly resembles the Son's in *Paradise Lost*, though contrasts are also apparent. Whereas Nisus tries to assume the blame for the crimes perpetrated by him and another, the Son assumes responsibility for the sin of all human beings despite having played no role in their Fall. As one would expect, the parallel thus represents a kind of superiority of the Christian over the pagan hero.[35] However, the parallel also opens up more complex questions about whether and in what sense either Nisus or the Son (or anyone else) may legitimately take ownership of another's actions. Milton's logic is not simply about the validity of individuals' speeches, but about the nature of the actions they perform.

In *Paradise Lost*, Milton presents one divine figure accepting an assignment from a superior — indeed, omnipotent — one. This could seem like a special case, about which examples from life and literature could seem to offer little precedence for deciding the freedom of the action of the subordinate agent. Nevertheless, we should recognize that in many logic books in addition to Milton's there is discussion of closely analogous cases in which humans behave in accordance with divine injunction. For example, the logician Zachary Coke notes that "the Creatures though they be instruments in respect of God, yet have they their action distinct from Gods," and that "unto such instruments often is given the efficacy of the principal Agent, as Preachers are said to convert and save souls when the Lord doth these by them."[36] As when Milton cites the example of Nisus, for Coke there is an easy elision from formal argument to actions undertaken in the real world. It is, moreover, hardly coincidental that he is discussing the "conversion" of pagans at the same time he is illustrating the logical procedure of converting terms in a proposition — any more than it is coincidental that the word "convertite" appears in the speech of Nisus, where it signifies both a sword being thrust into a sacrificial victim and the procedure of logical manipulation being elucidated in the "Analytic Praxis." Logic may be used to analyze both real-world missionaries and literary heroes because logic is always already present in the real world and in literature.

Throughout chapter 4 of *The Art of Logic*, Milton describes the causal mechanisms underlying actions, whether they are performed by humans in response to humans or at the behest of God. In the paragraph immediately following his analysis of the Nisus and Euryalus episode from the *Aeneid*,

Milton introduces fundamental questions about freedom and determinism, observing at the outset that a cause is either "impulsive, in some way impelling and moving the principal, or it is instrumental" (35). The question with respect to *Paradise Lost* is, in making the Son his "instrument and subordinate worker of his gracious will," does God rob him of his free will?[37] Milton is as careful as Coke about how one should attribute responsibility to "secondary" actors. One way in which he does so is by emphasizing the importance of the inner experience of the actor. Utilizing the typical terminology of Ramist logic, Milton describes inner motivation and outer impulsion as two kinds of cause, namely, the *proegumenic* and *procatarctic*. In his analyses, it is the former that has the most power — or, at least, the most moral force. For example, he explains the inner (*proegumenic*) and outer (*procatarctic*) causes of Christ's death as follows: "Long ago the proegumenic cause of the death of Christ was the ignorant zeal of the Jews; the procatarctic cause was the violation of the sabbath and the seditious assemblies with which he was charged. It should be noted, however, that where a proegumenic or internal cause is lacking, there the procatarctic or external cause has no power" (*Art of Logic*, 37). Without one's inner conviction, outward force is ineffective. If God's promise of grace and his request that someone enable it to take effect is the procatarctic cause, it has no power without the Son's inner experience of zeal on behalf of humankind. Milton adds further corroboration to such a view when in the same chapter he discusses causation with specific reference to God's prior will for an action subsequently carried out by another agent. While it is true that even when God is the first cause "absolutely," and that "others, called *secondary* and so forth, depend on the first or the prior causes, and each is a kind of effect," Milton advises that "these divisions of causes in logic need not be zealously followed out, for the whole force of arguing is contained in the proximate cause" (39). The implication of Milton's view is that one is responsible for one's actions — even if God himself has commanded them. I suggest, then, that we take the Son at his word when he says that he "freely" casts off his divinity.

Milton's Ramist textbook does not simply contain "logic" as we usually understand the term. Embedded within it is also a theory of the will that corresponds to what Milton says elsewhere in works such as *Areopagitica* and *De doctrina Christiana*. It is significant that the Son's offer of self-sacrifice alludes to such a discussion within the logic handbook, given critical debates that have ensued about his agency. In the council in heaven, Milton represents God making logically sound arguments that constrain the behavior of the Son — so that it seems the Son *must* sacrifice himself in accordance with God's plan. In *The Art of Logic*, during a discussion of analogous cases, Milton nevertheless emphasizes that being so constrained is insignificant in comparison to one's mental response to one's predicament. God creates a situation in which the Son has to act, but in that situation the Son freely chooses to offer himself as a sacrifice to redeem fallen human beings. Milton's conception of logic rests precisely on this kind of recognition: not simply of the abstract truth or falsity of a proposition, but when and how one is obliged to act in accordance with it.

Conclusion

In *Paradise Lost*, as in his political and theological works, Milton uses Ramist logic to justify his opinions. The shortcomings of his method from the standpoint of the history of logic are evident. Its technical armature is, comparatively speaking, rudimentary. Insofar as it is oriented toward debate rather than objective proofs, one could even dismiss Ramist logic as a kind of rhetoric in disguise. Many have done so. Nevertheless, it should be recognized that a "rhetorical logic" is not the same as mere rhetoric. In calling his method "logic," Ramus caused people to think about how his arguments might or might not meet the standard of reason, and indeed to interrogate the meaning and limits of reason itself. The presence of rival systems of logic in seventeenth century England further encouraged theoretical speculations about logic rather than its unreflective employment. Insofar as Milton's *Paradise Lost* interrogates the limits of logic through his poetic representation of different forms of circular argumentation, he should be seen as part of a general cultural trend that subjected logic to skeptical inquiry.[38] It is useful to remember that the central cultural debate since the Reformation, in which rival theologians found scriptural warrant for the fundamental authority either of the pope or of Scripture alone, had been characterized as "the famous circle of the Church and Scripture."[39] The cultural recognition that the famous circle could not be closed through rational argument did not prevent the formulation of logical defenses of Protestant and Catholic ideas. At their best, writers were clear on those principles about which they would brook no disagreement. For Milton, that principle is the inviolable freedom of rational agents, which he affirms in his political books and even his textbook of logic. In the end, Milton's *The Art of Logic* ought to be read not only as a series of technical procedures for making any sort of argument, but at least in part as an ethical treatise meant to facilitate decisions that result in actions within the sociopolitical world. In Milton's view it is a basic misunderstanding of the purpose of logic to use it to explain away the significance of such actions.

PART TWO

———※———

RELATIONSHIPS

CHAPTER 4

---※---

Growing Up with Virgil

MAGGIE KILGOUR

Like many other critics of his generation, C. S. Lewis assumed that the *Aeneid* was the most important classical model for *Paradise Lost*. This was partly because Renaissance readers saw the *Aeneid* as the quintessential epic and Virgil, the "god of poets," superior even to Homer.[1] K. W. Gransden asserted that "only the *Aeneid* offered the proper blue-print for *Paradise Lost*," providing the model for its structure, style, and even scenes.[2] For Lewis, however, Virgil's real significance lay in his revolutionizing of Western literature. He changed the nature and purpose of epic: "With Virgil European poetry grows up. For there are certain moods in which all that had gone before seems, as it were, boys' poetry, depending both for its charm and for its limitations on a certain naivety, seen alike in its heady ecstasies and in its heady despairs, which we certainly cannot, perhaps should not, recover." Virgil similarly transforms his readers; as Lewis continues, "No man who has once read [the *Aeneid*] with full perception remains an adolescent."[3]

As he so often does, Lewis draws attention to an important matter. While his comment may sound somewhat quaintly idiosyncratic, it is part of a long tradition of reading Virgil's works as a whole and the *Aeneid* in particular as a story of maturation. Like others, Milton was interested in Virgil's epic as a narrative of poetic and psychological growth. Early Greek poets had generally worked within a single genre, which they assumed was determined by the poet's own fixed and unchanging character: the amorous man wrote

83

love lyrics, the wise and serious poet wrote epic, the bilious/splenetic one wrote invective — or possibly criticism.[4] While the later Hellenistic writers, whose experimentation greatly influenced the Roman Augustan poets, moved among genres, Virgil's practice made both poetic and personal identities dynamic and progressive. His major works were seen as forming a triad or *rota* (wheel) that linked poetic, personal, and social growth as parts of a natural process: the generic progression from the *Eclogues* through the *Georgics* to the *Aeneid*, from humble to grander genres, reflected the growth of the individual from youth to old age, and the transformation of societies from pastoral to agricultural and, finally, to urban worlds.[5] This story of development was then recapitulated in Virgil's final work. In Fulgentius's influential reading of the *Aeneid*, the shipwreck in book 1 represents birth (which is therefore appropriately followed by Aeneas's meeting with his mother); the dalliance with Dido in book 4 and the games of book 5 are adolescence; with the death of Palinurus, "*postposito lubricae aetatis naufragio*" (the shipwreck of unstable youth is now over and done with) and in book 6, Aeneas descends to the underworld to be initiated into knowledge.[6] The last books show his attainment of maturity achieved through the conquest of the passions, first figured in Dido, usually read as representing erotic desire, and then climactically in Turnus, whom Fulgentius read as "*furibundus sensus*" (furious rage).[7] By overcoming these destructive emotions, Aeneas undergoes a radical metamorphosis. Appearing in book 2 as an old-style Homeric hero who seeks individual honor through a glorious death in battle, he is hammered in the course of the poem into a new figure: the self-denying leader who sacrifices his own desires to serve his nation. As a reward for this transformation, the hero who begins the poem as a loser on the side of the defeated Trojans is transformed into a Roman who will conquer Italy, and so foreshadows the Augustus whose Rome will rule the world.

It is not surprising, therefore, that Virgil was so central in pedagogy from his own time on, seen as a means of turning uncouth children into not only ideal rulers but also well-behaved subjects who could master their passions.[8] For Thomas Elyot, his works provided a full curriculum appropriate to every stage of a pupil's development:

> And veryly (as I before sayd) no one auctour serueth to so dyuers wittes, as
> doth Uirgile. For there is not that affect or desire, wherto any childes fantasy is

dysposed, but in some of Uirgils warkes may be fou[n]den matter therto apt &
propise. For what thing can be more famyliar than his bucolikes? nor no warke soo
nyghe approcheth to the commune dalyance & maners of chyldre[n], & the praty
co[n]trouersies of the simple shepeherdes therin conteyned, wonderfully reioy-
ceth the chylde that hereth it wel declared, as I knowe by mine owne experience.
In his Georgikes, lorde what pleasant varietie there is.... And in the laste bokes
of Eneidos, shal he finde matter to minister to hym audacytie, valiaunt courage
and polycie, to take and susteyne noble enterprises, if any shall be nedefull for
the assailynge of his enemyes. Finally (as I haue sayde) this noble Uirgile, like to
a good norise, giueth to a child, if he wyll take it, euery thynge apte for his witte
and capacitie. Wherfore he is in the ordre of lerninge to be preferred before any
other autor latine.[9]

For later writers and thinkers, therefore, Virgil does not mean only certain
episodes or techniques; his stories shaped their understandings of their
development as writers and indeed individuals. As Charles Martindale
notes generally, "classical influences go much deeper, involving patterns of
thought and feeling that . . . have defined the preoccupations and sensibilities
of our culture, and that thus affect some of the most important experiences of
our lives."[10] Virgil's work, and specifically the story of Aeneas, informs modern assumptions that development and progress come from the overcoming
of obstacles and temptations through hard work and self-sacrifice — a model
that sounds, of course, highly Miltonic. Virgil's plot is central to Augustine's
representation of his own spiritual growth. In charting his conversion from
Virgil to Christianity, Augustine converts the *Aeneid* into a story of conversion in which, like Aeneas, he must renounce a beloved Dido who is now
the pagan Virgil himself. Aeneas's transformation from Trojan into Roman
easily turns into a Pauline putting off of the old man and putting on of the
new as, ostensibly rejecting Virgil's narrative, Augustine internalizes and
spiritualizes it.[11] Virgil's narrative of development still subtly shapes our
inner landscapes; tellingly, Freud, who had a lifelong fascination with Rome
(albeit an ambivalent one, as in his youth he had idolized the Carthaginian
Hannibal), took as the motto for the *Interpretation of Dreams* Juno's threat
in *Aeneid* 7.312: "flectere si nequeo superos, Acheronta movebo" (if I cannot
persuade heaven, then I'll raise hell).[12]

But there is another aspect of the Virgilian narrative of growth that has
also left its imprint on our sensibilities. The story of progress is shadowed

by the poet's sympathies for those left behind in his grand narrative who are not allowed to grow up or who refuse to become part of the process.[13] If Aeneas's journey demands self-sacrifice, it also requires the sacrifice of others. Each of Virgil's three works ends with a death that enables progress: in Eclogue 10 the love elegist Gallus succumbs to the power of love and is left behind to die in Arcadia, freeing the speaker to begin his move into a Georgic mode; in *Georgic* 4, the death of the poet/lover Orpheus, caused by the worker Aristaeus, who embodies the work ethic of the poem and prefigures Aeneas, lets the poet himself move forward; and in *Aeneid* 12, the Italian Turnus is slain to confirm Aeneas's new authority and, indeed, identity.[14] Virgil admires the might of Rome even as he knows that it is built on a pile of displaced and dead bodies: the exiled shepherds of the *Eclogues*, Dido, the lovers Nisus and Euryalus, Pallas, Lausus, Camilla, and finally Turnus and perhaps even Aeneas himself. Maturation crushes beauty, vitality, and, above all, love. It involves a kind of stripping away, a version of the pruning of young elms described in *Georgic* 2.368–70, where Virgil advises farmers: "tum stringe comas, tum bracchia tonde / (ante reformidant ferrum), tum denique dura / exerce imperia et ramos compesce fluentis" (then strip their locks and clip their arms — ere that they shrink from the knife — then at last set up an iron sway and check the flowing branches). The underlying anthropomorphism of the natural world, in which trees have arms and hair, suggests the violence here; the image will be recalled in *Aeneid* 3, when Aeneas breaks off shoots to build a shrine to his mother only to discover, with understandable astonishment, that what he took for local shrubbery was his cousin, the metamorphosed Polydorus. The cost of this process is not just for the losers but also for the winners themselves. Virgil remembers the Greek tragedies that had demonstrated that the Trojan War had destroyed the victors as much as the victims. Agamemnon's homecoming was not a huge success, and in *Aeneid* 11, Diomedes, one of the blood-thirstiest of all the Greeks, refuses to continue fighting the Trojans, saying that "infanda per orbem / supplicia et scelerum poenas expendimus omnes, / vel Priamo miseranda manus" (we, the wide world over, have paid all manners of penalties for guilt in nameless tortures, a band that even Priam might pity [11.257–59]). In the process of becoming a *winner*, Aeneas *loses* everyone he cares about personally:

his wife, his father, his lover — even his old nurse has to die before he reaches Italy to show that he has truly grown up and become completely independent. (His mother, of course, hardly speaks to him, despite his poignant attempts to reach out to her.) If Aeneas is allowed to keep his son, it is because an heir is a dynastic necessity to ensure continuity. For him, maturation brings an individuation that is equivalent to alienation, including that from the self since, ironically, such individuation depends on the total repression of the individual's personal desires. It seems a particularly lousy deal.

Finally, who or what does Aeneas really become at the end of the poem? Fulgentius and others said that in slaying Turnus, the hero was overcoming the *furor* with which Turnus is associated.[15] Yet in the act of killing his furious enemy, Aeneas is himself described as "furiis accensus et ira / terribilis" (fired with fury and terrible in his wrath [12.946–47]); Lactantius therefore complains: "Quisquamne igitur hunc putet aliquid in se virtutis habuisse, qui et furore tamquam stipulo exarserit, et...iram fraenare nequiverit?" (How could anyone, therefore, think that Aeneas had anything of virtue in him: one who kindled with fury like straw...and could not restrain his anger?).[16] Is Aeneas overcoming his emotions or giving in to them? Has he really changed at all from the furious Trojan who, during the fall of Troy, seemed as enflamed as the city itself? The poem ends with an extended close-up of the consciousness of Turnus, shifting our attention and sympathy to the loser at the moment that he meets death and his shade leaves his body. The chillingly abrupt ending — which lacks the comfort of closure afforded by the burial of Hector's body in the *Iliad*, Virgil's primary model for this part of the poem — seems ominous for the future of Rome, a future that Virgil knows will include civil war. The final scene does not emphasize growth and progress but returns to the pattern of premature death that haunts the poem, and indeed Roman history, as Anchises's triumphant vision of the future in book 6 ends abruptly in lamentation for the death of Augustus's nephew and heir Marcellus.[17] If Turnus's death makes possible the future of Rome, it is a future that will repeat the past by taking the lives of young men. There is something about the founding of Rome that stunts progress and new developments; the fact that all roads lead to Rome may not be a good thing if they also just end there.

While this other voice of Virgil has been clamoring for attention in recent years, critics have debated whether it was heard by earlier readers.[18] As David Wilson-Okamura's superb study of Virgil in the Renaissance shows, scholars clearly were aware of some of the darker aspects of the poem but largely chose to ignore them.[19] However, as Wilson-Okamura dryly observes, critics are generally a conservative bunch, happy to overlook innovation and retreat into the security of familiar errors. (Of course, he is talking only about critics in the Middle Ages and the Renaissance.) Poets are a different matter, more sensitive to and indeed interested in probing the conflicts and contradictions of Virgil's story. This is especially true of Milton, for whom Lewis's description is particularly apt. With Virgil, Milton grows up. More importantly, however, through Virgil Milton thinks about what it means to grow up.

The importance of Virgil to Milton's early growth as a poet is obvious from the numerous echoes and allusions in the early Latin and English verse. Many critics have noted how the 1645 *Poems* narrates the development of what Louis Martz describes as "the rising poet, the predestined bard."[20] Each half of the double volume, divided roughly between English and Latin poems or, more precisely, between modern and ancient languages, is arranged so that, as Martz shows, "the over-arching structure runs from poems of early youth to poems that enact a movement towards the broader visions of maturity."[21] The model for this self-fashioning is clearly Virgil, whose reputed sexual purity is also congenial to Milton's great theme of chastity, and who provides the motto for the volume as well as many of the characters and images.[22] The English half opens with the Nativity ode, which draws on Virgil's Eclogue 4 to celebrate not only the birth of Christ but also Milton's own poetic beginning. The Latin section also opens with Elegia 1, a poem that places the poet in the Virgilian sequence, as the topic of exile recalls Eclogue 1, though playfully, as Milton's pleasant exile from school makes poetry possible. Two Virgilian pastoral elegies, *Lycidas* and *Epitaphium Damonis*, bring each half to a close and announce the poet's next move up the *rota*. As in Virgil, the poet's progress depends on the death of others. This sounds rather ghoulish, recalling Northrop Frye's famous description of a young Milton who "had been practicing since adolescence on every fresh corpse in sight,"[23] but partly reflects the fact that poets conventionally develop their craft by writing elegies, as Virgil did in Eclogue 5. Still, for Milton as for Virgil, such deaths enable the poet's growth in other ways as well. Like those of Virgil, Milton's speakers identify with but ultimately detach themselves from figures who represent an aspect of themselves they must abandon in order to mature: in *Lycidas*, Edward King, and, in *Epitaphium Damonis*, heartbreakingly, Milton's best friend, Charles Diodati. Both poems address the poet's development as he confronts the mortality that threatens it. While *Lycidas* traces the transformation of the drowned young man into the "Genius of the shore" (183), this symbolic death and rebirth also transforms the poet who in the last eight lines separates himself from his past pastoral life and gestures toward the ottava rima of epic.[24] The moment recalls especially the end of *Georgic* 4, when the speaker looks back from some distance at his former bucolic and georgic selves as he prepares to enter the world of the epic. In a similar way in *Epitaphium Damonis* the loss of Diodati shatters the ideal and protected world of Milton's youth and brings an end to the poet's first phase of development through the shattering of the pipes of pastoral poetry (157–60). But what appears at first to be the end of his career turns into a new beginning, as the poem rises toward the metamorphosis not only of Diodati, who is now in heaven, but also of the speaker whose epic future is shadowed here as he speaks of possible subjects for his poetry (163–71). The death of his closest friend, which seems to prematurely end the poet's career, is ultimately the means by which Milton also ascends.[25] While the final image of the poem shows a transfigured Diodati in heaven, the speaker sneaks himself up there, too, in a pun on the last word, "Thyrsus" (219): literally, the Bacchic wand, but also echoing the Virgilian name, Thyrsis, that Milton has given himself in the poem. Diodati's death reassures him that he will get to heaven through his writing.

Both the English and the Latin halves of the 1645 volume, then, tell the same story. While poems like *L'Allegro* and *Il Penseroso* in English and Elegia 6 in Latin speculate on the different kinds of writer Milton might be and so seem to leave future directions of development open, the overarching narrative seems overdetermined from the start. Whether he writes in English or Latin, the young Milton is on a Virgilian route. Such doubling and overdetermination seems itself Virgilian; as often noted, Virgil sees history as an echo chamber of reverberating events in which history repeats itself according to foreseen patterns set by Jove and the Fates. All roads do lead to Rome.

The symmetry of this *gemelle liber* (double book; "Ad Joannem Rousium," 1) is broken, however, by the inclusion of *A Mask* at the end of the English half. The work stands out for many reasons, including the fact that it has no Latin counterpart. In Martz's reading of Milton's Virgilian rise, it is therefore treated as a work apart. But in many ways *A Mask* is the perfect encapsulation of the Virgilian narrative. As the *Aeneid* recapitulates the story of growth told in Virgil's early works, *A Mask* repeats and completes the process of development told in the two parts of the volume. It bridges the two parts, giving the collection a center that epitomizes and consolidates the process told in both languages. As William Shullenberger reminds us, *A Mask* is an initiation rite, dramatizing both the Lady's transition from childhood to womanhood, and Milton's transition to the epic that the masque constantly points toward.[26] The longest piece in the volume, and a shift to a completely new genre, drama, *A Mask* is an ambitious leap forward from the short poems. It is a summary of the classical and English literary traditions, a retrospective on Milton's progress so far and a blueprint for his future. The masque genre can barely mask Milton's eagerness to get to this next stage of his career. Epic elements keep intruding. It is haunted by the shades of Milton's own future: the line "What never yet was heard in Tale or Song" (*Mask* 44) — which is basically a highly conventional claim of originality — seems eerily proleptic of the more famous "Things unattempted yet in Prose or Rhime" (*PL* 1.16), while the debate between Comus and the Lady rehearses the confrontation between good and evil in *Paradise Lost* and in *Paradise Regained*. But the epic elements also point the poem toward the past. The Lady is a version of the typical epic questor, whose journey is impeded by evil forces. She looks back to Odysseus, who resisted Comus's mother before her, and Spenser's Guyon and especially his Britomart, who is also on a path of chaste womanhood. Yet even more strikingly, the Lady's journey is like that of Aeneas. Unlike Odysseus, but like Aeneas, she is going not to an old home but a new one; she leaves England for Wales on a journey that is both a story of personal growth and part of the expansion of empire.[27] The link to the story of Aeneas is reinforced by the role of Sabrina, the water nymph who helps the Lady cross the river that symbolically divides her two states, and who is herself of Trojan descent; associated with chastity, like the Lady and Virgil, she is summoned by her genealogy as: "Virgin, daughter of *Locrine* / Sprung of old *Anchises* line" (922–23).

The story of Sabrina reminds us that, though Milton himself was skeptical of the myth in *The History of Britain*, the English, like the Romans and indeed all other Renaissance nations, claimed to be descended from the Trojans.[28] As Aeneas established Rome, the Trojan Brute founded England—a myth that reinforced the belief that Virgilian models had particular relevance for the English. For Spenser, England repeats Roman history, as is clear in the history of Britain in *Faerie Queene* 2, in which Sabrina plays a very small, though telling, role.[29] Copying Virgil, who made the history of Rome a repeated battle against and conquest of savage (and often semihuman) forces, Spenser imagines England to be a nation that is constantly threatened by but eventually overcomes dangerous monsters. However, the people who repel foreign invaders succumb to enemies within: traitors, and especially their own lustful desires. The latter is the case of Sabrina's father, the Trojan Locrine, who conquers all foes except his own passions; giving in to lust, he is killed by his jealous wife. The illegitimate daughter of his affair, Sabrina is an innocent victim who is also murdered by the enraged queen.

By using this minor character, who in Spenser appears and dies in a single stanza (*Faerie Queene*, 2.10.19), for the crucial role of liberating the Lady, the young Milton creates a genealogical link between his own budding epic ambitions, Spenser, and beyond them both, Virgil. It is an august literary family tree for the rising poet. But Milton seems also to be noting Spenser and Virgil's presentation of history. In rewriting Spenser, Milton makes Sabrina's death a suicide, a revision that emphasizes the theme of social and individual self-destruction that troubles Spenser's story of Britain.[30] It is a theme that haunts Virgil as well, and one that is appropriate for a country whose other major myth of foundation involved fratricide (the story of Romulus and Remus) and which had just been through the civic suicide of civil war. At the beginning of the *Aeneid*, Aeneas has suicidal tendencies, seeking glorious death in battle as befits a classical warrior. As Aeneas learns to become a new kind of hero, however, Virgil projects these early self-destructive impulses onto Rome's enemies and, especially, women — Dido, Amata, and Cleopatra — who take their own lives.

Spenser, however, disturbingly makes such women part of the history of Britain in the forms of Cordelia and Bunduca (Boadicea) (*Faerie Queene* 2.10.27–32, 54–57). Although he admires their bravery and heroism, he also presents such traits as evidence of the self-destructive impulse that is a part of England's classical inheritance and was perhaps particularly disturbing for a country ruled by a female monarch whose famed virginity was bringing the Tudor dynasty to a dead end. Milton, by revising Sabrina's death as a suicide, makes her part of this pattern (he may also be remembering that in Spenser Bunduca kills herself at the Severn; see *Faerie Queene* 2.10.54–55).[31] Like that of similar Virgilian figures, Sabrina's death enables the hero's progress. The stage direction makes clear the dynamics here: "Sabrina descends, and the Lady rises out of her seat" (*Mask* 921–22 s.d.). But as a boundary figure who represents geographical divisions (England and Wales), Sabrina also marks the limits of the Virgilian tradition in the poem, the place at which Virgilian development reaches its dead end.

A different future for the Lady is suggested by the vision of heaven in the Attendant Spirit's last speech and, in particular, by the figure of Psyche who with her husband, Cupid, and twin children, Youth and Joy, inhabits the highest paradise to which the Spirit now returns (*Mask* 1003–11). Psyche does not, of course, appear in Virgil or even, despite what many think, Ovid. Her story is a late myth, first appearing in the second century in Apuleius's *Metamorphoses*, better known as *The Golden Ass*. As the original title makes clear, Apuleius's work consciously recalls Ovid's epic.[32] But like Ovid's *Metamorphoses*, it is also a response to Virgil's narrative. Like Virgil, Apuleius tells a story of growth through loss, trial, temptation, and ultimately recovery. The beautiful Psyche is taken to paradise by her lover, whom she does not know is Cupid, only to lose both husband and home when she is persuaded by her envious sisters that he is a monster who will devour her. Like Aeneas, she is sent into exile and has to make her way home. Through suffering and trial she wins back the paradise that was at first simply given to her. But in so doing she learns also that in union with another she is not consumed but strengthened. Love is not, after all, a monster — the destructive force in Virgil that in the *Eclogues* and *Georgics* spreads madness and leads to the death of Gallus and Orpheus, and which in the *Aeneid* threatens individuation and progress — but a god, who raises his beloved to divinity. Psyche is therefore an anti-Aeneas who grows not through the rejection of love but through its power. Becoming part of a couple, her ultimate goal is not individuation but relationship or, rather, individuation in relationship.[33]

As many have noted, much of the final description of the heavenly gardens in *A Mask* anticipates Milton's presentation of a paradise centered around a happy couple. This brings me back finally to where I started: the role of Virgil in Milton's epic. *Paradise Lost* is also a story about growing up, as it traces the development of Adam and Eve and of the world itself. Eden is like Virgil's Rome: originally bounded by walls, it is fated to expand to include the entire universe. Just as Virgil's Jove imagines Rome reaching to the stars and becoming "imperium sine fine" (*Aeneid* 1.279), Milton's God suggests a future time when earth will "be chang'd to Heav'n, & Heav'n to Earth, / One Kingdom, Joy and Union without end" (*PL* 7.160–61).[34] The garden is itself a place of growth that looks back to the Virgil of the *Georgics*.[35] As Virgil, and indeed any gardener, knows, in order to grow, nature must be cut back — as the image of pruning I cited earlier suggests. Left to its own devices, nature runs riot and destroys itself; so Virgil warns us, "*poma...degenerant*" (apples degenerate [2.59]). For this reason also, Milton's Adam and Eve must tame the "Wilderness of sweets" (*PL* 5.294) that, weeping "odorous Gumms and Balme" (4.248), is "Wilde above Rule or Art" (5.297); the gardeners wander

> where any row
> Of Fruit-trees overwoodie reachd too farr
> Thir pamperd boughes, and needed hands to check
> Fruitless imbraces: or they led the Vine
> To wed her Elm; she spous'd about him twines
> Her marriageable arms, and with her brings
> Her dowr th'adopted Clusters, to adorn
> His barren leaves.   (5.212–19)

While the labor in the garden is like that in Virgil, the imagery here is very different from Virgil's vocabulary of amputation, cutting off, and clamping down, as Milton emphasizes gardening as a process of union. Here too the anthropomorphism of the vine and elm suggests the deep interconnection between humans and nature, joined by an act of marriage. Paradisal gardening is both a product of and a form of marriage, a natural wedding, in which the union between Adam and Eve generates and symbolizes the process of growth.

While Aeneas's story also is one that leads to marriage with the Italian Lavinia, the *Aeneid* never reaches the happy wedding day (left to be told in Maffeo Vegio's *Aeneid* 13).[36] That future marriage is envisioned coldly as the engrafting of primitive Italian vigor onto a somewhat decadent and even effeminate Trojan race, while sex only appears through violence — the union of Nisus and Euryalus in death, the symbolic deflowering of the latter and of Lausus and Pallas. For Virgil, moreover, gender differentiation is essential to Aeneas's development. When they first meet, Dido and Aeneas are mirror images of each other: exiles who are founding new countries, good rulers, generous, noble. At the same stages in their individual stories, they are distinguished only by nationality and gender. Renaissance readers believed that the story of the historical Dido, who had been famed for her chastity and lived long before Aeneas fled Troy, had been appropriated and twisted by Virgil to explain the origins of the conflict between Carthage and Rome. But Virgil's version is influential in offering a central myth for the origins of sexual difference in which two characters who are originally alike develop antithetically.[37] Aeneas's progression requires Dido's regression from a model ruler and lawgiver into a raving madwoman, a mixture of Medea and Cleopatra. *Aeneid* 4 claims that men and women develop in opposite directions: men acquire self-control as women become hysterical and suicidal.

The presentation and development of Milton's couple offer a striking contrast to the Dido and Aeneas of *Aeneid* 4. Though originally one flesh, they are not identical to begin with. They are, therefore, also unlike Du Bartas's Adam and Eve, who are so similar that "hardly, one / Could have the Lover from his Love discride, / Or knowne the Bridegroome from his gentle Bride."[38] The difference is, of course, famously expressed in the authoritative affirmation of gender hierarchy in book 4: "both / Not equal, as thir sex not equal seemd" (*PL* 4.295–96). As Karen Edwards notes, "The peculiar grammatical construction, 'both / Not equal,' insists upon the sameness of Adam and Eve even as it admits some unspecified degree of difference."[39] At one level the two are the same, even as at another they are different. Their actions and speeches show that from the very start Adam and Eve have distinct characters and develop in different ways. Where the introverted Eve seems initially happy and self-sufficient in her solitude, the extroverted Adam immediately craves and seeks others. Yet despite this and Eve's stressed subordination, their roles seem fairly flexible. Like most couples, the two lovers also have different memories of their courtship and union that are suggestive of the personalities Milton will create for the newly separated halves. They are dynamic characters who develop even in the brief time we see them before the Fall as they learn from Raphael, their work, and, most of all, each other.[40] Although in retrospect the fact that Eve speaks first on the last day seems sinister, it is also a sign that the two are changing. Like everything in the garden, they grow.

The glimpse of Edenic growth is, of course, a brief one, cut off by the Fall, which thrusts the couple into a world much more familiar to us in which sexual hierarchy is now clearly codified as a rigid division of labor. Men and women now develop differently, as Adam learns history through divine revelation, Eve through dreams. Divided by gender, full of hard work, the newly fallen world has a Virgilian shape. As often noted, the vision of history in books 11–12 draws on Anchises's presentation of Rome's future in *Aeneid* 6, the model for all such epic genealogies. For Milton, however, the imperial march of Rome has become a futile cycle of self-destruction, manifested also in Adam and Eve's despair and desire for immediate death. Like Virgil's women, Eve contemplates suicide. As often noted also, her offer of self-sacrifice, "On me, sole cause to thee of all this woe, / Mee mee onely just object of his ire" (*PL* 10.935–36), echoes *Aeneid* 9.427–28, in which Nisus offers himself in place of his beloved Euryalus: "Me, me, adsum qui feci, in me convertite ferrum, / …mea fraus omnis" (On me — on me — here I am who did the deed — on me turn your steel…mine is all the guilt). In Virgil, Nisus's attempted self-sacrifice only leads to the death of both lovers, beginning a new phase of savage killing in the Italian war. Adam, however, dissuades Eve from that course of action, sensing that it is no longer necessary. Eve does not need to play that role because it has already been taken by Christ, who in book 3 offers himself as substitution for humankind: "Behold mee then, mee for him, life for life / I offer, on mee let thine anger fall" (*PL* 3.236–37).[41] Christ's self-sacrifice repeats, completes, but also ends the recycling of self-destruction that seems eternal in Virgil.

Christ's offer means that as they leave paradise Adam and Eve may stay together. Though they are now deeply divided from each other and sentenced to antithetical forms of labor, they are still joined, "hand in hand" (*PL* 12.648). As the angels descend to send the couple out from their pastoral life into the next georgic stage, the final scene modulates into a shadowy crepuscular tone reminiscent of Virgil. Milton describes the angels in a rich simile:

> as Ev'ning Mist
> Ris'n from a River o're the marish glides,
> And gathers ground fast at the Labourers heel
> Homeward returning.   (12.629–32)

The figure of the laborer suggests the couple's entry into the georgic world of hard work. Like the exiled shepherds in the *Eclogues* who seek shelter in the darkness as *"maioresque cadunt altis de montibus umbrae"* (longer shadows fall from the mountain heights [1.83]), Adam and Eve are exiled into a darkening world in which they have to search for a "place of rest" (12.647).[42] Expelled from Eden, they arrive now at the point at which Virgil's career and Milton's 1645 *Poems* start, when they too must begin growing up, not with Virgil, but with each other, as Virgil's isolated wanderer becomes Milton's alienated but still united couple. Fortunately, their path is not that of Aeneas, but that of Psyche, who sets out to earn for herself through trial and labor the paradise she was first simply given, and who will be helped through the power of love.

CHAPTER 5

———※———

Reason, Love, and Regeneration
in *Paradise Lost*, Book 10

DANIELLE A. ST. HILAIRE

The regeneration scene in book 10 of *Paradise Lost* has been a site of critical contention, and, in particular, readers have disagreed about where to place the responsibility for Adam and Eve's initial repentance and thus their subsequent steps toward regeneration. Joseph Summers famously gave the credit to Eve's love when she begs Adam's his forgiveness (10.914–36), which Summers views as a type of God's own forgiveness, and for many critics this argument continues to carry the day.[1] Georgia B. Christopher, however, provides a strong, if lonely, voice of dissent to the tradition of reading Eve as the hero of regeneration. Aiming to put an end to what she called such "romantic" and "sentimental" readings of the poem, Christopher argues that "Eve's loving gesture of reconciliation (which is far more self-serving than selfless, anyway) has no direct bearing upon Adam's return to faith." For Christopher, reading the poem through the writings of Luther and Calvin, Eve cannot be responsible for regeneration because, as the beginning of book 11 asserts, God's a priori prevenient grace is the cause of the fallen pair's repentance: if God is preeminently responsible, then Eve cannot also be the eminent cause.[2] Since Christopher's article, Dennis Danielson has convincingly demonstrated the Arminianism of *Paradise Lost* and particularly of the regeneration scene, which, he argues, "place[s] within the context of divine grace the limited but real freedom we have seen operating."[3]

Recognizing the cooperative nature of grace in the poem eliminates the logical necessity of dismissing Eve as a cause of regeneration, and so it is perhaps unsurprising that, while many discussions of Eve at the end of book 10 still cite Christopher's account, critical consensus has continued to point to Eve's "sounder emotional nature," her "humility powered by love," and her "selfless wish to suffer for Adam" as the engine driving Adam and Eve's reconciliation with God.[4] Yet I would like to return to Christopher's warning against making Eve the hero of regeneration and her love the means, not because such a reading obscures God's agency in regeneration but because overemphasizing emotion at the expense of reason, and foregrounding individual heroism, underemphasizes the role of mutuality, relationship, and collaboration in the scene. The prevenient grace God offers to his fallen creatures, the means to start on the path of regeneration, is the power of freedom: freedom requires the exercise of right reason, which is only enabled by collaborative action. I will argue that love in *Paradise Lost* consists in the use of reason for the benefit of another. But this means that the poem cannot make either Eve or Adam into the hero of regeneration because regeneration is not the work of heroic individuals: it is by its nature a kind of relationship, an undertaking that requires mutual acknowledgment, mutual striving, mutual engagement with the other.

The moment many have called Eve's heroism, her poignant "Forsake me not" speech, concludes with Eve saying she

> to the place of judgment will return,
> There with my cries importune heaven, that all
> The sentence from thy head removed may light
> On me, sole cause to thee of all this woe,
> Me me only just object of his ire.[5]

Where many readers have found a loving self-sacrifice, Christopher instead hears only a "wail." Eve "will risk anything," she argues, "rather than be left totally alone": thus, "her offer is an unconsidered and almost instinctive gesture of self-preservation."[6] Christopher's reading of Eve perhaps seems harsh — Daniel Doerksen accuses her twice of being an unsympathetic reader[7] — but Christopher picks up on the self-serving element of Eve's speech that subsequent readings have either ignored or passed over too quickly. Christopher notes that, prior to her offer of sacrifice, Eve asks Adam, "forlorn of thee, / Whither shall I betake me, where subsist?" (10.921–22), suggesting that Eve's greatest fear is to be left ultimately alone without Adam (which is also the fear that leads her to offer the fruit to Adam in book 9). More than this, however, Eve's words also evince solipsistic thinking. Immediately prior to her offer, Eve says to her husband,

> on me exercise not
> Thy hatred for this misery befallen,
> On me already lost, me than thyself
> More miserable; both have sinned, but thou
> Against God only, I against God and thee.   (927–31)

Eve will ask God for all the punishment because, she argues here, she deserves all the blame. But her desire to take all the blame does not seem to grow entirely from a desire to shield Adam from God's punishment but rather — at least in this moment — from a desire to shield herself from Adam's vitriol: she wants him to stop directing his "hatred for this misery" to her. Her argument for why he should do so — that she is "more miserable" than he is — furthermore attempts to diminish Adam's own suffering by comparing it to hers, as if their suffering were a competition in which the victor gets to demand the other's forgiveness. As Regina Schwartz points out, "Eve is overzealous here, owning more fault than is her due, and without a warning voice, she is susceptible to lapsing into narcissism again, the narcissism — 'me, sole…mee mee only' — of self-pity."[8] In trying to persuade Adam to take pity on her, Eve imagines her pain to outweigh her husband's and so treats herself with pity. In this context, her offer of self-sacrifice appears to be more about escaping her own misery — and perhaps proving to Adam that she suffers more than he — than it is about a heroic act of love for her husband.

Eve's words furthermore resonate ominously with other utterances of despair elsewhere in the poem. Where Summers compares these lines to the Son's offer at 3.236–41 to die for humanity's sins ("Behold me then, me for him, life for life / I offer, on me let thine anger fall") in order to claim that Eve is engaging in "the imperfect, if unconscious, imitation" of "the loving offer" the Son makes for humanity,[9] I would argue that Eve's words in book 10 more closely resemble the proximate and considerably less heroic words of her yet unregenerate husband. In his previous soliloquy, Adam had displayed the same sort of solipsistic overtones and momentum toward self-serving intents, claiming,

> all my evasions vain
> And reasonings, though through mazes, lead me still
> But to my own conviction: first and last
> On me, me only, as the source and spring
> Of all corruption, all the blame lights due;
> So might the wrath.   (10.829–34)

Here Adam, like Eve, overstates his fault for original sin, ignoring his partner's participation in the act, and this overstatement leads him to ask that, since all the blame is his, all the punishment be his as well.[10] As in Eve's speech, Adam's desire to be the sole recipient of God's punishment at this moment seems to grow more from a sense of the situation's hopelessness than from love for another. Adam claims that he has tried to escape his sense of guilt through "evasions" and "reasonings" but is nevertheless in all cases brought back "to [his] own conviction." In other words, he returns to a "declaration of [his own] guilt" but also to the "mental state or condition of being convinced" that all paths lead to his guilt.[11] Adam, like Eve after him, feels trapped in and by his misery, and so death — which Adam as yet views as the product of God's wrath[12] — appears as the only escape from the intolerable sense of his sinfulness.

Mary Ann Nevins Radzinowicz describes Adam in these lines as "plunged in despair. He has understood God's justice but been unable to feel his mercy."[13] If this is true of Adam's offer of self-sacrifice, then it is true also of Eve's. Both are driven to a desire to die by the self-pity of "me, me only," by a solipsism that leads them only to their own convictions and offers death as the sole remedy. This suggests that Eve is not in fact "respond[ing] first to 'prevenient grace'" when she approaches Adam in her distress, any more than Adam is in his soliloquy; her inner state is just as despairing as his.[14] But this is not to say that Eve does not provide what Rachel Falconer calls "the *peripeteia* of the whole work, reversing its spiral downwards, and initiating the process of regeneration."[15] The mechanism by which she does so simply has less to do with her interior state and more to do with the providential structure of regeneration in the poem.

To know when Adam and Eve first start to move toward regenerative thinking and action, it is helpful to look to book 3, where God describes the process whereby fallen creatures may begin to make their way back to him. God explains:

> Man shall not quite be lost, but saved who will,
> Yet not of will in him, but grace in me
> Freely vouchsafed; once more I will renew
> His lapsèd powers, though forfeit and enthralled
> By sin to foul exorbitant desires;
> Upheld by me, yet once more he shall stand
> On even ground against his mortal foe.   (3.173–79)

God's gift to his fallen creatures, the "grace" he offers, is the renewal of their "lapsèd powers." These "powers" enable humanity to return to an even playing field against Satan and his followers, suggesting, as Benjamin Myers argues about these lines, that the power God announces will be restored by this grace is the ability to *choose*: "prevenient grace places the human will's power of choice back on the balanced scales, so that the alternative decision between good and evil becomes an authentic possibility."[16] What sets fallen humanity on the path toward regeneration is the restoration of the freedom that God earlier insists is necessary for all his creatures (3.102–11).[17]

The return of humanity's "lapsèd powers," however, is not sufficient for regeneration. This freedom is instead part of a process by which a fallen being finds his or her way back to God. God describes this process a few lines later:

> And I will place within them as a guide
> My umpire conscience, whom if they will hear,
> Light after light well used they shall attain,
> And to the end persisting, safe arrive.
> This my long sufferance and my day of grace
> They who neglect and scorn, shall never taste;
> But hard be hardened, blind be blinded more,
> That they may stumble on, and deeper fall;
> And none but such from mercy I exclude.   (3.194–202)

Once he has renewed their lapsed powers, God explains, his creatures can walk one of two paths. One path could lead them to choose to follow the guidance offered by conscience, figured as a "light" in line 196. By doing so, they will find themselves offered yet more light, which in time will help them, if they persist, to "safe arrive" at God's kingdom in heaven. The other path could lead them to choose to "neglect and scorn" God's "day of grace." If following conscience means hearing the voice of God within and looking to God's light, then the choice to scorn what God offers leads to blindness — the removal of God's light, the guidance of conscience — which in turn leads the creature away from God and his mercy.

In this sense, God's creatures *by his grace* are enabled to become once more "Sufficient to [stand], though free to fall" (3.99). As the light metaphor makes clear, however, their ability to persist again in this state of freedom is contingent upon their making the right choice. The fallen being's ability to receive additional light depends on whether that light is "well used" in the first place, meaning they choose to hear the guidance of conscience; those who instead "neglect and scorn" lose that light. When light is no longer offered, the ability to choose to follow that light disappears — and with it free choice. Freedom in *Paradise Lost* is thus, as William Walker notes, conditional.[18] It does not consist merely in choice, but in *right* choice. The "lapsèd powers" God restores cannot be merely the ability to make any choice, but the ability to choose what is right. Being free in *Paradise Lost* means having access to the guidance of reason.

The poem, therefore, insists upon the connection between reason and freedom. God explains earlier in book 3 that he gave his creatures freedom of both "will and reason," adding that "reason also is choice" (3.108). Similarly, Adam tells Eve that "what obeys / Reason, is free" (9.351–52), and Michael tells Adam that "true liberty" "with right reason dwells / Twinned" (12.83, 84–85). But reason is not unerring, which Adams recognizes when he warns Eve to

> bid [Reason] well beware, and still erect,
> Lest by some fair appearing good surprised
> She dictate false, and misinform the will
> To do what God expressly hath forbid.   (9.353–56)

Appearances can be deceiving, Adam notes, and by following those deceitful appearances, reason can lead the will astray. To prevent this, he says,

Eve must bid her reason be "erect," a word which by its etymology recalls Adam's claim in the previous line that "reason [God] made right" (9.352) as well as Michael's later reference to "right reason." What makes reason "right," Adam's words to Eve suggest, is that it is directed: "erect" derives from the Latin root *regere*, which means "to guide" or "direct."[19] Specifically in this case, Adam tells Eve to keep her reason guided by what God has asked of them, to avoid doing "what God expressly hath forbid." For the fallen creature, the guide of reason is, as God explains in book 3, conscience. Right reason — reason guided by conscience — signifies the being's freedom because right reason enables him or her to make the right choices and thereby to continue to receive God's light. *Right* reason goes hand in hand with freedom.

The poem provides an instructive negative example of the relationship between right reason, freedom, and regeneration in Satan's famous book 4 soliloquy. Here Satan shows he is capable of conceiving of the possibility of repenting, which would be to follow the guidance of conscience. However, his misuse of reason ends up shutting off his ability to make a right choice for himself, a choice that would lead him back to God. Satan begins by hypothesizing that he "could repent and could obtain / By act of grace [his] former state," but then immediately reasons that this repentance would not work:

> how soon
> Would height recall high thoughts, how soon unsay
> What feigned submission swore: ease would recant
> Vows made in pain, as violent and void.
> For never can true reconcilement grow
> Where wounds of deadly hate have pierced so deep:
> Which would but lead me to a worse relapse
> And heavier fall.   (4.93–101)

Satan's prediction of his hypothetical future self shows the archfiend using his reason, but not "rightly." He assumes his "high thoughts" are a necessary outcome of a return to his former "height"; yet earlier in his soliloquy he already noted the fallacy in this line of thought, concluding that his free will, not his height, led him to fall in the first place (4.58–66). He also builds into his prediction the presupposition that his "submission" would be "feigned," and therein excludes any other possible outcome that might result from a *true* submission to God. His claim that "never can true reconcilement grow / Where wounds of deadly hate have pierced so deep" furthermore shows a lack of understanding of the "grace" he invokes in line 94. Thinking only of himself when he says that there can be no reconcilement, Satan chooses to ignore that reconcilement *is*, of course, possible for God, manifest in the very "act of grace" that would restore Satan's "former state" in the first place.[20] He does not understand — or chooses to ignore — God's justice and how it works or could work. At best, then, Satan is inconsistent in his logic. At worst, his logic is circular: the assumptions upon which he concludes the inevitable failure of his repentance presuppose that failure.

The logic of Satan's "wrong reason" leads him to conclude that he has no choice — that is, that he has no free will. He finishes by including God in his fallacious line of reasoning: "This knows my punisher; therefore as far / From granting he, as I from begging peace" (4.103–04). Having decided he cannot properly repent, Satan furthermore decides that the decision is not really his, anyway: God stands in the way of his repentance, too, so there is no point in even trying. Once he has decided that the path of repentance is closed to him, evil then becomes not a positive choice but the only choice, something thrust upon him: "all good to me is lost; / Evil be thou my good" (4.109–10). Satan embraces evil here after he has decided the only other option — return to good — "is lost" to him, and his use of the passive voice construes his loss as something done *to* Satan rather than *by* Satan. As Harold Skulsky notes of this scene, "Not only doesn't Satan 'seem' on the available evidence to have the power of choice, he doesn't 'seem' to have it even to himself."[21] The romantic heroism of Satan's book 1 assertion that "The mind is its own place, and in itself / Can make a heaven of hell, a hell of heaven" (1.254–55) has proven only half-true: Satan cannot find a way to make a heaven of hell and instead discovers that he has no choice but to make a hell of his own mind: "Me miserable! Which way shall I fly / Infinite wrath, and infinite despair? / Which way I fly is hell; myself am hell" (4.73–75). When Satan bids "farewell hope" after concluding that "All hope [is] excluded" (4.108, 105), he gives up not just on the possibility of having choices but specifically of having *right* choices — choices made by a reason that follows God's "umpire conscience," which in this case counsels Satan to repent. Without the ability to truly consider good possibilities, choice becomes meaningless, so that by book 9 "Evil be thou my good" has been transformed into "all good to me becomes / Bane" (9.122–23).[22] All illusion of choice here has been stripped away, so it is no surprise when Satan finds himself later in the speech "*constrained* / Into a beast, and mixed with bestial slime" (9.164–65; my emphasis).

Satan's misuse of reason means the loss of the freedom that reason is supposed to uphold. The poem thus presents in Satan a clear picture of what it means for a fallen creature to "neglect and scorn" God's "day of grace." Though Satan sees the possibility of repentance on Niphates's top, he chooses not to treat it as a genuine option, instead using his reason to move him away from, rather than toward, the one right choice available to him. As a result, he falls into greater and greater sins, becoming increasingly blind. Such are the thoughts of the unregenerate mind, manifesting the effects of a will and reason that have become, in God's words, "Useless and vain, of freedom both despoiled" (3.109). In considering Adam and Eve's regeneration in book 10, we can look to Satan's book 4 failures to identify the moment at which Adam and Eve depart from his erroneous course. To the extent that Adam and Eve use their reason erringly, they remain unregenerate. When, however, they begin to act with true freedom — that is, when their reason offers them a right choice and directs them to make that choice — they begin the path of return back toward God.

Both Adam's book 10 soliloquy and Eve's attempt at reconciliation initially manifest Satan's solipsism, the same kind of despair, and the same inability to conceive of or imagine or reason their way toward good options to remedy their state, seen in Satan's book 4 soliloquy. Just as Satan finds that "Which way I fly is hell," Adam's "evasions vain" lead only back to his "own conviction": both are stuck in a solipsism born of a lack of freedom. Not surprisingly, Adam's reasoning leads him to the same place it led Satan, as Adam concludes that his situation is hopeless:

> Thus what thou desir'st
> And what thou fearst, alike destroys all hope
> Of refuge, and concludes thee miserable
> Beyond all past example and futúre,
> To Satan only like both crime and doom.   (10.837–41)

A reader recalling book 4's soliloquy reads Adam's giving up "all hope" here with the knowledge that what follows Satan's "farewell hope" is his conclusion, "Evil be thou my good" (4.108, 110), and so Adam's hopelessness in book 10 puts him dangerously close to confirming his moral similarity to Satan in both "crime and doom."[23] Eve's "me than thy self / More miserable" likewise echoes Satan's "Me miserable," culminating, like Adam, in her own "conviction" for a crime whose only sentence is death. Adam's subsequent criticism that Eve is "Unwary, and too desirous, as before, / So now of what thou knowst not" (10.947–48) indicates that she, too, reasons in error when she offers to go before God. That she is just as unable as Adam to come up with a right choice for their situation reveals that she has yet to regain the freedom God's grace offers.

At the same time, however, the narrator makes quite clear that Eve's speech is indeed a turning point for the fallen pair:

> She ended weeping, and her lowly plight,
> Immovable till peace obtained from fault
> Acknowledged and deplored, in Adam wrought
> Commiseration; soon his heart relented
> Towards her.   (10.937–41)

In book 9, Satan's "relentless thoughts" drive him to destroy despite knowing that his actions mean his own destruction (9.130), and in his book 10 soliloquy Adam appears similarly unable to relent in his self-condemnation. That Eve's words cause Adam's heart at last to relent suggests an important shift in his interior state. This alteration, Mandy Green argues, suggests through the etymology of the word — "re + lentare, to make flexible, to bend, to become soft again" — a hint of God's promise to "soften stony hearts" (3.189).[24] But it is Adam, in his response to Eve's speech, and not Eve herself, who first shows signs of the rehabilitated reason necessary to the process of regeneration. By noting that Eve is "Unwary, and too desirous, as before, / So now of what thou knowst not," Adam in one moment acknowledges both her past sin and that her present line of reasoning is running toward that sin again, demonstrating for the first time since his fall his ability to distinguish a right argument from an erroneous one.

The pattern repeats itself as Adam and Eve continue their dialogue. Because "miserable it is / To be to others cause of misery" (10.981–82), Eve suggests they refrain from propagating their curse in their progeny by either abstaining from sex or by killing themselves before they have any children. Again, Adam comprehends the mistake, arguing how suicide or "wilful barrenness"

> cuts us off from hope, and savours only
> Rancour and pride, impatience and despite,
> Reluctance against God and his just yoke
> Laid on our necks.   (10.1042–46)

Here again Adam sees in Eve's despairing proposal not just an error in rational decision making, but a repetition of their original sin: disobedience against God.[25] And in correctly reasoning out the problem, Adam for the first time since their fall implies that hope does, in fact, exist and that their failure to find that hope had grown out of their faulty reasoning rather than from a hopeless situation. This recognition enables Adam to conclude they should pray to God for forgiveness (10.1086–92), a moment indicating God's providential promise from book 3 that he will, by his grace, "soften stony hearts / To pray, repent, and bring obedience due" (3.189–90). With right reason comes right choices. The scene illustrates that after Eve confronts Adam with her despair, he reverses course so that instead of reproducing Satan's reprobate line of reasoning, Adam undoes it. He enables both himself and Eve to experience freedom again by first discovering and then choosing to follow the light of conscience.

—❈—

I have emphasized Adam's role in the early stages of Adam and Eve's regeneration to demonstrate the importance of reason in this process because the theology of the poem identifies right reason, the power that produces creaturely freedom, as the mechanism by which fallen beings can find their way back to God. This is not to say, however, that Adam's reason, rather than Eve's love, is responsible for regeneration. Choosing between love *or* reason — or between Adam *or* Eve — in assigning the source or cause of regeneration in the poem misses the extent to which the theology of regeneration in *Paradise Lost* treats right reason as a necessary component of love and of faith, and treats relationship rather than individual effort as both the means and end of grace. This connection between reason and loving relationships is given dramatic form in book 10's regeneration scene, but it is first described by God in book 3. Before he explains that his grace will manifest itself in the creature's freedom, God defends the idea that the freedom of his beings is necessary in the first place:

> Freely they stood who stood, and fell who fell.
> Not free, what proof could they have given sincere
> Of true allegiance, constant faith or love?
> Where only what they needs must do, appeared,
> Not what they would, what praise could they receive?
> What pleasure I from such obedience paid,
> When will and reason (reason also is choice)
> Useless and vain, of freedom both despoiled,
> Made passive both, had served necessity,
> Not me.   (3.102–11)

God explains that freedom, though it enables beings to fall away from him, nevertheless is necessary for three reasons: (1) it enables "proof...sincere / Of true allegiance, constant faith [and] love"; (2) it enables God to "praise" because what they "do" is what they "would" do — their actions are a manifestation of their inner states; (3) it enables God to receive "pleasure" from their "obedience." The interconnected progression indicates that "obedience" and service are, for God, predicated on "true allegiance...faith [and] love." To give "proof" means to make a trial of something, as Raphael's later paraphrase indicates, but "proof" also means to provide evidence.[26] To prove their inward allegiance, faith, and love, God's beings need to make that inward state appear through what they do. Outward manifestation of "obedience" equates to service. This is not an unthinking, servile obedience but, rather, this service is what one who feels "true allegiance,...faith [and] love" *would do*; that is, it is the activity produced by the inner state of "true allegiance,...faith [and] love." Raphael's earlier lessons to Adam resound here, as Raphael had explained, "freely we serve, / Because we freely love" (5.538–39), and he describes God as "whom to love is to obey" (8.634).[27]

God's words in book 3 are significant for two reasons. First, they illuminate the connection between reason and love in *Paradise Lost*. What enables inner love to manifest itself in obedience, God indicates, is the freedom of "will and reason." Following an Augustinian and Thomist tradition in which love "is partly a matter of feeling, but it is primarily a matter of will," Milton's God specifies that love requires action.[28] Since what directs the will to act is reason, as Adam explains to Eve at 9.353–56, then the role of reason in the poem is to manifest love in the world through action. It makes little sense, therefore, to assign to reason *or* to love the power to initiate the process of regeneration in book 10: love without reason has no power to act in the world, while reason without love is not right reason and is not properly directed because it will not be seeking to obey he "whom to love is to obey."

Second, and perhaps more important, God's words at 3.102–11 indicate that the teleology of freedom in *Paradise Lost* is relationship. As God describes it, the purpose of freedom is to enable beings to have allegiance, faith, and love toward him, and as a result to perform deeds consistent with those emotions. Absent this freedom, God could only say that they "served necessity," meaning they do not "serve" another at all but rather "furnish what is requisite for" necessity, in the same way we might say that 5,280 feet "serves" a mile.[29] Allegiance, faith, and love all aim at another—we have allegiance *to* someone, faith *in* someone or something, love *for* someone—just as obedience and service do, at least in the sense God means when he says he wants them to serve him. God indicates that inner states and outward actions serve the purpose of creation: to be able to enter into a loving, faithful relationship with him. As Russell Hillier argues, love for God is bound up with love of one's fellow creatures in *Paradise Lost*, both before and after the Fall, so that the freedom of will and reason are the means by which God enables beings to enter into meaningful relationships with one another, to do the service that is the "proof" of allegiance, faith, and love.[30]

The importance of relationship in *Paradise Lost* sheds light on God's subsequent distinction between the fates of his angelic and human creations. God explains that Satan and his crew

> by their own suggestion fell,
> Self-tempted, self-depraved: man falls deceived
> By the other first: man therefore shall find grace,
> The other none.   (3.129–32)

His words perhaps have the appearance of an edict, wherein God decides
to save humanity because of mitigating circumstances that do not apply
in the case of the fallen angels, but Diane McColley suggests instead that
"these words are prophecy, not decree."[31] God does not say that he will *offer*
grace to humanity and not to the fallen angels; he says only that the fallen
angels will not *find* grace, placing the determining factor in regeneration in
the hands of the creatures rather than in their creator. Given that the Son
claims that "Grace…finds her way,…/ To visit all thy creatures, and to
all / Comes unprevented" (3.228, 230–31), grace in the poem appears to be,
as the Arminians would have it, universal. But this universal grace extends
beyond just humankind insofar as it is offered to all "creatures," a category
that would include Satan and all of the other angels. If this is the case, when
God differentiates the manner of Satan's fall from Adam and Eve's, he is
not doing so to explain why he gives grace to one party and not to the other,
since he offers grace to all. Instead, God explains the cause and effect of
providence, why one party *will find* grace, and not the other.[32]

The key difference lies in the manner of their deception: those who are
"self-tempted" will not find grace, while those who are "deceived / By the
other" will. As God's earlier discussion of the necessity of freedom suggests,
this is because freedom is relational. Satan's problem is that he has fallen
out of relation to any other and instead has fallen into a relationship exclusively with and within himself. Satan's oft-noted narcissism, manifest most
clearly in his attraction to his "perfect image" in Sin (2.764), replaces his love
for another. Insofar as his love for God was the proper use of his freedom,
turning his love inward, away from an external being — especially when that
being is God — corrupts his free will, suggesting that freedom is a "use it
or lose it" kind of capability.[33] Satan errs in misusing free will, not just in
disobeying God but also in removing himself from the kind of relationship
that his free will is for. He himself renders his free will useless. In this sense,
to be thus excessively or exclusively self-loving may lead to choices that, in
turn, leave one "self-depraved." Adam and Eve, however, fall because they

are "deceived / By the other first." Though they choose to disobey God, and so make a wrong choice, they never go so far as to choose to drop out of all relation to another. This crucial difference means that, whereas Satan at the critical moment in book 4 has already chosen to isolate himself from both God and the peers with whom he once found allegiance by deciding in book 2 that "this enterprise / None shall partake with me" (2.465–66), Adam and Eve only temporarily isolate themselves from each other in book 10, and, though they find dialogue difficult to initiate, they do. As William Shullenberger argues, "Even in their falling, Adam and Eve fall together, and it is in their disposition toward the other as an embodiment of the self that leads the self beyond itself that they discover the possibility of grace."[34]

Adam's book 10 repetition of Satan's book 4 logic exposes this difference between being "Self-tempted, self-depraved" and being "deceived / By the other first," insofar as the scene reveals the difference between the precondition of freedom — reason — acting in isolation, versus reason confronting an other. By themselves, both Satan and Adam reason erringly, justifying their own sense of misery rather than directing their reason outward to find a way to reestablish their connection with God. But whereas the self-tempted Satan earlier chooses to deny himself the presence of others, Adam, who fell to be with Eve (9.896–916), is not completely alienated from her by the Fall. He has another person outside of himself who confronts him, and this confrontation makes the difference that enables Adam and Eve to "find grace" where Satan found none. After Eve speaks to Adam, the narrator states that peace between them could only be "obtained from fault / Acknowledged and deplored," but the events of the poem reveal that this must be a collaborative endeavor rather than the act of a single being. Both Satan and, before Eve approaches, Adam acknowledge and deplore their own faults, without finding peace. Satan acknowledges that God "deserved no such return" from him, and notes that he "justly rues" his decision (4.42, 72), just as Adam ends his soliloquy in terms presaging Eve's, convicting himself of his guilt and lamenting his misery. However, when Eve acknowledges and deplores her own fault, she achieves "peace" not because she engages in superior acknowledgment and deploring, but *because she is not the only one* acknowledging and deploring. Adam's "commiseration" quite literally indicates mutual lamentation. More importantly, Adam acknowledges Eve's fault not just by agreeing that she is guilty but also by criticizing her for being too quick to offer up her life.

The error Adam reproves in Eve's proposal is the same error Adam appeared incapable of rooting out in his own logic, when his self-conviction led him also to ask that he might receive the entirety of God's wrath. His solipsism is a maze his own mind cannot escape, but, seeing that solipsism in Eve, he recognizes the mistake in the reasoning that kept turning them both down the path of despair. His "conviction" suddenly disappears as his resolution to die turns to irresolution in the face of another, and what had seemed an impossible problem now becomes a starting point, a moment from which the pair can move forward and back to God. The same process happens when Eve suggests abstinence or suicide as a way to avoid passing on their curse. In his earlier soliloquy, Adam has considered the same premise that leads Eve to her suggestion — God's command to *"Increase and multiply"* is to him "death to hear! For what can I increase / Or multiply, but curses on my head?" (10.730–32) — and this leads him only to despair. Once he hears this idea coming from Eve, however, and sees where it leads her, Adam comprehends the mistake, which directs him to search for an alternative that will serve both God's will and the fallen pair's relationship.

In making the case that Eve's love is responsible for regeneration, Green notes the failure of Adam's reason in his book 10 soliloquy, arguing that the speech shows that finding "the way out of this tortuous, twisting maze clearly lies beyond the reach of reason alone."[35] But Adam's problem before Eve appears is not that he is overreliant on reason but that the object and sphere of his reasoning is only himself, making him vulnerable to reason that "dictate[s] false, and misinform[s] the will," to return to Adam's book 9 warning. Part of the purpose of the reconciliation scene in book 10 is to show the difference between misdirected, misguided, and isolated reason — reason directed only at the self rather than at God and others — versus the productive ways and means of "right reason," directed toward serving another in acts of allegiance, love, and faith.

Both Adam and the narrator explicitly note the difference that otherness makes. After he censures Eve's desire to die for him, Adam continues,

> But rise, let us no more contend, nor blame
> Each other, blamed enough elsewhere, but strive
> In offices of love, how we may light'n
> Each other's burden in our share of woe.   (10.958–61)

We have already seen Adam striving — and failing — to "light'n" his own burden; but when he strives to lighten another's burden, his reason provides better insight. When he is guided by love directed outward, his "stony" heart begins to "soften" (3.189). That this is specifically a mental striving on behalf of the other is made clear by the narrator after Eve's suggestion of mutual suicide, when we are told that "Adam with such counsel nothing swayed, / To better hopes his more attentive mind / Labouring had raised" (10.1010–12). The laboring of the mind brings hope, but only because it is "attentive," an adjective indicating both that Adam's mind is "observant" — in this case, observant of Eve's proposal — and that it is "assiduous in ministering to the comfort or pleasure of others."[36] His mind stands in service to her.

If the teleology of reason's freedom is to enable God's creatures to choose to serve him and his other creations, Adam's "more attentive mind," which seeks to serve Eve, demonstrates he has started to function again as one of God's creatures, having indeed found grace — or at least using well the light God has provided him — which will bring yet more light. This is not to say, however, that Adam is the sole agent of regeneration. While the narrator focuses more on the interior working of Adam's mind than of Eve's, Adam's entire ability to use right reason depends on his engagement with Eve, who shows the same reasoning ability — both unregenerate and improving — by giving voice to the same ideas Adam considers. Indeed, she is the first to try to come up with a solution to the problem of the curse laid upon them when she suggests abstinence. That her plan contradicts God's will, as Adam notes, demonstrates that her reason is not yet sufficiently "right"; yet in trying at all to find a way out of their misery, she provides Adam with a model for what it might mean to use reason to serve someone other than himself. And when Adam comes up with the plan to repent, Eve demonstrates her mental capacity's return to freedom by choosing to go with him. In this way, while Adam perhaps shows the regeneration of his right reason first by being the first to discover the right action, the process by which both arrive at the choice to repent is in every way a collaborative one, and one that simply could not work if the other were not present.

Thus, the problem with assigning the cause of Adam and Eve's regeneration to a heroic act of love on Eve's part is that doing so occludes both the importance of reason in manifesting love in the world and the extent to which such manifestations of love must be collaborative, the product of a relationship rather than of individual heroism. Due in large part to Satan's perspective on Adam and Eve in book 4, which differentiates the couple according to "their sex" — "For contemplation he and valour formed, / For softness she and sweet attractive grace" (4.296, 297–98) — many readers of the poem treat Adam as the reasoning half of the relationship and Eve as the emotional one, and so likewise treat reason and emotion themselves as separate faculties. But when God states in book 3 that free will is necessary to "give proof" of "allegiance, constant faith or love," he makes reason the means of showing love. If love is proven in the act of service, that service must be aimed at the good of the other, and only reason can discern what choices will achieve that good. Eve is not loving properly when she offers to die for Adam because she has not yet been able to discern an action — a "service," to use God's word — that would be good for him. When, however, considering Eve's proposal leads Adam to the conclusion that they should "strive / In offices of love" for each other, laboring with minds and hearts attentive to each other to find better hopes, he signals that their dialogue will enable them to give proof of a love that genuinely secures the other's good.

CHAPTER 6

―――※―――

Preferring His Mother's House

Jesus at Home and in Exile in "Paradise Regained"

MARGARET JUSTICE DEAN

Though an early defender of divorce for incompatibility in England, Milton himself never divorced, nor did his parents divorce. Neither as an adult, nor as a child, was he ever forced to choose, as many today have, between his father's and his mother's houses. However, in *Paradise Regained* Milton's Jesus chooses his mother's house over his father's. At any rate, that is how I read the final two lines of the brief epic: "hee unobserv'd / Home to his Mothers house private return'd." Fewer than 100 lines earlier, the Son had been placed on "his uneasie station" above the temple, supposedly his "Fathers house." Many scholars have noted the contrast between the projected return of Samson's body "Home to his Fathers house" at the end of *Samson Agonistes* (line 1733) with Jesus's return "Home to his Mothers house" at the end of *Paradise Regained,* and a few have noted the curious addition of this last detail to the temptation accounts in the Synoptics.[1] The contrast between these two "houses" marks a significant distinction between the co-published poems. But no scholar of whom I am aware has discussed the tension between these two parental houses within *Paradise Regained* itself.

Locations are significant in *Paradise Regained*: the plot of the poem culminates in Jesus's exalted placement atop the temple in Jerusalem and concludes with his quiet choice to return home. These locations have seldom been examined in the context of Luke's narrative of Jesus's childhood, despite the poem's five allusions to his early trips from home to temple.[2] Both are places of obedience and prayer for Jesus; according to Milton's theological treatise, his presence, obedience, and prayers there sanctify both. Nonetheless, Jesus's submission to his parents and sufferance of Satan's temptations do not constitute groveling abasement. Just as when he allows himself to be crucified, when Satan brings Jesus to the temple his submission to humiliation becomes an occasion for his exaltation.[3] At the conclusion of *Paradise Regained*, Jesus's choice to return to Mary's house reaffirms his choice of incarnation, sanctifying the human condition and the "house" in which it dwells.

In her essay, which follows this one, Maura Brady discusses the fate of the garden of Eden in *Paradise Lost*, as explicated by the archangel Michael to Adam, "To teach...that God attributes to place / No sanctitie, if none be thither brought / By Men who there frequent, or therein dwell" (*PL* 11.836–38). Michael's lesson about the misattribution of sanctity to place is reinforced in *Paradise Regained*. Satan *attributes* sanctity to place; Jesus *brings* it. As he has in *Paradise Lost*, in *Paradise Regained* Satan fixates on a hierarchy of location. His attempts to promote this hierarchy are a recurrent theme in his temptation of Jesus, but Satan's attribution of sanctity to place prevents him from discerning the sanctity that accompanies Jesus to any place.[4] Thus, Satan is blindsided by his own exaltation of Jesus at the temple. From his first dialog with Jesus to his last in the brief epic, Satan's words suggest a hierarchical valuation of place: "Sir, what ill chance hath brought thee to this place?" (*PR* 1.321). "I to thy Fathers house / Have brought thee, and highest plac't, highest is best" (4.552–53). Jesus, however, refuses to attribute hierarchical value to place, as is evident in his rejection of Satan's proffers of food from exotic locales, power over ancient empires, even rule over Jerusalem and the temple itself. Instead, Jesus chooses to return to Mary's house, a quotidian and private place with no imperialistic, dynastic, or religious pretensions. His return to the place, not some attribute intrinsic to it, is what sanctifies it.

1. Nazareth versus Jerusalem

As in the Gospel accounts, readers are reminded that Nazareth in Galilee is Jesus's hometown. The narrator describes Jesus as coming "From *Nazareth*" (*PR* 1.23) to his baptism in the Jordan; Mary calls Nazareth "our dwelling many years" (2.79–80); God the Father describes Mary as living "in Galilee" (1.135). Because he subscribes to hierarchical value of place, Satan ("As one in City, or Court, or Palace bred" [2.300]) denigrates Jesus's home and hometown as being like the wilderness, a backwater, a place of privation and obscurity, unsuitable to either Jesus's education or his destiny:

> Thy life hath been private, most part spent
> At home, scarce view'd the *Galilean* Towns,
> And once a year *Jerusalem*, few days
> Short sojourn; and what thence could'st thou observe?
> The world thou hast not seen, much less her glory.[5]   (*PR* 3.232–36)

As a corollary to Jesus's hometown, Satan diminishes Jesus's connection with and preference for those living there, including his mother. Satan promotes Jesus's affiliation with King David and Jerusalem, the city of David, while disparaging his connection with lesser people and places. Satan calls King David "Thy Father...By Mothers side thy father" (3.152–80). This genealogical reading of Jesus's connection to King David betrays a superficial understanding of Jesus's status as both David's son and lord.[6] Both Matthew's and Luke's accounts indicate that David is Jesus's forefather through Joseph, who is a descendant of David and Jesus's legal, but not biological, father.[7] By asserting Jesus's "right" to King David's throne through the maternal line, Satan, like the Archbishop of Canterbury in act 1 of Shakespeare's *Henry V*, insinuates Jesus's need to enlist Satan's aid, take up arms to assert this weak dynastic claim, and secure his seat in Jerusalem (3.154–55).[8]

While promoting Jesus's claim to David's throne, Satan blurs the distinction between the Davidic dynasty and the temple when he speaks of "thy Fathers house" (3.175, 282; 4.552). The shared terminology for dynasty and temple adheres because both use this biblical designation and both are associated with Jerusalem (3.282–83, 4.544–46).[9] Satan more frequently refers to David as Jesus's father (3.153, 154, 175, 282, 353) than he does to God the Father (1.486; 3.110, 219; 4.552); additionally, at least two of these references (those to "thy Fathers house") could refer to either. According to Satan, Jesus's claim must be secured in Jerusalem, the seat of David and his dynastic empire, as well as the locus of the temple (3.234, 373, 383; 4.108, 379, 480, 552). Satan exploits the slippage between houses and fathers to tempt Jesus to end ambiguities and clarify his affiliations. He attempts to rouse Jesus to declare himself along one or another conventional line of authority: to feed and free his people, to claim David's throne and empire, or to reveal his unique status as God's son, itself understood in dynastic terms, from the temple in Jerusalem.[10] Dynasty and temple, in other words, merge in Satan's rhetoric and in his understanding of the significance of the temple as a physical location.

The ascending order and loci of Satan's temptations suggest his hierarchical perspective on place. He presents wilderness and city, home and temple as opposed in value. He exults in his place on earth (*PR* 1.44–47, 2.124–25) and boasts that he has been granted leave to reenter heaven's courts. But he fails to convince Jesus, who rebukes Satan's notion of the intrinsic value of particular places by reminding him of his placement in hell. Jesus observes that even when Satan is temporarily allowed to return to heaven, he cannot participate in the "joy" of that "happy place," "so [Satan is] never more in Hell then when in Heaven" (1.416–20). Jesus brings sanctity within himself to any place, be it the wilderness, the temple, or Mary's home.

As he does in bringing Eve to the foot of the forbidden tree in *Paradise Lost*, one of Satan's stratagems with Jesus is to move the temptee to a place suitable to his temptation. He tempts Jesus to distrust the Father's provision in the wilderness by placing a banquet before the fasting Son; he offers Jesus earthly power and glory in mountaintop visions of various ancient cities and empires. At the conclusion of these displays, Satan reveals his materialist valuation of place by telling Jesus, "know also thou, that I / On what I offer set as high esteem" (4.159–60). This movement of temptee by tempter is most evident in his final temptation to presumption, when Satan places Jesus atop the pinnacle. Given his adherence to hierarchy of place, Satan probably aims for the temple from the onset. He has observed Jesus there on earlier occasions. "Fair" Jerusalem, which both the narrator and the gospel

of Matthew entitle "The holy City" (*PR* 4.545; Matt. 4:5), is, in Satan's estimation, the ideal place to tempt Jesus. This is what makes the actual exaltation that occurs on the pinnacle and Satan's fall there so ironically powerful.
Even more important is Jesus's choice to come down from that height, walk
away from the temple and Jerusalem, and return to his mother's house in
Nazareth. The point of this final action, as we will see, is to underline a key
element of Reformed teaching about what confers true sanctity on any given
place. Jerusalem is no more intrinsically holy than Nazareth; the temple is
no holier than Mary's home, but Jesus's presence brings sanctity to these
places.

2. TEMPLE AND CHURCH

As Brady's essay explains, Reformed teaching on the irrelevance of place
to sanctity was well established by Milton's time. However, in order to
endorse the established church at the expense of the Separatists, English
commentators of Milton's day generally follow William Perkins in qualify-
ing Matthew's designation of Jerusalem as the holy city. Perkins's influential
commentary on the temptation of Christ, *The Combat betweene Christ and
the Divell displayed*, published posthumously in 1606, for example, asserts,
"Now if Jerusalem at this time were the true church of God then, then may
wee well say, that in England God hath his true church."[11] Perkins and
many of his followers agree that by Jesus's time Jerusalem was a place of
corruption, but as a place where God's worship had been lawfully practiced
and the Church instituted, the city, and especially the temple, could still be
designated holy, as it was by the evangelist in Matthew 4:5. Furthermore,
some later commentators exceed Perkins in suggesting that city and temple
retained a residual, intrinsic sanctity of place. Typical of these is Bishop
Lancelot Andrewes, whose *Seven Sermons upon the Temptations of Christ*
grants intrinsic holiness to city and temple: "[Satan] brought [Jesus] to Jerusalem, the holy City: for that addition is given it…he brought him into the
Temple, where even the very ground was holy."[12] Based upon such establishment premises, some commentators on the temptation scene assert that
Satan selects the temple location to exploit any false security on Jesus's part:
Satan attempts to blindside Jesus in a place intrinsically holy, deemed secure

from temptation.[13] Concurring with this hierarchical view of place, Satan assumes Jesus will reveal himself at this exalted and holy locale. The narrator's and Satan's repetitions of comparative forms of "high," some five times in nine lines (*PR* 4.545–53), indicate this emphasis on hierarchy. Instead, Milton's poem has Satan blindsided by Jesus's exaltation at a temple made extrinsically, temporarily holy. His presence at the temple does not sanctify Jesus: Jesus's presence sanctifies the temple. Because of this sanctification of the temple, Jesus must be exalted there, and Satan expelled.

Of the many seventeenth century English commentators I reviewed for this essay, the observations of Thomas Taylor seem most relevant to Michael's lesson on sanctity of place in *Paradise Lost* and Jesus's words and actions in *Paradise Regained*.[14] As a disciple of Perkins and an Anglican clergyman himself, Taylor endorses Perkins's discussion of "the holy citie" and the Church of England, but he refrains from admitting any residual sanctity there: "*Jerusalem* is called the *holy citie*, not because of any holinesse in the place: for no place as a place is more holy then other.... [Nor is there] inherent holinesse in the place, onely for the present the presence of God appearing after a speciall manner, makes a speciall holinesse to bee ascribed unto it. Neither is it called *holy* in respect of the people and inhabitants: for the faithfull citie was long before this become an harlot."[15] Milton, like Taylor, allows for the possibility of places becoming sanctified, but, as Brady's argument suggests, he refrains from endorsing the established church as the new temple. While Milton may condone the notion of a place temporarily housing sanctity, he has the archangel Michael insist on the extrinsic nature of such sanctity and he reinforces this conception of holy places in *Paradise Regained*. Jesus's exaltation at Herod's temple blindsides Satan because, as Taylor observes, "onely for the present" [Jesus's] "presence... appear[s there] after a speciall manner," bringing temporary sanctity to the place. This sanctity, extrinsic to the temple itself, "lifts Jesus up" in exaltation above the temple, even as in Jesus's childhood Simeon and Anna have done, and ironically, now Satan himself is compelled to do. The narrator's prophecy in book 1, "But contrary unweeting he fulfill'd / The purpos'd Counsel pre-ordain'd and fixt / Of the most High" (*PR* 1.126–28), is fulfilled in the Son's exaltation and Satan's humiliation in book 4. Despite his schemes,

Satan's notions of hierarchy of place coupled with his appropriation of the temple serve the purposes of "the most High." The city, the temple and Satan, despite their mutual corruptions, are forced to work in concert in the exaltation of the Son of God.[16]

Noam Reisner discusses temple symbolism in *Paradise Regained*; he also notes the seventeenth century association of Herod's temple with the Church of England and decries scholarly neglect of "the typological significance" of the temple. He maintains that "the idea of the temple as a type, or metaphor, for the body of Christ functions as the interpretive *locus* of the poem" and that "Milton's use of temple imagery in *Paradise Regained* finally emerges as a powerful trope for the very spirit of reform and instruction that so often animates his poetry."[17] As I observe, above, Satan conflates the phrase "Fathers house" so that it refers to Herod's temple, the Davidic dynasty, or both. Satan uses this phrase as he attempts to spur Jesus's hierarchical ambitions, dynastic or clerical, and the phrase retains its association with hierarchy. Like many Reformed Christians of his time, Milton had no love for the established church. As an anti-Laudian, Milton comes to regard the Church of England as more "Nebuchadnezzar's Palace" than God's temple.[18] He sees it as an arm of "the Antichristian temple," which in Puritan estimation was the Roman Catholic Church. Reisner comments, "In *An Apology against a Pamphlet*...Milton attacks the Laudian introduction of the litany on the grounds that it has its roots in the popish liturgy, as he says, 'still serving to all the abominations of the Antichristian temple.'"[19] Reisner argues that Milton, like "the more tolerant conformists of the Caroline mainstream" of the time, also uses "the word 'temple' as a euphemism for the episcopal English church." But for Milton, the use of "temple" for the established church had associations with Roman Catholic or even pagan practices. Milton's positive use of the term is encapsulated in the proem of *Paradise Lost* when the narrator asserts that the spirit of God "prefer[s] / Before all Temples th' upright heart and pure" (*PL* 1.17–18). Milton's negative use of "temple" may also be seen in Jesus's reference to Satan's "Temples" (*PR* 1.449), Jesus's disparagement of hero worship "with Temple, Priest and Sacrifice" (*PR* 3.83), and Samson's initial refusal to present himself at the temple of Dagon,

"Present at Temples at Idolatrous Rites" (*SA* 1378). Reisner refers to these alternate usages when he concludes, "On one level, then, the temple for Milton is at once the body of the risen Christ as well as the battleground for Reformation."

Russell Hillier supplements Reisner's observations on the typology of the temple by noting that Milton's study of Josephus's *The Jewish War* would have informed him that the Holy of Holies was "vacant" in Herod's temple. Besides its corrupt administration — as noted by Jesus himself in John 2:16 — and builder, Herod's temple contained neither the Ark of the Covenant nor God's presence.[20] These corruptions, as well as its associations with the established English church, made Herod's temple less worthy and less comparable to "the Church militant" than Solomon's in Milton's estimation.

Milton regarded Solomon's temple as the more perfect type of what the church should be. Even so, while commenting in *The Reason of Church-Government* on the earlier temple's precise design as detailed in Ezekiel 40–48, he emphasizes its abrogation and supersession by the church: "Did God take such delight in measuring out the pillars, arches, and doores of a materiall Temple, was he so punctuall and circumspect in lavers, altars, and sacrifices soone after to be abrogated, lest any of these should have been made contrary to his minde? Is not a farre more perfect worke more agreeable to his perfection in the most perfect state of the Church militant, the new alliance of God to man?" (YP 1:757). Perhaps Milton's most significant prose discussions of the ideal temple are found in his explication of 1 Corinthians 3:16 in *De doctrina Christiana* in his chapter "Of the Holy Spirit:" "*The temple of God. The temple of the Spirit.*... It is because the Father and the Son, not only the Holy Spirit *live in us*...that we are called *the temple of God*. So in I Cor. vi.19...we are called *the temple of the Spirit.*... Paul explains more fully in what sense we are called *the temple of the Spirit* in Eph. ii. 22: *you, too, are built together in him to be the home of God through the Spirit*" (YP 6:290–91). Here, and throughout his poetry, Milton's emphasis is on the superiority of the new temple, one not made with hands. Citing Ephesians 2:22, Milton asserts that the renewed human being is to become the temple, "the home of God through the Spirit."

3. HUMILIATION AND EXALTATION

His hierarchical view of place and appropriation of Herod's temple are not the only causes of Satan's amazement and fall there; his failure to discern and apply the predictive pattern of humiliation and exaltation in Jesus's life is yet another. Jesus's incarnation has rendered him subject to a cycle of humiliation and exaltation, especially the former.[21] This cycle becomes evident in Jesus's two childhood trips to the temple in Jerusalem as described in Luke, chapter 2. Furthermore, these two childhood trips share five characteristics, which form a pattern; this pattern is in turn replicated in a final trip in book 4 of the brief epic. While he claims to have been observing Jesus from his birth (1.66–69, 4.503–09), Satan, and a few readers as well, have overlooked the cycle and the pattern, and their significance. Before examining this pattern, a brief look at Milton's understanding of the relationship between humiliation and exaltation should help readers discern the presence of the cycle.

De doctrina Christiana describes numerous aspects of the Son's incarnation as humiliations, and several of the humiliations the Son suffers in *Paradise Regained* fit these descriptions. Even those that are not specifically detailed are mentioned in the course of the poem: his birth (1.65–66, 134–40, 234–39), circumcision (1.254–58), flight into Egypt (2.75–76), obedience to the whole law (which includes submission to parents) (1.207–08), poverty (1.234–35, 2.411–15), manual labor (2.414–15), baptism (1.21–28 and throughout), temptation (throughout), Passion (1.263–65, 3.190–94, 4.386–88, 4.477–80) and death (1.264, 4.388).[22] The Son suffers humiliation in the brief epic from beginning to end.

As Milton explains in his theological treatise, however, "Christ's humiliation is followed by his exaltation" (YP 6:440).[23] Milton understands the Son's life on earth as essentially a string of humiliations, punctuated with occasional exaltations (such as the ones immediately following his baptism, transfiguration, the attesting voice from heaven at the end of Jesus's public ministry, his Resurrection and Ascension — all of which fit the Son's and/ or Milton's definitions of exaltation).[24] A work emphasizing Jesus's human susceptibility to temptation, *Paradise Regained* details these humiliations.[25] Jesus's triumph over Satan is the exaltation that takes center stage in the poem, and in the course of the narrative Milton concentrates on Jesus's paradoxically exalting subjection to Satan's displays of power. Satan's physical power over the Son is one explicit instance of humiliation.[26] By undergoing incarnation, the Son has been "made a little lower than the angels" (Heb. 2:9). Remarkably, he refrains from using supernatural power to resist Satan's incursions.[27] Additionally, his poverty, isolation, and hunger serve as avenues for Satan to further the Son's humiliation. Satan, as an archangel, is not subject to these humiliations, but his power over the Son is temporary and limited.[28] He cannot deliver the Son to death until the time is ripe. The Son must suffer Satan's affronts to prepare for his ultimate humiliation on the cross and for the same reasons: to obey and please the Father, reject Satan's aid and humiliate him, and "earn Salvation for the Sons of men."[29] Viewing Jesus's exaltations with alarm and envy while overlooking many of his humiliations, Satan misses the predictable cycle of humiliation and exaltation in Jesus's life.

Satan does not simply neglect this cycle; rather, in carrying Jesus to the temple, Satan, who is fixated on glory as well as hierarchy of place, fails to discern the explicit pattern of *both* humiliation and exaltation established during Jesus's earlier family trips to the temple. According to *De doctrina Christiana*, which refers specifically to these trips in Luke, chapter 2, Jesus is humiliated by his subjection to his parents, the Law, and circumcision at the temple (YP 6:439–40). Furthermore, his parents are humiliated by their loss of control over Jesus and their amazement at the temple. All Satan seems to remember from Jesus's childhood visits is Jesus's recognition and exaltation; Satan alludes to Jesus's recognition as a 12-year-old to urge him to "Be famous then / By wisdom" (4.215–26). His passionate response to Jesus's exaltation at the beginning of book 1 (36–38) may be read as typical of his earlier responses to Jesus's exaltations in the temple. Satan has overlooked the humiliations suffered by the Son and his parents, as detailed above. His neglect of humiliation in the cycle of humiliation and exaltation, to which the Son is subject, prepares the way for Satan's humiliation.

The poem's five specific allusions (1.209–14, 255–58; 2.87–92, 96–99; 4.215–21) to two passages in the gospel of Luke (2:33–39, 41–51) serve to prefigure and provide an ironic backdrop for Satan's humiliation and Jesus's exaltation at the temple.[30] These allusions establish a fivefold pattern, which illustrates the cycle of humiliation-exaltation and anticipates the action at the pinnacle. In Luke, chapter 2, Jesus's parents present him at Herod's temple in Jerusalem in order to fulfill the ceremonial law. This particular occasion is referenced in *Paradise Regained* by Jesus in 1.255–58 and Mary in 2.87–92. Later in the same chapter in Luke, Jesus's parents take him to the temple in Jerusalem as part of their Passover celebration; there he discusses theology with the resident teachers. This occasion is referenced in the brief epic by Jesus in 1.209–14, by Mary in 2.96–99, and by Satan in 4.215–21.[31] Milton's poem frequently alludes to Luke's narrative of Jesus's childhood in order to engage five characteristics of action; these characteristics establish the fivefold pattern I describe here. This pattern is, in turn, replicated in Jesus's final trip to the temple in *Paradise Regained*; the pattern also illustrates the cycle of humiliation/exaltation to which Jesus's incarnation subjects him, as well as anticipates Satan's own humiliation, as follows:

1. Jesus is brought to the temple by those who are authorized by God to have physical control over him. This physical control over the Son, like Satan's permitted physical control of him during the temptation, is an example of humiliation from Milton's perspective.

2. Once they have brought him there, his carriers lose control of him at the temple because of his unique interior sanctity. In Luke 2:28, Simeon takes Jesus from his parents. In Luke 2:43, Jesus lingers in the temple without his parents' permission. This loss of control over the Son, like Satan's loss of control of him at the temple pinnacle, is an example of humiliation for his carriers from Milton's perspective.

3. His carriers get more than they bargained for by bringing Jesus to the temple; they are "amazed" at what transpires there. In Luke 2:33, his parents marvel at the prophecies of Jesus's messiahship. In Luke 2:48 and 50, both the theologians and his parents are amazed at Jesus's knowledge, understanding, and violation of custom.[32] This exaltation of the Son, like Satan's amazement at the temple pinnacle, is also an example of humiliation for his carriers from Milton's perspective.

4. Because Jesus brings sanctity to the temple, not vice versa, he is recognized and exalted there, but not by those who brought him. Each incident informs readers more than carriers. From Milton's perspective, exaltations must follow recognition of Jesus, like Satan's ironic exaltation of the Son at

the pinnacle immediately following the narrator's use of Jesus's name and Jesus's citation of Deuteronomy 6:16.

5. Following these incidents, Jesus returns to his parents' home in Nazareth (Luke 2:39, 51). This submission to human authority by the Son, like his return to Mary's home in Nazareth following the temptation, is an example of humiliation from Milton's perspective. Furthermore, Milton's addition of Jesus's return to Mary's home at the conclusion of his tempta-tion, an incident commensurate with the synoptic accounts, but not spe-cifically recorded in them, suggests his engagement of this fivefold pattern because a return to his parents' home in Nazareth is specified in Luke's account of his childhood visits to the temple.[33]

The poem's five allusions to Jesus's temple visits in his childhood estab-lish a pattern that prepares readers for Satan's temporary physical control of Jesus, Satan's loss of that control, Satan's humiliation and amazement, Jesus's exaltation at the temple, and Jesus's quiet return home afterward. However, this pattern does more than anticipate action; it reinforces sig-nificant Miltonic themes by emphasizing Jesus's interior holiness and his mature choice of incarnation, which includes enduring the cycle of humili-ation and exaltation until he returns to session at the right hand of God the Father in a final exaltation.[34]

In the action of *Paradise Regained*, Satan's placement of Jesus above the temple exalts Jesus and humiliates Satan, but Satan's action also drama-tizes Jesus's supersession of the temple. Noting that the gospel of John pro-vides central themes for *Paradise Regained*, Reisner observes, "another key Johannine subtext to shape the poem is the idea that the imagined destruction of the Jerusalem temple prefigures the death, Crucifixion, and Resurrection of Christ's 'fleshly tabernacle.'"[35] In *Reason of Church-Government*, Milton comments on the replacement of Solomon's temple with "Christ's body, which is his Church": "Should not [God] rather now by his owne prescribed discipline have cast his line and levell upon the soule of man which is his rationall temple, and by the divine square and compass thereof forme and regenerate in us the lovely shapes of vertues and graces, the sooner to edifie and accomplish that immortall stature of Christs body which is his Church, in all her glorious lineaments and proportions" (YP 1:757–58). Solomon's temple may prefigure the church, but Christ's body is the church, which has replaced all temples made with hands. In the prose passage above, Milton calls "the soule of man [God's] rationall temple." This concept is reinforced in *Paradise Regained* when Jesus refers to "Godlike men [as] The Holiest of Holies" (4.348–49) in his condemnation of Satan's promotion of Greco-Roman philosophy and rhetoric.

4. PLACES OF PRIVATE PRAYER

Satan's hierarchical view of place as well as his ignorance of the cycle of humiliation and exaltation are causes of Satan's amazement and fall at the temple, but his underestimation of private prayer is yet another. Because Jesus brings sanctity to any place he "frequents," and he frequents the temple, his presence and prayers there sanctify it (as both the archangel Michael and Thomas Taylor affirm), rather than vice versa. Herod's corrupt temple cannot contaminate Jesus. Milton argues that this sanctifying presence is not only true of Jesus but "every good Christian" as well. In *Reason of Church-Government*, Milton's discussion of church discipline ridicules the prelatical notion that the mere "touch of a lay Christian" could "profane" any temple furniture:

> as if the touch of a lay Christian who is never the lesse Gods living temple, could profane dead judaisms.... But when every good Christian thoroughly acquainted with all those glorious privileges of sanctification and adoption which render him more sacred then any dedicated altar or element, shall be restor'd to his right in the Church....not fearing lest...something unholy from within his own heart should dishonour and profane in himselfe that Priestly unction and Clergy-right whereto Christ hath entitl'd him. (YP 1:843–44)

Milton blasts the prelates for claiming as exclusively their own the privileges of all Christians and demeaning the status of the laity, who have been restored by God and whose human nature Jesus himself has assumed: "thus have they [the prelates] made common and unclean, thus have they made profane that nature which God hath not only cleans'd, but Christ also hath assum'd" (YP 1:845). In the same publication, during his discussion of the contrast between temples in Jerusalem and "the Church militant," which has abrogated all temples, Milton contrasts the detailed descriptions of temple construction in Ezekiel 40–48 with those "patch't" and "varnish't" "imbellishings of mans imagination," the prelates' discipline (YP 1:757). Not only do the sanctified bring sanctity to any place they frequent or dwell, just as Jesus does, but also his body has become the new temple, the church.

In *Reason of Church-Government*, Milton may in essence be offering a preface to *Paradise Regained*; he describes "the deliberat and chosen counsell of Christ in his spirituall government, whose glory is in the weakenesse of fleshly things to tread upon the crest of the worlds pride and violence by the power of spirituall ordinances." Milton asserts "the prime end of Christs comming in the flesh, that is to revele his truth, his glory and his might" in "the spirituall force of his bodily weaknesse" (YP 1:849–50). This sounds like the Father's description of the Son's spiritual weapons at the onset of the brief epic, "the rudiments / Of his great warfare...To conquer...By Humiliation and strong Sufferance: / His weakness shall o'recome Satanic strength" (PR 1.157–61). "The spirituall force of [Christ's] bodily weaknesse" is what Milton foregrounds in his brief epic. Satan appears to be in control: he manipulates the weather; he does most of the talking; finally, he lifts Jesus up and places him atop an exposed and corrupted place, but "the rudiments of his great warfare" (the power of private prayer in any place) amaze and topple Satan.

Herod's temple, as Satan knows well, is "empty"[36] and "violated" (PR 3.160), but it too can be sanctified by Jesus's presence and prayers. As part of his argument for separate essences of God the Father and of the Son of God in *De doctrina Christiana*, Milton notes Christ's recognition of even Herod's temple. Countering contemporary exegesis of Malachi 3:1b,[37] Milton describes Christ's human body as both a temple and the church, in which God the Father is honored alone: "These words denote, in prophetic language, the Lord's entrance into the flesh, or into the temple of the body, as in John ii. 21. For the Jews sought to worship no one in the temple except the Father. Christ himself, moreover, in the same chapter, called the temple his Father's house, not his own....Lastly, [Christ] shall come into his Church, which the prophets usually refer to figuratively as the temple" (YP 6:232–33). In *Paradise Regained* even Herod's temple has been sanctified by Jesus's presence, so it also must exalt him, as his childhood incidents there suggest.

In her essay in this volume, Brady cites Milton's discussions of prayer in *De doctrina Christiana*. She notes that Milton allows for any place and any time as potentially suitable for private prayer and that such prayer is often silent in order to render prayer even more private. Interestingly, she also observes that Milton finds some places and some times "particularly suitable." Particularly suitable places include a private chamber, a mountain top, and the temple in Jerusalem; particularly suitable times include evening, morning, and midday (YP 6:671–74, 704, 708). In *Paradise Regained* Jesus prays (or recalls praying) in each of these particularly suitable places and times. He meditates in silence and seclusion in Mary's house, which, Milton assumes, would include a private chamber (1.229–30, 260–69); similarly in the wilderness, which includes a mountain top (1.229–30, 290–99; 2.110; 3.251–63); and he stands in an attitude of private prayer on the temple pinnacle (4.562). He prays in the evening (1.500–03); at midday (2.291–92); and, finally, Jesus prays in the morning just before his final encounter with Satan. This last time frame, overdetermined in the poem, is marked by both the narrator (4.432–33) and Satan, who greets Jesus, "Fair morning yet betides the Son of God, / After dismal night" (4.451–52). Brady comments in this volume on Milton's ambiguity concerning these parameters of prayer, "having established both need and precedent for private prayer, and having cleared a private place [and time] for this purpose, [he] leaves it open and undesignated." Yet, the brief epic seems to prefer these "particularly suitable" times and places for prayer.

Jesus's very presence can bring sanctity to any location, but in *Paradise Regained* he brings sanctity to place and sustains his relationship with the Father by the practice of private prayer there. According to *De doctrina Christiana*, "Christ generally prayed alone and by himself" (YP 6:671). In *Paradise Regained*, Jesus brings sanctity to his home and even Herod's temple by dwelling, frequenting, and praying there in private. Similarly, his presence and prayers also bring sanctity to the wilderness. During his wilderness meditations, Jesus remembers his earlier ones in Mary's house, where she encourages them (*PR* 1.229–30). Later, Mary comments about her son's childhood in Nazareth, "his life / Private, unactive, calm, contemplative" (2.80–81). Jesus himself describes the sustenance of private prayer, "[I am] fed with better thoughts that feed / Mee hungring more to do my Fathers will" (2.258–59). Following the final storm sequence in the poem, the narrator comments on the effect of Jesus's private prayer: "ill wast thou shrouded then…yet only stoodst / Unshaken…while thou / Sat'st unappall'd in calm and sinless peace" (4.419–25).

The poem alludes to Jesus's private prayers in the wilderness and in Mary's house, but specifies none at the temple. Like Samson, whom the Hebrew Messenger describes in the temple of Dagon, "with head a while enclin'd, / And eyes fast fixt he stood, as one who pray'd" (*SA* 1636–37), Jesus stands quietly in an attitude of silent, private prayer on the pinnacle of the temple. Milton's depiction of Jesus's private prayer is commensurate with the precepts of Milton's treatise, which offers locations for "private prayers [in] a place where we can be unobserved.…It is hypocritical to offer private prayer in public.…It was, however, lawful to offer private prayers…[especially if they are silent] in the temple at Jerusalem" (YP 6:671, 673–74). Neither Milton's Jesus nor Milton's Samson offer audible private prayers at public temples because to do so would be hypocritical according to *De doctrina Christiana*. Satan disdains Jesus's prayer life, exclaiming, "the Wilderness / For thee is fittest place" (4.372–73). Vanita Neelakanta, connecting Jesus's practice with Puritan devotional literature, comments on Satan's intrusion into and animosity toward Jesus's private prayer, "The materialization of Satan in desert-as-closet reinforces the concerns of closet devotional literature that the devil abhors solitary prayer."[38] Unable to anticipate the power of prayer as one of "the rudiments / Of [Jesus's] great warfare," Satan lifts him up to the highest point of the temple, where Jesus stands and withstands Satan in private prayer.[39]

5. Incarnation and Exile

Satan urges dynastic ambitions on Jesus by reiterating his supposed need to seize "*David's* Throne" (*PR* 3.153, 169, 357, 383; 4.108, 379, 471). Earlier, Satan called Jesus "[David's] true Successour" and offered him installation in "*David's* royal seat" (3.373). Jesus may accept the title of "*David's* true heir" (3.405), but his accession can only be accomplished as Solomon's was in God's "providence."[40] When Jesus rejects Satan's offer and the dynastic implications of his "Father *Davids* house" (3.282), Satan turns to the clerical implications of "thy Father's house" in "the holy City." The fiend carries Jesus to the city of David, where he attempts to incite his clerical ambitions to cleanse and rule from the temple as suggested by Jesus's stated preference for "*Sion's* songs" and "the Law of God" (4.347, 1.207). David's "true heir," like Solomon, will build the temple, the one that abrogates all others.[41] Any of the ambitions that Satan attempts to arouse in Jesus — to free his people, to rule as David's heir, or even to claim the highest place in the temple (all of which Jesus had considered in his youth [1.202–26]) — have failed to tempt the mature Son.[42] Nonetheless, Satan persists in his materialist/political perspective as he places Jesus on the pinnacle in Jerusalem.

Satan tempts Jesus to indulge in a false dichotomy: residence in Nazareth results in humiliation; in Jerusalem, exaltation. Not only is "his Mothers house" antidynastic and private, it is also located in the obscure backwater of Nazareth. As he has from the onset of the brief epic, Satan implies that Jesus has been in exile from Jerusalem, the locus of both the throne of David and his "Fathers house," the place where his ambitions, gifts, and stature can be realized (*PR* 3.380–85). Satan accuses Jesus of hiding his "God-like Vertues…Affecting private life" (3.21–22) and urges Jesus on to fame and glory in Jerusalem, topped by the hierarchy of the temple. Satan presses Jesus to grab "Occasions forelock" and begin his "endless raign" at home in the holy city in his Father's house (3.173–74); instead, Jesus chooses home in exile, in his mother's house.

Despite Satan's insinuations, Jerusalem is neither the place of Jesus's true home nor his throne, but neither is Mary's house in Nazareth because any place on earth is still physically apart from the Father. In *Paradise Regained*, Jesus is *both* in exile *and* at home in Mary's house until he returns incarnate to sit on his heavenly throne in the New Jerusalem, the true holy city, where the only temple consists of the Father and the Son.[43] Like Satan, Jesus is in exile from his native heaven; like Satan, Jesus has chosen to station himself on earth. But unlike Satan's fixation on hierarchy of place and defiance of heaven, Jesus chooses a humble place on earth to please heaven. Satan seeks an earthly sanctuary from his hell within, but Jesus brings within himself a paradise, a place of private prayer, which sanctifies his earthly station.

Jesus's choice of incarnation includes voluntary humiliation, suffering spiritual opposition, and exile. His choice to return to Mary's house suggests his mature decision to continue his submission to incarnation. Mary Beth Rose asserts, "Jesus' relation to Mary is the sign and symbol of his humanity."[44] I add that this symbol is further emphasized by the startling phrase Milton inserts into the final line of *Paradise Regained*: "Home to his Mothers house." Her house in Nazareth has become a symbol of his incarnation; it is the "darksom House of mortal Clay," which the Son chooses as his residence in "Ode on the Morning of Christ's Nativity." Milton alludes to the permanence of Jesus's incarnation throughout his works, but especially in this ode, which takes as its subject not the Nativity but the Incarnation.[45] In the ode, the Son *lays aside* his "glorious Form," *forsakes* "the Courts of everlasting Day," and *chooses* a human body as his residence (emphasis mine; stanza 2, lines 8–14). Robert Entzminger comments of the Son in *Paradise Regained* that he has already "voluntarily surrender[ed] his heavenly throne for . . . 'a darksome House of mortal Clay.'"[46] It is a physical location, a dwelling place but, more important, a state of being.[47] Mary's house cannot refer to a dynasty. It cannot spur imperialistic or clerical ambition, but it remains a place of humiliation, prayer, and obedience chosen by the Son in order to please God the Father. Furthermore, as scholars from Barbara Lewalski to Russell Hillier have observed, Jesus's choice to humble himself in incarnation anticipates his final humiliation on the cross.

By choosing incarnation, Jesus, like his follower Paul, suffers humiliation and exile there because while he is "at home in the body, [he is spatially] absent from the Lord . . . [he is] willing rather to be absent from the body, and to be present with the Lord" (cf. 2 Cor. 5:6–9).[48] Jesus's incarnation has exiled him [spatially] from the Father's bosom and right hand to become "Son both of God and Man." Milton deals directly with this significant aspect of Christian theology in both his poetry and his prose. In *Paradise Lost*, as one example, God the Father speaks of this spatial separation and the cycle of humiliation and exaltation implicit in it when he responds to the Son's request for incarnation:

> I spare
> Thee from my bosom and right hand, to save,
> By loosing thee a while, the whole Race lost
>
> . . . .
>
> Therefore thy Humiliation shall exalt

With thee thy Manhood also to this Throne;
Here shalt thou sit incarnate, here shalt Reign
Both God and Man, Son both of God and Man,
Anointed universal King.   (*PL* 3.288–317)

In a second example, which points to the centrality of the incarnation in Milton's theology, he explicates Paul's discussion of the paradox of incarnation in chapter 13 of *De doctrina Christiana*, "Of the Death Which Is Called the Death of the Body." This chapter argues for the unity of the body and the soul to demonstrate that the death of the soul is included in the death of the body. Near the end of the chapter, Milton offers selections of his own translation of 2 Corinthians 5:1–20 as the "ninth passage" buttressing his argument for the unity of body and soul (YP 6:413–14). Here, Milton translates the first part of verse 1 as, "*the house of this tabernacle*" (the body), which is opposed to "*a building* and *a home*" (not made with hands, eternal in the heavens). He follows Theodore Beza in indicating this "home" will clothe Christians "in the heavens." Milton further explicates verses 8 and 9: "*to be absent from the body and to be present with the Lord*, must, in fact, be understood as a reference to our final and perfect beatitude [in verse 8] ... and the word *ekdemeo* in the ninth verse should be interpreted as an indication of our eternal removal to a heavenly existence" (YP 6:413).[49] In this passage, Milton employs Paul's discussion of the soul's physical location (at home in heaven and absent from the earthly body or at home on earth in the earthly body and absent from heaven) demonstrating that location has no effect on an individual's relationship with God because, as Milton affirms with Paul, "we strive, whether living at home with God or away from him, to be accepted by him" (YP 6:414; 2 Cor. 5:9). What is significant in Milton's prose argument for the purposes of this essay is the motivation behind the individual's choice to remain in "the *earthly house* of this life," as Milton translates verse 1 in a second, briefer discussion of 2 Corinthians 5 in *De doctrina Christiana*.[50] Whether in heaven or on earth, the individual's motive is "to be accepted by [God]." Milton's explication of these verses applies to Jesus's relationship with God in *Paradise Regained*, especially as the "Angelic Quires" extol his victory near the end of the brief epic. The angels emphasize the Son's constancy of motive and consistency of action, regardless of locale:

> True Image of the Father whether thron'd
> In the bosom of bliss, and light of light
> Conceiving, or remote from Heaven, enshrin'd
> In fleshly Tabernacle, and human form,
> Wandring the Wilderness, whatever place.   (*PR* 4.596–600)

Jesus's "fleshly Tabernacle" is the new temple; it is also both his home and place of exile.

Jesus's incarnation will abrogate the empty and corrupt temple, soon to be utterly destroyed.[51] However, Jesus's choice to return to Nazareth also emphasizes his spatial separation from his Father's "bosom and right hand, to save...the whole Race lost." On earth, Jesus has been spatially "remote from Heaven, enshrin'd / In fleshly Tabernacle." Jesus's choice of location, whether at home in heaven or in exile at home in Mary's house, is motivated by his desire to please the Father. Because his choice demonstrates this motive, Jesus's return to Mary's house both "expresses" his status as "True Image of the Father...The Son of God," and establishes "a fairer Paradise for Adam and his chosen Sons."[52]

Jesus brings sanctity to "his Mothers house" (not vice versa). Though Herod's temple will be abrogated during Jesus's life on earth, like Mary's house it also is sanctified by his presence and prayers there. Until Jesus begins his public ministry, his home and preferred location for private prayer remain "his Mothers house." Jesus's return to his home in Nazareth reminds readers of his choice of incarnation, with its attendant life of humiliation and obscurity, his submission to the continuing cycle of humiliation and exaltation until he reascends to heaven, forever clothed in his "fleshly Tabernacle" of incarnation.[53]

By choosing to dwell there, Jesus restores the sanctity lost at the Fall to the human body as the temple of the Holy Spirit.[54] This temple, and place of private prayer, is the "paradise within thee, happier farr," which the archangel Michael promises Adam (*PL* 12.587). In the co-published *Samson Agonistes*, Manoa asserts he will carry Samson's dead body in a public funeral train, "Home to his Fathers house" in marked contrast to Jesus's choice in *Paradise Regained* to return privately "Home to his Mothers house." Samson's remains enjoy public acclaim and a heroic tomb on earth, in his father's house, but Jesus chooses to continue his incarnate life of humiliation that, as the cycle of humiliation and exaltation indicate, will conclude with divine exaltation of his human body at his Ascension and session at the right hand of God the Father. In the presence of the Father, Jesus will remain differentiated from him. Jesus, still incarnate in his glorified human body, will again face the divine Father in perfect obedience and love.[55] Milton's Jesus, like his Adam and Eve, accepts the human state of displacement and exile, but instead of accepting inevitable expulsion from an external paradise as Adam and Eve do, Jesus chooses to leave one in order to attain "a fairer Paradise" for "Adam and his chosen Sons" in "his Mothers house."[56]

PART THREE

———✳———

PLACES

CHAPTER 7

—⁂—

"An Iland salt and bare"

The Fate of the Garden in "Paradise Lost"

MAURA BRADY

From its opening reminder that with the Fall came "Death...and all our woe, / With loss of *Eden*" (*PL* 1.3–4) to the final image of Adam and Eve walking "hand in hand with wandring steps and slow, / Through *Eden*" as they leave the garden (12.648–49), *Paradise Lost* seems to assert nothing more unswervingly or with greater certitude than that paradise is lost. The poem delivers this lesson pointedly — and poignantly — when, in book 11, the archangel Michael descends from heaven to pronounce the sentence of exile. As if to underscore the message, he reveals to Adam that the garden will be inundated in the flood of Noah:

> all the Cataracts
> Of Heav'n set open on the Earth shall powr
> Rain day and night, all fountains of the Deep
> Broke up, shall heave the Ocean to usurp
> Beyond all bounds, till inundation rise
> Above the highest Hills: then shall this Mount
> Of Paradise by might of Waves be moov'd
> Out of his place, pushd by the horned floud,
> With all his verdure spoil'd, and Trees adrift
> Down the great River to the op'ning Gulf,
> And there take root an Iland salt and bare,
> The haunt of Seals and Orcs, and Sea-mews clang.
> To teach thee that God attributes to place

No sanctitie, if none be thither brought
By Men who there frequent, or therein dwell.[1]   (11.824–38)

In spite of the angel's subsequent tender of a "Paradise within thee, happier
farr" (12.587), the spectacle of the garden swept out to sea is one of the
most deeply affecting scenes in the poem, as critics often note.[2] Much of
the episode's resonance, as I hope to demonstrate, derives from a profound
ambivalence at its heart the depths of which have not hitherto been sounded,
although they are suggested by a persistent tension running through the
criticism. On the one hand, Michael's claim that the devastation of paradise teaches that "God attributes to place / No sanctitie, if none be thither
brought" (11.836–37) has inclined many critics to assimilate the episode
to Reformed theology's emphasis on personal sanctity — the cultivation of
an inward disposition toward holiness — and, by implication, to parallel
Reformed efforts to uncouple holiness from particular times and places.[3]
On the other hand, however, the poem's abiding preoccupation with place,
from the initial topographical descriptions of hell to its many geographical
allusions to its evocative and precisely detailed descriptions of the garden
itself, appear to strain against lessons about the irrelevance of place.[4] The
poem exhibits a lingering attachment to place that seems to call for explanation, which critics have made by pointing to the poet's own experience of
political exile, to the isolation effected by his blindness or, more generally, to
the culture's loss of intimacy with the natural world.[5]

    In this essay, I will demonstrate that the "Iland salt and bare" is a striking
image of both devastation and conservation, a key locus of the poem's ambivalence about place and sanctity, a vexed matter in Reformation England. The
emerging body of criticism on this theme in Milton's work suggests that his
views on this subject, as on others, shifted over time. In her instructive essay
on Milton's engagement with the *genii loci* of medieval Christianity, Alison
Chapman argues that the apotheosis of Edward King as the "genius of the
shore" in *Lycidas* effectively rewrites the Catholic landscape of the west coast
of England and Wales, "replac[ing] the kind of *genius loci* so familiar to
Catholics with one amenable to nonconformist Protestants."[6] However, the
situation with regard to place and sanctity in *Paradise Regained* is different,
as both Vanita Neelakanta and Margaret Justice Dean demonstrate. Places
in *Paradise Regained* are "religiously potent," Neelakanta observes, but they

serve as replenishment rather than as permanent abode.[7] In her essay in this volume, Dean convincingly argues that while the Son's presence sanctifies the places he frequents, including the temple, he also supersedes the temple, and indeed any other place he might sanctify with his presence. *Paradise Lost* may represent a transitional stage between these two polarities in Milton's thinking about place. In her important study of the links between hope and place in Milton's work, Mary Fenton argues that place still matters after the Fall, not for personal territory and empire, as Satan would have it, but as a location where humans might faithfully and charitably cultivate the paradise within *and* the places where they will dwell with God.[8] Fenton links the desert island relic of paradise explicitly to the desert of *Paradise Regained*, where "Jesus will symbolically re-energize the wasted place that paradise has been rendered and will become the site of a 'fairer Paradise' for humanity."[9]

If Milton's views of place and sanctity shift over time and thus evince complexity, or even ambivalence, perhaps we should not be surprised. The work of recent historians has begun to reveal just how problematic the subject was, particularly for the second and third generation of Reformers. Revisiting the influential Weberian argument that the Reformation inaugurated the "disenchantment of the world," Alexandra Walsham and Andrew Spicer show that by the beginning of the seventeenth century Reformers had begun to resanctify many of the sites in England, Wales, Scotland, and Ireland that were targeted for destruction in the first wave of the Reformation.[10] Walsham documents the process of "reform[ing] the landscape" that continued throughout the seventeenth century well into the eighteenth, a process that featured the reconfiguring of some holy wells as therapeutic spas, new interpretations of the earth's geology and of ancient monuments, and the emergence of new rites of consecration for places of worship. She concludes that, during this period, "the sacred was not so much eroded as reconfigured and relocated: the way in which it was present in the world was redefined rather than wholly denied."[11]

As I hope to show here, the island formerly known as paradise represents a similar reconfiguration of place and its relationship to sanctity. The figure of the island has received scant attention in critical discussions of book 11. The commentary typically emphasizes the devastation wreaked by the flood-waters to demonstrate that paradise is "utterly destroyed," "obliterated," or "demolished," and implicitly assimilates the island to this demolition.[12] Yet although paradise is no longer a paradise after the flood, it endures as a *place*, a location with a defined topography and natural boundaries, one that serves, moreover, as a "haunt" for living creatures. The gesture is an uncommon one in Reformed writing, as we shall see; sixteenth century Reformers developed the theme of paradise inundated, but their readings of Genesis clearly marked the garden for destruction, not dereliction. Moreover, although Michael's gloss on place and personal sanctity in book 11 is usually read by critics as hewing closely to early Reformed teachings on place and holiness, the views Milton expresses on the matter in *De doctrina Christiana* equivocate in ways that contrast with these earlier precepts and parallel his choice to preserve paradise as a desert island in *Paradise Lost*. When aligned with earlier Reformed writings, then, the "Iland salt and bare" emerges as an intriguingly ambivalent figure, one that serves not only to remind readers of the paradise that was lost but also to hold open the category of sacred place itself, and the possibility that it might one day be resanctified by its inhabitants to participate in their experience of the divine.

Milton among the Reformers: The Garden of Eden in the Flood

Milton's version of the inundation of paradise participates in a long and complex tradition of commentary, myth, literature, and cartography on the afterlife of the earthly garden, as Joseph E. Duncan demonstrated some years ago.[13] Questions of what paradise was and what happened to it after the Fall were debated from early Christian times. From late antiquity through the Middle Ages, it was generally regarded as a real place on earth, the location of which had been rendered hidden or inaccessible by the Fall; it was thought to lie behind a ring of fire, sit atop a high mountain, or to be cut off from the rest of the earth by a vast expanse of water or desert.[14] These interpretations were the result of attempts in the twelfth and thirteenth centuries to reconcile Christian belief in a real earthly paradise with the newly recovered and reconstructed Aristotelian natural philosophy.[15] Belief in the continued existence of paradise on earth, however, began to decline in the early sixteenth century as exegetes dedicated to the literal reality of the garden of Eden recast its inaccessibility in temporal rather than geographical terms and advanced the thesis that although paradise had once existed as a real place on earth, the flood of Noah had wiped it out. While scholars have debated the reasons for the decline of the tradition of paradise extant, Alessandro Scafi argues convincingly that the historical garden emerged in response to a resurgence of allegorical interpretations of paradise during the Renaissance, and that it appealed to exegetes because it skirted unresolved philosophical contradictions that had long been posed by the idea of an earthly paradise.[16] During the sixteenth and seventeenth centuries, most defenders of paradise extant were Catholic, while advocates of the theory of paradise inundated were, on the whole, Protestant.[17] Thus, Duncan concludes that Milton, "in emphasizing the destruction of paradise, reflected the solid Protestant opposition to the views of Bellarmine and other Catholic writers."[18]

Milton, as we shall see, aligns himself in general with mainstream Reformed opinion about the fate of paradise. However, his account departs from these in one important respect: the garden of Eden is not obliterated by the flood in *Paradise Lost* as it is in other commentaries, but it is transformed into a different kind of place altogether. Close comparison of *Paradise Lost* with two key Reformed texts will show that Milton's preservation of the desert island may not align quite as neatly with "solid Protestant opposition" to views of paradise extant as Duncan claims.

Although several earlier commentators had suggested that Eden was devastated in Noah's flood, Luther's argument on this point in the *Lectures on Genesis* proved to be foundational to subsequent Reformed commentary.[19] Luther asserts emphatically that the garden was altogether obliterated by the floodwaters, an insistence that would appear to be driven by the need to take an unequivocal position on this much-debated question, and to defend against erroneous theories of paradise extant and allegorical paradise. In the section devoted to Genesis 2:8 ("And the Lord God planted a garden in Eden towards the east, in which He placed the man whom He had formed"), Luther offers his historical paradise as a head-clearing tonic for readers overwhelmed by a confusing jumble of esoteric interpretations. He sketches the tradition of paradise extant as a thicket of countless opinions that threatens to entangle ("amaze") commentators: "At this point people discuss where Paradise is located. The interpreters torture themselves in amazing ways. Some favor the idea that it is located within the two tropics under the equinoctial point. Others think that a more temperate climate was necessary, since the place was so fertile. Why waste words? The opinions are numberless" (*Lectures on Genesis*, 88).[20]

Luther then lays out his own reading in unambiguous terms designed to arrest the useless proliferation of possible locations for paradise, clarify the historical nature of the place, and fortify readers against "senseless discussions": "My answer is briefly this: It is an idle question about something no longer in existence. Moses is writing the history of the time before sin and the Deluge, but we are compelled to speak of conditions as they are after sin and after the Deluge.... For time and the curse which sins deserve destroy everything. Thus when the world was obliterated by the Deluge, together with its people and cattle, this famous garden was also obliterated and became lost. Therefore it is vain for Origen and others to carry on senseless discussions."[21] Luther's flat assertion of the garden's destruction is plainly offered as an antidote to traditional views of its continued existence. Furthermore, his introduction of Origen, a third century Christian theologian known for his allegorical readings of Scripture, indicates that he intends his historical paradise to speak to those who might find a figurative interpretation alluring: "The distance between the rivers troubles Origen, for he has in mind a garden area of the size they are among us. Therefore he turns to allegory. Paradise he takes to be heaven; the trees he takes to be angels; the rivers he takes to be wisdom. Such twaddle is unworthy of theologians, though for a mirthful poet they might perhaps be appropriate. Origen does not take into consideration that Moses is writing a history and, what is more, one that deals with matters long since past." Therefore, he concludes, "when we must discuss Paradise now, after the Flood, let us speak of it as a historical Paradise which once was and no longer exists."[22]

After Luther, other Reformed commentators moved quickly to adopt the view that paradise had been eradicated by the flood.[23] The predecessor to whose work Milton's *Paradise Lost* has been linked most directly, however, is the Huguenot poet Guillaume Du Bartas. His poems "La semaine ou création du monde" (1578) and "La seconde semaine" (1584), translated by Josuah Sylvester in 1608 as *The Divine Weeks and Works*, have been shown to have influenced *Paradise Lost*.[24] Like Luther, Du Bartas firmly asserts that paradise is no longer a place on earth and frames its demolition as an answer to skeptics who might be tempted by figurative interpretations of the Bible to doubt that it was ever a real place. He introduces the garden at the beginning of the "Seconde Weeke" of his *Divine Weekes and Works*, in the section entitled "Eden." Here is the passage, as rendered by Sylvester:

> A certaine place it was, now sought in vaine;
> Where set by grace, for sin remov'd againe
> Our Elders were: whereof, the thunder-darter
> Made a bright sword the gate, an Angell porter.
> Nor think that *Moses* paints fantasticke-wise
> A mistike tale of fained Paradice:
> ('Twas a true Garden, happy plenties horne,
> And seat of graces) least thou make (forlorne)
> An Ideall *Adams* food fantasticall,
> His sinne suppos'd, his paine poeticall.
>   . . . .
> But if thou list to guesse by likelihood,
> Thinke that the wreakfull nature-drowning floud
> Spard not this beauteous place which formost saw
> The first foule breach of Gods eternall law.[25]

Paradise, insists Du Bartas, is a "true Garden" and not "fantasticke," a "mistike," or "fained"; the multitude of erroneous figurative readings indicated here suggests that he regards them as both grave and powerfully seductive. The scope of the danger, moreover, extends to Adam himself, who might by this reckoning seem merely "ideall" rather than real. Like Luther, Du Bartas clearly wants to steer his readers toward a literal reading of the garden of Eden while heading off any doubts that might be raised by speculation about its present-day location. He adumbrates the scene in terms that indicate nothing less than the complete obliteration of paradise from the face of the earth:

> Thinke that the most part of the plants it puld
> And of the sweetest flowers the spirits duld;
> Spoild the faire gardens, made the fat fields leane,
> And chang'd (perchance) the rivers channell clean:
> And thinke that Time, whose slippery wheel doth play

> In humane causes with inconstant sway,
> Who exiles, alters, and disguises words,
> Hath now transform'd the names of all these fords.
> For as through sinne we lost that place; I feare,
> Forgetfull, we have lost the knowledge where
> 'Twas situate; and of the sugred dainties
> Wherewith God fed us in those sacred plenties.   ("Eden," 189–200)

The garden is emphatically lost, through sin, time, and the flood. Nothing of it survives.

There is a certain ambiguity in Du Bartas about the particulars of the garden's fate that appears to stem from the necessity of evoking a "true Garden" in descriptive terms without prompting readers to speculate about specifics. Luther gave grudging license to the "mirthful poet" to indulge in allegorical interpretation, but Du Bartas, resolutely literal, will have none of it. He would clearly prefer that his readers refrain from wondering about the details of its demise; "if thou list to guesse by likelihood / Thinke that the wreakfull nature-drowning flood / Spard not this beauteous place" ("Eden," 185–87). Such qualifications recall Luther, who offers his view as the best opinion among many on a question of very little importance: "The opinions are numberless. My answer is briefly this: It is an idle question about something no longer in existence."[26] Both writers' concerns are squarely on biblical interpretation; the certainty that paradise was a real place lost through sin is central, while any particulars that might be offered about its disappearance are, at best, speculative and, at worst, misleading.

Yet Du Bartas's account works against his claim that paradise was a real place by discouraging readers from imaginatively inhabiting it. His conditional language conspicuously brackets the description of the flora, the landscape, and the flood's devastation of paradise; if readers wish to "guesse *by likelihood*," they may suppose that the floodwaters "puld" the plants, "duld" the flowers, "spoild the faire gardens, made the fat fields leane, / And chang'd (*perchance*) the rivers channell clean" (*Eden*, 186, 189–92; emphases mine). Moreover, Du Bartas's decision to introduce the garden from a post-lapsarian perspective emphasizes its theological and exegetical dimensions at the expense of readers' imaginative experience of it as a place; their first approach to it is through a gate that is already guarded by cherubim and flaming sword ("Eden," 171–74). Du Bartas's garden is, from the beginning, a place already proscribed and already vanished.

The contrast with Milton's introduction of the garden is instructive. In *Paradise Lost*, as in Du Bartas's poem, it is proleptic, with the "loss of *Eden*" (1.4) established both in the poem's title and in the opening invocation, before the garden itself is shown. However, Eden's impending loss overshadows readers' approach to it less strongly in Milton's poem than in Du Bartas's. Our first view of the garden in *Paradise Lost* comes through Satan's eyes as he wings his way down from the "*Assyrian* mount" (*PL* 4.126) and "to the border comes / Of *Eden*, where delicious Paradise, / Now nearer, Crowns with her enclosure green" (*PL* 4.131–33). We subsequently dwell with Adam and Eve in the garden for six books of the poem before God instructs Michael to proscribe it and install "Cherubic watch, and of a Sword the flame / Wide waving" on the east side (*PL* 11.120–21). It is not until the final lines of the poem that Milton shows us what Du Bartas foregrounds from the beginning: paradise forbidden, "wav'd over by that flaming Brand, the Gate / With dreadful Faces throng'd and fierie Armes" (*PL* 12.643–44).

The emphasis on the garden as place in *Paradise Lost*, established through the poem's extended prelapsarian approach, emerges again with force and precision in book 11, in Eve's and Adam's laments for their erstwhile home (268–85 and 315–33), in Michael's gloss about place and sanctity (836–38), and in the relic of the "Iland salt and bare" itself (834). The contrasts with Luther's and Du Bartas's treatments of the episode throw Milton's emphasis on place into strong relief. Neither early Reformed writer posits anything like a desert island after the flood or draws a lesson like Michael's from the episode; both vehemently affirm the utter obliteration of the garden, and the terms in which Du Bartas does so seem designed to prevent readers from actually imagining paradise as a real place. The garden in *The Divine Weeks and Works* is gone so completely that it is almost as if it never existed.

What might be the significance, then, of Milton's pointed departure from Reformed opinion about the inundation of paradise? If his aim was to demonstrate that place has no relevance to personal sanctity after the Fall, then why did he not depict its utter dissolution, as earlier commentators had done? One answer may be that the image of the desert island serves to nullify, precisely and vividly, the prelapsarian functions of paradise. Designed initially as a human habitat, the garden can be said to have lost this meaning once humans are excluded from it, and the devastation that follows could serve to illustrate this loss, as both Lewalski and Gillies suggest.[27] The island may thus be read as an explicit image of ruin; as the flood strips away the features that marked it as "home" for Adam and Eve, the garden becomes a place too barren for human habitation, illustrating the consequences for the natural world of human sin and, to some extent, the deemphasis of place as a meaningful category of human experience.[28]

Insofar as it looks backward, then, the island may serve as a haunting reminder of what has been lost. However, two features of Milton's treatment in particular suggest that he has not finished with place and that it may in time acquire new relevance to sanctity. The first of these is the sense of contingency expressed in Michael's commentaries on paradise in the afterdays. The angel's gloss on the devastation of the garden, "that God attributes to place / No sanctitie, *if* none be thither brought" (11.836–37; emphasis mine), indicates that sanctity will not inhere in place itself after the Fall, but it also implies, as Karen Edwards observes, that any place will have the potential to be made holy through the sanctified spirit of its inhabitants.[29] The terms in which the angel presents it indicate that this properly sanctified spirit will depend on their ability to live upright and virtuous lives:

> onely add
> Deeds to thy knowledge answerable, add Faith,
> Add Vertue, Patience, Temperance, add Love,
> By name to come call'd Charitie, the soul
> Of all the rest: then wilt thou not be loath
> To leave this Paradise, but shalt possess
> A Paradise within thee, happier farr.   (*PL* 12.581–87)

Michael makes clear that both the "Paradise within" and its potential resanctification of place are not guarantees but possibilities that require human effort in order to be realized. In the order of operations he sketches, this inner disposition toward holiness comes first, serving as a source and sign for its resanctification of place. In her essay in this volume, Margaret Justice Dean argues that this is precisely what happens in *Paradise Regained* as Jesus's inward holiness sanctifies the places he frequents, including Herod's temple and, more significantly, his mother's house. The prospect of a paradise originating in the figurative holy place of the heart and moving outward to sanctify external place suggests that we ought to read the "Iland salt and bare" as a prospective figure, as well as a retrospective one.

The other aspect of Milton's handling of place that gestures toward some future relevance of place is the island's status as a relic. While it is true that the flood expunges the paradisal qualities of the garden and renders it unfit to serve as a home for human beings, what remains is *place* itself, a location with features both topographical (great river, gulf, island) and ecological (the land's "salt" barrenness, the animals "haunting" it) that identify it as a *type* of place on the earth. Against Luther's and Du Bartas's claims that the garden is no longer a place on earth, Milton's island emerges as a reliquary for human habitat, a spot that is "the haunt of Seals and Orcs, and Seamews clang," but with potential for rehabilitation. As Edwards notes, the island "will 'take root,' a phrase implying and promising growth."[30] If, at the poem's end, it is still too early to forecast the nature of such growth for this "salt and bare" land, it is nevertheless clear that the island will endure as a place after the floodwaters subside. The erasure of its garden elements — the trees, plants, and inhabitants that marked it as paradise — constitutes an emptying out of signifiers, while its perseverance as a blank place that will "root" after the flood points to the bare category of place, vitiated for now but awaiting possible revival.

The desert island's ambivalent bracketing of holy place affords some striking parallels with the complex dynamics of iconoclasm that Alexandra Walsham has identified in the responses of second- and third-generation Reformers to the ruins of former sacred sites that dotted the British landscape after the Dissolution. While many iconoclastic Protestants aimed to obliterate all traces of such places, others wished to preserve their remnants as evidence of the triumph of Protestantism over idolatrous Catholicism. However, as Walsham observes, because such sites often drew visitors and invited further ceremonies of destruction, iconoclasm "reproduce[d] the awe [it was] designed to dispel" and thus reconfigured these places as holy in a different way.[31] This strain of thought converged in unexpected ways with the competing view among some high churchmen that the ruins symbolized "shameful disrespect for the sacred" and were thus in need of preservation and protection from further acts of devastation and sacrilege.

By the beginning of the seventeenth century, the impulse to reconsecrate sacred sites and houses of worship had begun to emerge from this complex mixture of responses to the ruins in the landscape.[32] As a relic and reliquary of a formerly sacred place, the desert island of book 11 reproduces awe even while seeking to dispel it, and thereby resists efforts to limit its significance. It is a figure freighted with loss and regret, as ruined holy places were for some subsequent Reformers. As a chastening remnant in the postlapsarian landscape, it may also be read as a monument to human iniquity and its just punishment, a stern reminder of the wages of sin. And, as a place preserved and set apart, Milton's island leaves open the possibility of the resanctification of place.

MILTON AMONG THE REFORMERS:
THEOLOGIES OF PLACE

In order to underscore Milton's conspicuous bracketing of place in the figure of the desert island, I wish to draw attention to a parallel gesture in *De doctrina Christiana*. Tellingly, it concerns the matter of holy place and prayer and therefore offers a commentary on Michael's gloss on place and personal sanctity in book 11. Critical interpretations of *Paradise Lost* 11.824–38 that emphasize the supersession of external place by the "Paradise within" are in accordance with early Reformed theology, particularly Calvinism, which emphasized the divine omnipresence, rejected the notion that grace could be mediated by the material world, and argued that God had abolished all "distinction of places." This was not only a matter of theology but also of religious practice; since Reformed worship needed to be uncoupled from the Catholic calendar and consecrated spaces in order to flourish, early Reformers eschewed assumptions about the enhanced spiritual potency of particular places and times. Thus, both Luther and Calvin were at pains to disengage the quality of sanctity from particular places such as pilgrimage sites and churches, as well as from specific times of the day, week, or liturgical year. When read as a prelude to the relocation of sanctity from the external place of Eden to the interior "Paradise within," the devastation of the garden in *Paradise Lost* does indeed seem to resonate with sixteenth century Reformed teachings on sanctity and place.

It is somewhat surprising, then, to learn that the theology of place Milton sketches in his *De doctrina Christiana* does not readily align with this thinking. As we shall see, although he affirms Luther's assertion that all places are suitable for praying, and echoes Calvin's dictum (after Paul) that the worshippers themselves are the true temples of God, Milton also suggests that some places are more suitable than others without naming them explicitly. This gesture clears a place for prayer that stands alongside — and in tension with — pronouncements on the subject made by earlier Reformers.

In a sermon preached in 1544 at the dedication of the Castle Church in Torgau, Luther stipulates that congregants should be free to worship where and when they see fit:

> We should insist that we are the lords of the sabbath and of other days and places and not attribute special holiness or service of God to a particular day, as the Jews or our papists do. Therefore this house shall be built and appointed according to this freedom for those who dwell here in this castle and court or any others who desire to come in. Not that we are making a special church of it, as if it were better than other houses where the Word of God is preached. If the occasion should arise that people did not want to or could not assemble, one could just as well preach outside by the fountain or somewhere else.[33]

Luther pointedly refrains from using the language of sanctity, making it clear that he is not consecrating the church, or giving it any "special" designation at all, but "appointing" it as a place for worship. His chief concern is to make room for a congregation to worship freely, at times and places of their own choosing; this calls for the leveling of differences between places — church, house, fountain side — and times for prayer: "One can and one really should pray in every place and every hour; but prayer is nowhere so mighty and strong as when the whole multitude prays together. Thus the dear patriarchs gathered with their families, and anybody else who happened to be with them, under a tree, or put up a tent, and erected an altar, and this was their temple and their house of God."[34] The spontaneous group worship described in the example of the patriarchs above, and implied by Luther's suggestion that congregants might on occasion prefer to assemble outside the church, requires open, fluid places that emerge to meet the needs of the people as they arise. Churches, as houses where God's word is preached, are one place for prayer among many.

John Calvin argues more pointedly against the notion that sanctity inheres in churches of themselves: "These do not by any secret sanctity of their own make prayers more holy, or cause them to be heard by God. But they are intended to receive the congregation of believers more conveniently when they gather to pray, to hear the preaching of the Word, and at the same time to partake of the sacraments. Otherwise (as Paul says) [1 Cor. 3:16, 6:19; 2 Cor. 6:16] we ourselves are the true temples of God. Let those who wish to pray in God's temple, pray in ourselves."[35] Here, places are expressly denied the power to sanctify worshippers or their prayers. The reference to 1 Corinthians 6:19, in which Paul declares the body itself to be the temple of the Holy Spirit, reassigns holiness to an implicitly figurative "place" within the body of the worshipping subject. To temples themselves Calvin ascribes the mundane capacity of receiving congregants, and he has stern words for those who believe otherwise: "But those who suppose that God's ear has been brought closer to them in a temple, or consider their prayer more consecrated by the holiness of the place, are acting in this way according to the stupidity of the Jews and Gentiles. In physically worshipping God, they go against what has been commanded that, without any consideration of place, we worship God in spirit and in truth [John 4:23]."[36] In pointedly condemning belief in "holy" places and insisting on the properly interior nature of worship, Calvin offers a corollary to Luther's open and uniform spaces of worship; not only is sanctity not a property of place, but it rightly belongs to the hearts of true believers who worship God "in spirit and in truth."

When Milton writes directly about place and prayer in *De doctrina Christiana*, he begins by echoing Luther and Calvin. "Concerning places for prayer, every one is appropriate," he says.[37] What comes next, however, marks a departure: "In addition, in private prayer we are also permitted to be where it is more hidden: Matt. 6:6. 'go into your chamber,' and 14:23. 'he ascended a mountain to pray separately.' Indeed, to pray in a private way in public is hypocritical.... However, it was once allowed to hold private prayers in the sanctuary and the temple at Jerusalem."[38] Whereas Luther's congregants pray together out in the open, Milton points to the historical example of worshippers in the sanctuary and the temple of Jerusalem in order to validate his designation of private places for praying. Milton's concern to justify concealment during prayer and establish precedent for private prayers inside a church contrast markedly with Luther's open, undifferentiated spaces of worship and his express ban on the practice of "seek[ing] out secret corners to hide away, as the Anabaptists do."[39] According to Milton, it is "hypocritical" to pray publicly in the way one prays privately, and therefore public spaces do not suffice. He takes care not to directly condone private prayer in a sanctuary or a church; this is, he says, a practice that was at one time ("olim") permitted. Yet neither does he indicate where else worshippers might make their private prayers. Although Milton cites Matthew's recommendations of a private chamber or a mountain top, he declines to suggest in his own voice where else one might "also be permitted to be concealed" while praying.

Calvin, by contrast, takes one of Matthew's suggestions into his own text and elaborates on it. He defines prayer as an interior action that originates from within the worshipper, "an emotion of the heart within, which is poured out and laid bare before God, the searcher of hearts." As such, he concludes, the activity of prayer is best conducted in the silence of the worshipper's own heart, and in the seclusion of that most private of places, the bedroom.

> Christ our Lord, when he willed to lay down the best rule for prayer, bade us enter into our bedroom and there, with door closed, pray to our Father in secret, that our Father, who is in secret, may hear us (Matt. 6:6). For, when he has drawn us away from the example of hypocrites, who grasp after the favor of men by vain and ostentatious prayers, he at the same time adds something better: that is, to enter into our bedroom and there, with door closed, pray.... For he did not mean to deny that it is fitting to pray in other places, but he shows that prayer is something secret, which is both principally lodged in the heart and requires a tranquility far from all our teeming cares.[40]

Milton draws close to Calvin in condoning private places for prayer. Tellingly, however, while both writers cite Matthew 6:6, only Calvin develops its recommendation in his own voice. For him, the bedroom's suitability as a place for prayer derives from its inherent privacy; in a world of places, it is the analog closest to the human heart, the original prayer chamber. By contrast, Milton lets Matthew give this example while he himself points instead to the historical examples of the sanctuary and the temple of Jerusalem. In

Paradise Regained, as Dean demonstrates in her essay in this volume, Milton will do more to connect prayer with the private places suggested by Calvin. In *De doctrina Christiana,* however, having established both need and precedent for private prayer, and having cleared a private place for this purpose, Milton leaves it open and undesignated.

Turning from proper *places* for prayers to proper *times* for them, Milton's ambivalence is even more pronounced: "Moreover, there is no time for prayer that is not fit.... On the other hand, chiefly evening, morning, and midday are fit."[41] On the one hand, he acknowledges with Luther and Calvin that every time is suitable for prayer. On the other, however, he singles out times that are *particularly* appropriate and names them ("evening, morning, and midday"). In this, he goes further than he does in talking about place, where he differentiates without specifying. Yet in both cases the gesture encompasses mutually exclusive alternatives; all times and all places are equally suitable for prayer, *and* certain ones are especially suitable. In making this gesture, Milton appears to balance a commitment to early Reformed teaching about holiness and place against a sense that this is not, perhaps, the whole story.

Indeed, the emergence of rites of consecration in seventeenth century England and Scotland documented by Andrew Spicer indicates that Reformed views on place and sanctity were evolving and multivocal during this period. Although the reconsecration movement gained momentum under William Laud, it also predated his tenure and was endorsed by some moderate Calvinists.[42] That Milton was likely aware of this trend is suggested by Laud's consecration of a new chapel at Hammersmith in June 1631, shortly after his father's relocation of the family there.[43] By 1667, Milton was surely no friend to episcopal rites of consecration, but it appears that in some cases a congregation's use of a place for worship was thought sufficient to consecrate it without the need for the formalities of a bishop.[44] If Milton's thinking about place and sanctity in the 1630s hewed more closely to Laudian views, as Chapman's analysis of *genius loci* in *Lycidas* would suggest, then the desert island of *Paradise Lost* may represent just how much distance he had put between those earlier views and his more mature thinking on the subject by the 1660s. In leaving the ruins of paradise standing, reconfigured as a bare and haunted place, he overwrites Catholic, Lutheran, and Laudian notions about what makes a place holy with his own Reformed image of a place scoured clean in hopeful readiness for the sanctifying presence of one who brings a heart devoted to God.

In contemplating the "Iland salt and bare," it is hard not to think of the potent places of *Paradise Regained*, especially the "Desert wild" to which the Son withdraws to discern "how best the mighty work he might begin / Of Saviour to mankind" (*PR* 1.186–87). At the close of *Paradise Lost,* however, this lies in the future. As a set of open brackets, the desert island points back to the loss of sacred place and ahead to the possibility of recuperation. Like the silence into which Milton lapses as he contemplates place and sanctity in *De doctrina Christiana*, it enacts a simple posture of watchful meditation. The imagery of devastation, taken together with the contrastive language of "tak[ing] root" and of habitat, suggest a willingness to suspend expectations about the future of place and to dwell for the time being in hope, which, as Mary Fenton argues, is for Milton "a dynamic force that aspires toward the heavenly and yet remains connected to a definite physical space."[45] The image of the desert island touches both the sorrow of exile and hope for the future, but it is perhaps most eloquent of all as a figure for the ground in between: the places where humans must dwell for now, and the quiet, poised attentiveness they will need as they watch and work for whatever still matters about place in a fallen world.

CHAPTER 8

———— ⋙⋘ ————

Images of the East in *Paradise Lost*

TALYA MEYERS

The Middle Eastern and Asian presence in Milton's *Paradise Lost* differs from that of the poet's epic predecessors in two fundamental ways. First, for Milton, these widely varied places largely reside under the monolithic category of "Eastern": they are other and exotic, and references to them tend to be similar in affect and tone. Second, Milton's consolidated East, as Benedict Robinson says, "is finally altogether literary and metaphorical: a set of orientalist allusions from an impossibly wide array of moments and sources are grafted onto a story in which there are no Saracens or Egyptians, in which Islam and Egypt do not exist, and in which the only real Eastern site is that most equivocal place, Eden."[1] Milton's figurative East draws upon images of general and even clichéd luxurious excess, imperial splendor, and mercantile bounty to guide our readings of Satan and Eden. Moreover, late in the seventeenth century, when England occupied an increasingly prominent position on the world stage, had established a strong trade presence, and was beginning to think of itself and the surrounding world in imperialist terms (even though the Middle Eastern and Asian world, from Istanbul to Cathay, contained a large number of powerful and influential governments, as he was well aware), Milton harnessed the imaginative power of an increasingly familiar East for new ends. The vast and varied world of the Middle East and, to a lesser extent, southern and eastern Asia and Africa that Europeans confronted in the sixteenth and early seventeenth centuries

157

is imaginatively colonized for a European and Christian story that leaves nonfigurative Easterners out of the equation entirely.

However, there is more to Milton's East than a collection of evocative images. Scholars who have addressed the oriental presence running through *Paradise Lost* have tended to treat its motifs and images separately. For example, Satan is famously compared to a monarch of Persia or Mughal India. Critics have also seen correlations between Satan's arrival in Eden and that of a European colonizer to a rich, commercially viable, and very Asian- (or, according to some, American-) looking place. This essay connects some of Milton's many evocations of the Orient, tracing a narrative of figurative language that runs alongside Milton's literal narrative and that reveals uncomfortable parallels between Eden and Pandaemonium, and between Eden and an East with which Europe, although it might be increasingly familiar, was certainly not comfortable. Ultimately, Milton never defuses — nor do I think he intends to — the tension between Eden as an Assyrian garden and Eden as the cradle of Christianity and thus of the West, or between a Satan who is spiritually weakened under his oriental splendor and a Satan who, like an Eastern superpower, is physically, culturally, and geographically a significant force. Rather, prelapsarian Eden is perched precariously between East and West, and if it falls with Adam and Eve, it falls irrevocably East.

Here we have the essence of Milton's Eastern images: strictly speaking, they are not essential to his plot, but they are essential to understanding the poem and, in particular, what happens to Eden. Without reading Eden as falling toward Easternness, we miss a vital aspect of Milton's theodicy and his sense of the world after the Fall. And it is unsurprising, and not coincidental, that Milton's figurative narrative suggests an Easternness that is never ultimately contained.

Milton is the inheritor of a long tradition of European epic and romance that takes as its subject European encounters with non-European peoples, especially those of the Middle East, North Africa, and Asia. In particular, many romances, as well as epics like the *Chanson de Roland* (twelfth century), Ariosto's *Orlando furioso* (1516–32), and Tasso's *Gerusalemme liberata* (1581), deal with "Saracens," an imprecise and, as the sixteenth century wore on, increasingly outmoded word for Muslims. The Muslims of these texts are frequently martial in nature and chivalric in their values and are, as a number of critics have commented, fundamentally like their Christian counterparts.[2] Even the Muslims of the *Gerusalemme liberata* — more sinister presences in a text with tremendous ideological investment in a historical Christian victory over the Muslims who had possession of Jerusalem during the First Crusade — are deeply pious. They truly believe that they are serving Mohammed and their enemies are themselves an infidel threat; they are given extensive narrative attention and subjectivity; and their nobility and bravery repeatedly divert the narrative's — and the reader's — sympathies from the triumph of the Christian cause. By comparison, the Saracens of Spenser's *The Faerie Queene* are narratively marginalized: rather than forming an essential part of Spenser's declared epic plotline, they roam independently of any larger martial or political structure and exist primarily to divert the knights from quests sanctioned by Gloriana, prophetic authority, or dream-vision. Their presence in the text also lacks the striking subjectivity that characterizes earlier epic Saracens, and, like many of Spenser's figures, they are stripped of their seeming personhood and made to serve Spenser's allegorical agenda. This marginalized and figurative component has important implications for Milton, as does the fact that Spenser's Saracens, unlike the vast and threatening Muslim armies of the *Chanson de Roland* and the Italian epics, are never collectively defeated or routed from Faeryland.

Luis Vaz de Camões's *Os Lusíadas* was published nearly a decade before the *Gerusalemme liberata*, in 1572. While it deals primarily with locations in southern India and sub-Saharan Africa (the latter of which was more closely associated in the period with European Atlantic holdings, to which it supplied a steady stream of slave labor, than with the East), its connection to Milton, with whose imaginative East it has much in common, makes it especially important in this context. Camões's non-European world, like Milton's, is large in scope. He takes as his subject the voyage of the Portuguese explorer Vasco da Gama to India at the end of the fifteenth century, an expedition that marked the beginning of a short period during which Portuguese control over many of the naval trade routes of the Persian Gulf and Indian Ocean rapidly expanded. As such, *Os Lusíadas* is the absorption into epic of recent, still-felt history. In the poem's last canto, the explorers listen to a prophecy in song foretelling Portugal's advancement into the Indian Ocean and the Persian Gulf. In addition, the nymph

Tethys offers da Gama's men a view into a globe through which they can view the spheres and earth and, more significantly, see as a whole the Orient and Africa, the "new regions of the East / You Portuguese are adding to the world."[3] These varied places transition seamlessly from one to the next in Tethys's guided virtual tour, characterized primarily by the commodities to be gained by access to them; the globe implies that the Portuguese eye — and thus its conquering potential — is able to hold these vast regions in a single glance even as the globe simultaneously makes the glance possible. For da Gama, Portuguese power in the Orient is a future close at hand; by the time Camões visited Africa and India as a soldier, this short golden age of seemingly endless potential expansion had been curtailed by the limitations of Portuguese material and administrative resources, and the story told in prophetic song was the nostalgic past.[4] The sweeping gaze of Camões's final vision of the exoticized non-European world, which stretches to include the Americas along with Africa and Asia, and his juxtaposition of past and future, have important consequences for Milton.

Spenser's Saracens may owe their marginalized plight to English fear of the empires of the Middle East, or to fantasies of greater military, cultural, or commercial prominence in the world, just as they owe their inclusion in the text to the epic/romance canon that precedes them. But the Middle East and Asia that the English confronted at the end of the sixteenth century were very different from the East as it was experienced and understood by late seventeenth century Europe, and England, too, had changed. In the late sixteenth century, the Middle East and Asia were by no means unknown, but they were still largely unfamiliar, with a growing body of knowledge, awareness, and involvement between Europe and these regions quickly replacing a long history of myth, rumor, and occasional but by no means comprehensive or widespread contact. The following century saw an increasingly globalized and connected world, one in which, as the historian John E. Wills explains, by the end of the seventeenth century, "there were not many peoples left in the world whose lives had not been drastically changed by the web of interaction and exchange."[5] Europeans, the English among them, had found footholds throughout the region; England had greater diplomatic clout and a strong trade presence, which helped and were helped by its colonial holdings in the New World.

At the same time, the Middle East and the Indian subcontinent were beginning a long period of transition that would soon provide Europeans with the opportunity to promote their own interests in the region and to exercise greater authority and control. Perhaps most important, the Ottoman Empire, which had been a source of envy, admiration, and fear throughout the sixteenth century, was beginning what was, increasingly clearly, a period of decline.[6] The Ottomans had made repeated attacks on European soil, and their view of their place in the world both mirrored and challenged the Europeans' (nascent and largely wishful) ideas of supremacy. As Leeds Barroll explains, "to them western *Europe* was the colonial frontier.... From the Ottoman viewpoint, rich and barbarous lands lay beyond their northern and western frontiers, and it was *their* sacred mission to bring religion, civilization, order, and peace to these alien peoples."[7] But, as Nabil Matar and Gerald MacLean argue, the Ottomans "lost their military edge in the final decades of the seventeenth century, and no longer posed a threat to British interests in the eastern Mediterranean," a change that brought with it a shift in English writing about the Turks from a stance of vilification and hostility to one of "curiosity and ease."[8] This combined with the replacement of English preconceptions of Islam, based primarily on Crusade mythology, with a familiarity accumulated from travel and captivity narratives, expedition reports, histories of Islam and of the Ottomans, and explanations (however prejudiced and disparaging) of Muslim theology and practice.[9]

Likewise, interaction between Europe and Safavid Persia — which was already experiencing a period of instability, although this probably would not have been apparent to Milton, and would ultimately collapse in 1736 — had taken off at the beginning of the seventeenth century, shortly after the rise to power of Shah Abbas. The increasing cooperation, motivated in part by a mutual history of conflict with the Ottoman Empire, led to a proliferation of traveler's accounts that, as Rudi Matthee explains, "lift[ed] the country out of the state of a fabled realm and turn[ed] it into a place explored and described from an experiential, empiricist perspective."[10] Interestingly, this greater familiarity and self-assurance seems not to have led, on the whole, to more nuanced or accurate representations of these places in literature. On the contrary, *Paradise Lost* reflects what Daniel Vitkus suggests was the changing state of affairs at the end of the seventeenth century: namely, that the sense of a region composed of many different cultures and identities gave way to a more abstract and integrated idea of "the Orient."[11] This results not in greater nuance but in the inverse: a growing series of self-serving clichés, deliberate attempts to exoticize, and figurative meanings that can be evoked in the service of European ideas about luxury, excess, barbarism, and, simultaneously, both weakness and power.

Nowhere is this more apparent than in representations of India — or, at least, what Europeans began to see as India. When Milton was writing *Paradise Lost*, the Mughal Empire, under the rule of the emperor Arangzeb, was an immensely powerful force, ruling over virtually all of the Indian subcontinent except for a relatively small portion of southern India (although it, too, would begin a long period of instability after Arangzeb's death in 1707 and eventually collapse). It was to this region along the coastline that England's own relatively insignificant presence at the end of the seventeenth century was largely contained. But as Shankar Raman observes, even if one takes into account that our modern conception of India involves the conflation of many different peoples and cultures, "a quick glance at a Renaissance map suggests that answering the simple question 'Where is India?' presupposes a later relation to the world that was only then beginning to emerge."[12] The issue of conceiving India in the period is further complicated by the fact that, as both Raman and Pompa Banerjee demonstrate, "India" in the early modern European imagination included not only the East and West Indies, but also other parts of Asia as well as Africa. Banerjee argues that this led to the understanding of India as "an amorphous landmass — an everywhere that is not Europe," and in turn to the identification of anything, anywhere, that is "Indian" as "the exotic other of Europe — the other which is subsumed into subsequent European colonial enterprises."[13] This was compounded — with profound consequences for Milton — by travelers who portrayed India as an exotic, corrupt, and even barbaric place.[14]

But that is not to say that the East was no longer taken seriously. In the case of the areas now known as East, Northeast, and Southeast Asia, this would not even have been possible. It is true that this region was, like much of the world, heavily affected by globalization and early colonialism. The Dutch in what is now Indonesia famously destabilized local power structures (such as that of the formidable sultanate of Aceh), massacred the Bandan islanders, and oppressed the people of the formerly Portuguese Moluccas (islands to which Milton refers and which had captured the European imagination even as their actual profitability declined). Other Southeast Asian governments were affected more indirectly by the rising tide of nationalities, cultures, religions, and goods that flowed through their land and influenced their people. Nor was this influence primarily negative — for example, the Nguyen regime, struggling against its newfound enemies (and former fellow statesmen), the Trinh, in what is now Vietnam, depended on trade for its continued existence.[15] But East Asia contained two great empires that provided an irrefutable challenge to European triumphalism or ideas about its own superiority; increasing awareness of their importance in recent decades has led to a widespread correction to a long academic tradition of European exceptionalism. A warring *daimyo* culture in the late sixteenth century gave way to a strongly centralized government in early seventeenth century Japan: the Tokugawa regime, which would continue into the nineteenth century. Japan ultimately rejected much of the transnational and transcultural trade that was beginning to reshape Europe, Africa, and Asia (although some small, heavily supervised trading was permitted); it forcibly expelled a European Christian missionary presence that had originated in the sixteenth century and, in the 1630s, instituted the Sakoku, a series of laws that all but eliminated the presence of foreigners in Japan and the freedom of Japanese citizens to travel outside the nation. For this reason, discussions of East Asian challenges to European ideas of superiority have tended to focus more extensively on China.

To overstate the sheer importance of China on the world stage and in the development of the system of exchange that so reshaped both East and West would be hard to do.[16] China, when Milton was writing *Paradise Lost*, was the product of thousands of years of successful and stable dynastic rule, and Chinese culture had been an important influence in the development of other Asian nations. The Chinese considered their empire to be the center of the world and thought of and referred to the nations of Europe as the "Far West," a fact to be taken into account when evaluating monolithic European conceptions of "the East."[17] As Robert Markley explains, "China was a tough target for a republican polemicist [like Milton] to attack: it was an ancient empire that had escaped the fate of the pagan regimes of the Mediterranean and Near East and continued to prosper; it boasted a written history that, in its antiquity, narrative coherence, and moral probity apparently rivaled the Old Testament; and it seemed, to many commentators besides Jesuit accommodationists, to provide an unassailable model of sociopolitical order and economic prosperity."[18]   Moreover, China's desire for silver was an essential component of European trading activity, and approximately 40 percent of the silver produced in the Americas in the seventeenth century eventually made its way to Asia.[19] England was eager to trade with China and devoted significant energy to the establishment of trade routes to the nation and acquisition of desirable Chinese goods, but as the Chinese were uninterested in the results of English manufacturing, the English were required to pay for their goods, both in China and elsewhere, with silver, which had significant consequences for England's own economic system. The citizens of China enjoyed a high quality of life, a significant national wealth, and a comparatively high level of technological sophistication.[20] In some cases, Chinese colonialism allied with or complemented European efforts: in the Philippines, for example, China was already a presence by the time of the Spanish arrival in the late sixteenth century; by the mid-to-late seventeenth century, Spanish and Chinese cooperation had been employed in a variety of ways to control the inhabitants of the islands and to turn a profit.[21] As Milton was composing *Paradise Lost,* however, the Manchus were busy relocating many of the coastal populations and destroying the abandoned villages in response to a series of internal conflicts that resulted in crushing maritime defeats. This maneuver essentially shut down Chinese trade completely until 1683.[22]

Eventually, the increasing European control over trade routes and revenues that arose from the decline of the Ottoman, Safavid, and Mughal empires led to irrevocable and frequently devastating changes throughout the region. Europeans who had established footholds were in a position to push their own interests and, increasingly, authority over the areas that they had originally entered as suitors of and even supplicants for trading privileges. The Chinese and Russian empires, likewise, continued to expand into central Asia throughout this period and would continue to be important presences in the region for much of its colonial history.[23] New competitors entered on the scene — among them the Japanese and German empires at the end of the nineteenth century — and European holdings would increase into the twentieth. What began as a desire for control over the flow of valuable Eastern goods both throughout the region and into Europe and the Americas became, over time, the more explicit government of Eastern peoples, their cultures, practices, and ways of life, as well as their resources. While most of this was still nascent in the late seventeenth century, *Paradise Lost*, with its more unified and othered conception of an East, its greater and more masterful sense of familiarity with the region and its peoples, and its lack of substantive engagement with actual Easterners, marks the beginning of this long transition.

Scholars have found it difficult to gauge the level of Milton's interest in Asian affairs. His East in *Paradise Lost* is more general and wide-ranging than Spenser's; far from being restricted to the Ottoman Empire and Persia, Milton includes references to a vast range of Eastern places, among them the Moluccas, India, and China. Certainly he was highly aware of the presence of a huge number of widely varied cultures throughout the Orient, in the context of his appointment as Secretary of Foreign Tongues, through his much-discussed enthusiasm for geography, and as an issue of more general contemporary interest. In the sixteenth century, the English had attempted to establish a relationship with the Russian czar that would allow them a trade route through Persia into China. Milton's *A Brief History of Moscovia*, first published in 1682, indicates the direction of his own historical interest "from the eastern Bounds of *Russia*, to the Walls of *Cathay*" and imagines Russia's geography in relation to the countries "adjoyning eastward, as far as *Cathay*" even as he acknowledges the "excessive love of Gain and Traffick" that prevents English expeditions to Russia from having heroic potential.[24] Markley points out Milton's fascination with the possibility of trade with China as a way to promote English prosperity even as the poet worries about the threat of Eastern luxury to the English character and about the wealth and stability of Asian empires.[25]

To write about the East in the works of Milton's epic predecessors is to focus primarily on representations of the Middle East or its peoples. In one sense, that focus need not alter much in a discussion of *Paradise Lost*. The majority of Milton's significant Eastern images draw upon the same region of the world. Not all of them do, to be sure. For example, although the exact position of Satan's earth landing after his journey through Chaos is not specified, it is frequently misread by critics as being China, for the simple reason that Satan's arrival is accompanied by an extended metaphor comparing him to a vulture that migrates from the Himalayas to the general area of the Gobi desert.[26] And on the journey through Chaos, Satan is compared to a merchant en route from India or the Moluccas — "Close Sailing from *Bengala*, or the Iles / Of *Ternate* and *Tidore*" (*PL* 2.638–39) — a reference laden, as we shall see, with colonializing baggage. But, for the most part, Milton's metaphorical East focuses on a relatively specific geographic region until the very end of the text. The reason for this is quite simple: the geographical space that is negotiated throughout *Paradise Lost* is, specifically, Eden, located imaginatively in the minds of Bible readers somewhere in the Middle East. Milton's references may be figurative, but they correlate to the general location of Eden in the Christian imagination, and, specifically, they connect the prelapsarian Eden imaginatively with the postlapsarian Eastern world with which it shares geographical space. However, that being said, it would be a mistake to see Milton's figurative East as being contained imaginatively to this immediate region, or to consider only the cultural, commercial, and political circumstances of that region without reference to the larger East. What becomes clear in the catalogue of "Earth's Kingdomes and thir Glory," which Michael shows to Adam so that his "Eye might there command wherever stood / City of old or modern Fame, the Seat / Of mightiest Empire" (11.384–87), is that this inherent Easternness is catching. The three dynamic and changing empires of the Middle East and the Indian subcontinent are not the only ones included — these seats of empire range not only "from the destind Walls / Of *Cambalu*" (11.387–88), the capital of the Mongol Empire, and Peking (Beijing) to Istanbul, but to kingdoms in Africa as well, and even, worryingly, to the Roman Empire, quintessentially a part of European history. As such, the Eastern potential implicit in Eden, once it makes its way to the surface, becomes a metonym for a larger network of non-European power, influence, and, as we will see, implied challenge to Western Europe.

If the East upon which Milton draws is more varied than that of some of his predecessors, it is nonetheless remarkably undifferentiated: images of the Mediterranean, India, the Moluccas, and so on seem largely to occur in related figurative contexts and to contain a similar imaginative force. Scholars have suggested that Milton's orientalism is a metaphorical critique of earthly monarchy in general and the Stuarts in particular, and his Orient is characterized less like a grouping of disparate cultures than like a general category of otherness.[27] Images of the Mediterranean and Asia abound in *Paradise Lost*, and these images are, MacLean observes, "oblique, learned, illustrative, polemical, *incidental* and surprisingly stereotyping" (italics mine); this lack of direct engagement means that "the recent resurgence of interest in England's intellectual and cultural relations with the Muslim world...has continued to pass Milton by."[28] But it is precisely the incidental quality of Milton's Eastern language that, to my way of thinking, associates him with an epic tradition that has received far more attention on this score. Spenser moves the Saracen warrior to a more marginal place in the text, and Milton takes this transition to its logical conclusion, creating an East that is pervasive but entirely located in the figurative. In his Eastern images, Milton's use of a long tradition of epic narrative that represents encounters with the Mediterranean and the greater Orient is evident. A few of these have proven especially provocative for Milton scholars and are frequently discussed: the image of Satan on his throne in Pandaemonium; the journey through Chaos; the sensuous and both foreign and familiar garden of Eden; and Eden's prophesied future. But it is the figurative narrative that these images create — one of contradictions and multiplicities of power and weakness, fallenness and uprightness, and past and future — to which I now want to turn.

If the descriptions of Satan and the devils in hell demonstrate a more solidly conceived idea of Easternness, they nonetheless employ the imaginative force behind representations of the Mediterranean in epic and romance texts and in earlier seventeenth century English writing. For example, the great hall of Pandaemonium is described as being "like a cover'd field, where Champions bold / Wont ride in arm'd, and at the Soldans chair / Defi'd the best of Panim chivalry" (*PL* 1.763–65). The description of Pandaemonium culminates with Satan

High on a Throne of Royal State, which far
Outshon the wealth of *Ormus* and of *Ind*,
Or where the gorgeous East with richest hand
Showrs on her Kings *Barbaric* Pearl and Gold.   (2.1–4)

As Balachandra Rajan points out, the image invokes imperial splendors
both past (Ormuz) and present (India, specifically the famously elaborate Peacock Throne in Delhi, on which Rajan suggests Milton may draw
both for Satan's throne and for the court of Pandaemonium.)[29] As Robinson argues, it is precisely the impressive splendors of Satan's kingdom that
render it flawed and problematic: "The monarchy of hell is 'Barbaric,' its
effort to fabricate a factitious heaven the measure of its fallenness: the shift
from 'gorgeous' to 'Barbaric' signals the distance between true splendor and
the false shows of a Satanic aesthetic."[30] Thus, we have a rather Miltonic
contradiction: the Orient is here represented at its most powerful, appeal-
ing, and refined, and yet this power and refinement is a sign of its ultimate
weakness, its inability to replace or to significantly threaten the true glory of
(Christian) heaven. Milton surrounds Satan with a consolidation of clichés
of a materially powerful and wealthy East, albeit in a form revealed to be
theologically weak and thus, ultimately, martially compromised.[31]

Nonetheless, the image remains one of power — to be specific, imperial
power — and it is the emperorlike Satan who offers to leave his own kingdom
in order to colonize the Christian Eden. Literary criticism generally treats
the Satan of Pandaemonium and the Satan who travels to Eden as separate entities, connected by similar figurative associations but not narratively
cohesive. Overwhelmingly, scholars have seen Satan's journey as that of a
European explorer, merchant, or colonizer: David Quint sees a connection
between the voyaging Satan and Vasco da Gama, the mercantile explorer of
Camões's *Os Lusíadas*; J. Martin Evans traces throughout *Paradise Lost* the
colonial discourse of the European conquest of the New World; Markley
argues for specific reference to, and criticism of, the Dutch monopoly of
the spice trade in the language of the journey through Chaos; and Su Fang
Ng finds in Milton's language a connection between mercantilism and war,
and thus a connection between Satan and European piracy in Asia.[32] There
is more than enough room in the journey to Eden for manifold, uneasily
eliding, and contradictory readings, and to these I wish to add another: in

imagining a Satan moving to conquer, we should not ignore what Bruce McLeod calls the "orientalist view of the ever-invasive East" with which Satan is associated.[33] We must remember that the Ottomans in particular had their own ideas about sacred duty and eventual supremacy, and that they had already made repeated attempts to gain control of European soil. Read as such, a very different picture emerges: Satan, at the height of his imperial gorgeousness, the leader of a powerful, culturally and intellectually sophisticated force, leaves Pandaemonium to colonize a place that, for all its Eastern associations, is like Faeryland, Jerusalem, or France in previous epics: a Christian, and thus to some degree European, place. Like Camões, Milton harnesses and mythologizes the imaginative power of what is, in this case, uncomfortably recent history.

This, at first glance, is easily overlooked. Satan traveling through Chaos is compared to a merchant leaving India or the Moluccas of Indonesia ("Close sailing from *Bengala*, or the Iles / Of *Ternate* and *Tidore* [*PL* 2.638–39]), and, as Markley points out, such merchants would presumably be en route to Europe, to the Dutch Republic.[34] As such, the image is one of Asian luxury and splendor infiltrating Europe rather than the other way around. However, Satan's and our first encounter with Eden is with the Middle East, an "*Assyrian* Garden" (4.285). That we first encounter Satan through Eden's eyes is a critical truism, although Anne Ferry objects to the idea that our vision is tainted by Satan's perception of the garden, since Satan's perspective is described by an external narrator who sees Eden "independently of Satan's point of view and describes it so that we will feel what Satan cannot feel."[35] Nonetheless, scholars frequently treat the exotic and commercial qualities of Eden as though our perspective at the beginning of book 4 were blurred with Satan's.[36]

Eden is a place of "Orient Pearl and sands of Gold," of "odorous," and, as has been frequently observed, valuable "Gumms and Balme" (4.238–48), but read against the image of a conquering emperor on a mighty throne, this begins to feel like descriptive sleight-of-hand. It may be an Assyrian garden, but it is also "a recognizably English setting," as Eric Song, building upon Barbara Lewalski's reading of Adam's "happy rural seat" (4.247) in light of the English country-house tradition, suggests.[37] Eden contains both the voluptuous Middle East and the virtues of rural Europe within it, qualities that we discover only when Satan arrives. What was, from the perspective of book 2, a Christian land under serious threat from an East-like Pandaemonium looks, at the moment of Satan's invasion, Eastern itself. There are even close linguistic correlations between, for example, the "Barbaric Pearl and Gold" of Pandaemonium and the "Orient Pearl and sands of Gold" of the newly infiltrated Eden. That Eden can be seen as a European place under attack by an Eastern threat is underscored in the simile used to describe Sin's and Death's building of the bridge between hell and earth:

> So, if great things to small may be compar'd,
> *Xerxes*, the Libertie of *Greece* to yoke,
> From *Susa* his *Memnonian* Palace high
> Came to the Sea, and over *Hellespont*
> Bridging his way, *Europe* with *Asia* joyn'd.   (10.306–10)

It is noteworthy that the "Libertie of *Greece*" was equally under Asian yoke in the seventeenth century. While ancient Greece was, to early modern England, the seat of classical knowledge and thus of Western civilization, most of modern Greece had been under Ottoman control since the late fifteenth century.[38] Through the association with Xerxes's conquest, Eden becomes an example of a successful oriental attack on the European world, a place in which an Eastern vision of supremacy over the West is actually made possible.

Thus, Eden's uncomfortably Eastern qualities prove to be ineradicable and point to the position that the present-day geography of Eden occupies in the imaginations of European readers. As Robinson argues, the terms used to describe Eden foretell its fall to come: "Eden is shadowed by the fraudulent paradises fallen humanity has built for itself, as its future history suggests."[39] Eden's geography is described in contemporary terms as stretching "From *Auran* Eastward to the Royal Towrs / Of great *Seleucia*" (4.211–12), and its landscape compared to various kinds of oriental richness and luxury; as such, it is weighed down both geographically and figuratively by its own future Easternness — and a particular vision of Easternness, at that. Robinson suggests that Pandaemonium and Eden exist in a relationship of mutual foreshadowing: "By the time Milton instructs us about the location of paradise, we are already familiar with Assyria.... The comparison of Pandemonium to Assyria and Cairo evokes an orientalist vision that transcends time, collapsing the empires of scriptural antiquity with the modern Islamic world.... Assyria was once Eden."[40] The collapse of past and future in *Paradise Lost* does not end there. In correlating Pandaemonium with Eden, the text anticipates for the latter an Eastern future in which it, like the early modern Ottoman Empire, is a threat to the West — a West to which it belonged in spirit, if not geographically, in its prelapsarian state. Fallen Eden, itself once the subject of an attack from an oriental invader, becomes in turn an outpost of oriental power. In the vision of history presented to Adam, Nimrod will lead a force of men that, like Satan's army of fallen angels, "Ambition joyns, / With him or under him to tyrannize, / Marching from *Eden* toward the West" (12.38–40). Here the past and future are collapsed and intertwined. Satan acts as Nimrod will act, just as Xerxes's attack on Greece provides a context for understanding the conquered Eden. Moreover, if the threat posed by Nimrod is, from Adam and Eve's perspective, the future, it is, for Milton's readers, the distant past; it is a looming threat on an imaginative spectrum but historically long since dispersed.

On the one hand, then, Milton's epic incorporates the increasingly familiar Eastern world into a Christian and European story (at least from the point of view of Christian Europeans; seventeenth century Muslims or Middle Eastern and Asian Christians would have disagreed) rather than writing an epic in which Middle Easterners or Asians are integral to the plotline, as his epic predecessors do. Moreover, he does so in a way that overlooks rather than emphasizes differences amid the variety of imaginative possibilities. The fact that this East exists as a series of illustrative images rather than as a real place to be experienced and understood — that it can be incorporated metaphorically into a subject in which it has no real part — suggests that the energy of the poet can now be concentrated elsewhere, that he no longer needs to confront this varied and uncontrollable place at all. On the other hand, though, the narrative formed by Milton's oriental images nonetheless suggests an uncontained and powerful world outside the boundaries of the text. Milton's East, even if it is more familiar and understood, and even clichéd, is still vital, unable to be encircled by European ambition or enterprise even if it can, through images, be contained in the European imagination. Even as epic changes and Europe's ideas about and relationship to the East undergo important transitions, the East remains a destabilizing force within European epic. Moreover, Milton's East, rather than being ultimately suppressed, gains traction until it becomes a literal part of the world to come — not simply an indication of future fallenness but a concrete part of the increasingly global world to which Europe now belongs.

I have referred to Milton's Eastern images as constituting a figurative narrative, one that begins with Satan as a figure of Eastern imperial splendor; moves through his colonization of an Eden that, even in its prelapsarian state, displays problematically Eastern traits; and ends with a prophetic vision of an Eden that now belongs both geographically and imaginatively to the East, and that, moreover, turns toward the Judeo-Christian West as a place of potential expansion. Eden is both the ancient home of Christian humankind and the contemporary Middle East, itself dominated by imperialism that both goes against Milton's political principles and signifies a colonializing — and thus threatening, however distantly or abstractly — power. Like Camões, Milton collapses past and future, creating a network of references that simultaneously serve as prophecy, point of reference, and memory, in which the future is the augury of the past and the ancient past moves forward to stand in parallel with recent history.

CHAPTER 9

———— ✺ ————

Alternative Histories and the New World
in *Paradise Lost*

JOSHUA LEE WISEBAKER

"For I know that this falls out infallibly, where two Nations meete, one must
rule, and the other be ruled, before a peace can be hoped for."
— *Thomas Morton*, New English Canaan

"It is as if the power of [*Paradise Lost*] to survive, to be translated and revised,
depended on it constructing its identity and its integrity at the edge of its own
time.... Its grasp on 'time' or history is loosened or running into a moment in
the future which it cannot yet fully conceive or represent but which is somehow
there in the work."
— *Homi K. Bhabha, "Afterword: An Ironic Act of Courage"*

In the opening pages of *An Historicall Description of the Iland of Britaine*,
William Harrison finds himself in the uncomfortable position of having to
reconfigure the world. Confronted with the "westerlie regions of late discouered (and now called America)," Harrison is forced to reconsider the
tripartite division of the earth traditionally attributed to Noah. The problem is a supremely novel one. Harrison notes that, "Not long before my
time, we reckoned Asia, Europa, and Africa, for a full and perfect diuision
of the whole earth.... But now all men...begin to doubt of the soundnes of
that partition." The world had quite suddenly grown to a remarkable extent,
and the novelty of the problem was matched or exceeded by its enormity.
Harrison estimates that "a no lesse part than the greatest of the three [Asia,
Europe, and Africa] ioined with those Ilands and maine which lie vnder the

north and Southpoles, if not double in quantitie vnto the same, are found out and discouered by the diligence of our trauellers." Potentially two-thirds of the world had escaped the notice of history, and the conclusion was unavoidable: "Hereby it appeereth, that either the earth was not exactlie diuided in time past by antiquitie; or els, that the true diuision thereof came not to the hands and notice of their posteritie, so that our ancestors haue hitherto...laboured in the Cimmerian darknesse, and were vtterlie ignorant of the truth of that whereabout they indeuoured to shew their trauels and knowledge in their writings."[1] Faced with this failure either of knowledge or transmission, Harrison revises the traditional model and creates a five-part world, adding the American continent and the Antarctic. The "writings" of antiquity were in sudden need of revision, and the shape and texture of the world was recast. At that historical moment, it seemed, everyone was living in a new world.

While the main thrust of Harrison's considerations involves geographical reconfiguration and reclassification, there are also deeper undertones. For one, this reevaluation of geographical divisions serves to recontextualize the historical narrative he is about to present, at least insofar as the stage of its occurrence has been reshaped. But what is more important, Harrison's brief meditation on America destabilizes received paradigms more generally, calling into question traditional notions of the physical world and of the past itself. America represented a lacuna in the record of antiquity, a geographical and historical blank space that demanded explanation. Indeed, in 1555 Richard Eden described the new continent and its inhabitants as "a smoothe and bare table vnpainted, or a white paper vnwritten, vpon the which yow may at the fyrst paynte or wryte what yow lyke."[2] But if the "vnwritten" continent demanded adjustments to prevailing geographical divisions, it also put pressure on prevailing models of historical process. Walter Lim remarks that the New World in the period "obtains much of its meanings from a theological framework and an apprehension of history mediated through a typological perspective."[3] While this is certainly true, the new continent also had a way of eluding these associations or at least challenging them. Francesco Guicciardini noted that "These voyages have not only confuted many things which had been affirmed by writers about terrestrial matters, but besides this, they have given some cause for alarm to interpreters of the Holy Scriptures," explaining that the apparent claim in Psalms for the global reach of the Gospel had been refuted by the Indians' ignorance of Christ.[4] The New World seemed to hang aloof from the structuring narrative of Scripture, and thus to implicitly call into question the totalizing temporal paradigm derived from it. At its most extreme, the emergence of the New World and its inhabitants had the potential to destabilize the very roots of human origins, giving rise to the polygenetic theory of human development that posited a descent from multiple Adams, a prospect that, as Anthony Pagden puts it, "struck at the basis of that most cherished of Graeco-Christian notions: the integrity of the human race."[5] In this context, it would be strange if the great Renaissance epic of origins and large-scale historical process did not have something to say on the matter.

The subject of this essay is Milton's engagement with the New World on the axis of temporality: the ways in which Milton situates America temporally within the narrative arch of *Paradise Lost* and with reference to the unfolding course of fallen history that extends into his own historical moment. While J. Martin Evans argues that the "colonial elements" in the poem act as a "continuous simile," bridging the "temporal and moral gap between Genesis and seventeenth-century England by 'likening' biblical to modern forms," I argue instead that the presence of the New World in the poem evokes a larger meditation on historical process that both contemplates the gap between biblical and seventeenth century events and also offers opportunities to depart from a historical trajectory that grows directly from that biblical narrative.[6] The terrain covered here is not altogether new. Critics have long been interested in the ways that conquest and imperialism inform Milton's depiction of history. David Quint, in his far-reaching study of the epic genre, argues that "political power" manifests itself in epic in its "capacity to fashion human history into narrative," into a "linear teleology" that defines history "as a coherent, end-directed story." Conversely, the losers in the imperial narrative "experience a [historical] contingency they are powerless to shape to their own ends." In *Paradise Lost*, Quint argues, the teleological experience of the epic winners is displaced onto the meta-narrative of divine providence while the romance narrative of the losers is manifested in both Satan's "cyclical" failures and in fallen human history itself.[7]

My argument seeks to relocate the nature of Miltonic temporality in the dynamics of a certain kind of encounter within the narrative of the poem, an encounter that, I will argue, comes to partially define the nature of the prophetic history outlined in the final books of *Paradise Lost*. We might say that where Quint is interested in narrative or historical trajectories, I am interested in the origin of those trajectories and the places in the poem that open up the possibilities for divergence, digression, alternative paths, and revisions within the overarching telos of divine providence. These origins and these opportunities occur in the encounter with various kinds of difference — whether ontological, cultural, or temporal — and in turn resonate with the discourse of difference being constructed in the colonial writings of the sixteenth and seventeenth century. As J. H. Elliot remarks, "Sixteenth-century Europeans . . . instinctively accepted the idea of a designed world into which America — however unexpected its first appearance — must somehow be incorporated. Everything that could be known about America must have its place in the universal scheme."[8] I suggest that what interests Milton about the appearance of the New World in *Paradise Lost* are the ways in which it *did not* fit into the "universal scheme" or, more precisely, in the ways that it suggested a potential fracture in the patterns of historical process. America operates in the poem as an undetermined variable in the historical narrative, both foregrounding the confrontation with difference, which is one of the poem's central concerns, and suggesting opportunities for divergence in the seemingly inevitable historical progression depicted in the prophetic books. If we take Thomas Morton's insistence, quoted in my epigraph, that the meeting of "two Nations" "infallibly" requires one to "rule" and one to be "ruled," as paradigmatic of contemporary beliefs concerning the confrontation with difference, Milton seems to be trying to think his way out of this narrative, to imagine new scenarios of interaction that can only be found, as Bhabha suggests, at the "edge of [his] own time," and it is here, at the fraying edges of history in the historical present, that he holds out the possibility for a new narrative trajectory by directing his readers to lessons from an imperial past.

The New World and its inhabitants make an early appearance in the course of Milton's fallen history. Roughly 100 lines after Adam "scrupl'd not to eat" and "thus 'gan *Eve* to dalliance move,"[9] with the fallen couple now clothed in their "Covering" of fig leaves as "if to hide / Thir guilt and dreaded shame," the epic narrator laments:

> O how unlike
> To that first naked Glorie. Such of late
> *Columbus* found th' *American* so girt
> With featherd Cincture, naked else and wilde
> Among the Trees on Iles and woodie Shores.   (*PL* 9.1113–18)

It is a strange moment to set foot on a new continent. The abruptness of the displacement, both geographical and temporal, is jarring. As epic simile this interjection seems notably abbreviated. While the association between "th' *American*" and Adam and Eve reached all the way back to Columbus and had been reiterated endlessly, this passage has all the feel of a strange interruption to the narrative flow of a passage central to the biblical story Milton is telling us. Paul Stevens argues that the simile represents Adam and Eve's descent into barbarity after their transgression against God; that they, like John Rolfe with his marriage to Pocahontas, have "gone native," becoming the "defining other of English or European culture."[10] While one can certainly see Stevens's point in the context, the language of the trope is remarkably neutral. Sharon Achinstein wonders whether we are to view the "authorial gaze" here as that of the "colonist," or that "of the political thinker exploring an instance of temporal and cultural difference."[11] It seems to me an apt way to characterize the problem. Even if we concede that, as Stevens argues, the trope is indicative of Adam and Eve's newfound barbarity, the question of what to do with it now that it has emerged is still left unanswered. The abruptness of the imagery and its relative detachment from the narrative flow of the passage seem to emphasize the comparison and draw it forth for the reader's active consideration. As in the fallen natural world, where the air "now / Must suffer change," variability, difference, and multiplicity have emerged at the lead edge of history (10.212–13). It also suggests a point of contact through time. What the Son found when he descended to Eden, Columbus, as representative of European society, has found again in the wilds of America, and the question seems to be what one is to do with fallen difference now that we are confronted with it.

As Evans notes, the passage bears a striking resemblance to perhaps the most famous visual representation of New World inhabitants in the period, Theodore de Bry's series of engravings appended to the 1590 edition of Thomas Hariot's *A Briefe and True Report of the New Found Land of Virginia*. There, as a kind of visual introduction to the Native American plates that follow, we find an engraving of Adam and Eve just before the moment of the Fall, both reaching to pluck apples from the tree of the knowledge of good and evil. In the background of this scene is the punishment for their imminent transgression — Adam works in the field while Eve nurses an infant after the pain of childbirth. As Evans argues, in both cases the message is clear enough: "The condition into which Adam and Eve fell through their disobedience is the condition in which the natives of Virginia, untouched by European civilization, still exist. The 'savage nations' of America are an image of unredeemed postlapsarian man, and vice versa."[12]

And yet in both instances the correlation between biblical and American imagery raises further questions, and those questions bear directly on the kind of narrative trajectory that might grow out of the encounter with the New World. As Andrew Hadfield remarks with reference to de Bry's engraving, "The meaning of the picture is ambiguous, as are its implications: has mankind rediscovered the Garden of Eden in the Americas…? And if so, is the European discovery of the peoples of the New World a violation, a forced entry into an earthly paradise which will eventually lead to its destruction?"[13] Bernadette Bucher suggests that to understand de Bry's "spatial syntax" we must first understand the temporal relations both within individual engravings and among multiple plates, which in some instances represent a larger temporal progression.[14] But at the same time that de Bry establishes tenuous connections between America and the biblical past, he leaves the future of that association frustratingly unclear. De Bry's engraving thus suggests a temporal movement outside of the field of its own representation. It sets in motion a linear temporal movement that gestures out to its European observer and yet does not, by virtue of the visual medium, clarify the nature of the very relationships that it suggests.

In Milton's simile we find similar ambiguities. While he circumscribes the American within the ontology of the fallen world, implicitly denying both the possibility that the Indians are unfallen and the polygenetic theory, the nature of the American presence is left ambiguous. While Stevens and Evans insist on a negative moral valence in the appearance of the Amerindian,

Milton remains conspicuously silent on how to read their presence in a way he does not in other instances. He tells us, for example, when Satan is lying, and reminds us that Adam and Eve's nakedness is morally commendable in a world of unfallen innocence. Here the moral orientation of the other is left undetermined, and this comprises a strategy of dealing with difference that recurs throughout the poem. What we are seeing in this simile is, after all, the emergence of multiplicity at the initiation of fallen human history, and Milton leaves the reader to puzzle out its significance with reference to the temporal progression that will soon come to dominate the narrative arc of the epic. The narratives of discovery, and the ways in which early modern authors filled in the lacuna of the American narrative, reveal that Milton gleans the raw materials for his history of difference in fallen human time.

Observers of the American discoveries were naturally anxious to locate the emergence of a new continent within the arc of biblical history. Richard Eden is an interesting figure in this sense. Eden played a prominent role in shaping English imperial aspirations a generation before his country made its first serious attempts to colonize the New World. In 1552, he became secretary to Sir William Cecil, who likely sought his help in planning the eastern expansion proposed by the Earl of Northumberland. It was to promote this project that Eden produced his first major work, *A Treatyse of the Newe India* (1553). In 1555, Eden translated large portions of Pietro Martire d'Anghiera's *De orbe novo decades* and other works as *The Decades of the Newe Worlde or West India*. His work influenced later colonial promoters like Richard Hakluyt, who in turn did much to encourage England's early colonial efforts.[15]

In the preface to Eden's translation of the *Decades*, the typological character and apocalyptic potential of the discoveries are stated in no uncertain terms. Eden declares here, at a moment of Anglo-Spanish amity, that while Moses, "as the minister of the lawe of wrath...was commaunded in his warres to save neyther man, woman, nor chylde, and yet brought no commoditie to the nations whom he ouercame and possessed theyr landes," the Spanish, "as the mynisters of grace and libertie, browght vnto these newe gentyles the victorie of Chrystes death wherby they beinge subdued with the worldely sworde, are nowe made free from the bondage of Sathans tyrannie."[16] The juxtaposition of Mosaic and Christian imagery and the parallel construction suggest typological fulfillment. Eden makes the typological connection between the ostensible proselytizing mission of Spanish colonialism and the Mosaic conquest of Canaan. In the same way that Christ serves as the fulfillment of Mosaic law, the discovery and the conquest of the Americas figures here as a Christian type of conquest of the Promised Land.

But Eden's biblical interpretation of the Spanish discovery and conquest of America is even more thoroughgoing, placing the colonization of the New World in a historical context that embraces all of salvation history. Eden observes that the West Indies have been delivered

> from the handes of owre commune enemie the oulde serpente who hath so longe had them in hys possession, vntyll the fulnesse of the gentyles be accomplysshed accordynge to the time prefinite by hym, who vnto the yeare after his incarnation. M.CCCC.lxxxxii. hath suffered the great serpente of the sea Leuiathan, to haue suche dominion in the Ocean and to caste such mystes in the eyes of men, that sence the creation of the world vntyll the year before named, there hath byn no passage from our knowen partes of the worlde to these newe landes.

Eden here depicts the discovery and colonization of the West Indies as an act of "gods vnsercheable prouidence," and the imagery partakes of a decidedly apocalyptic mood.[17] The defeat of the "serpente" connotes the ultimate fulfillment of history in the Revelation, the Second Coming, during which the corrupting hordes of Satan will be defeated once and for all. The "mystes in the eyes of men" that had concealed the reality of the new Eden span the analeptic and proleptic vision of history and implicitly bring that history to its eschatological completion.

But while Eden's interpretation of the American encounter is one of ultimate congruence with and fulfillment of "gods vnsercheable prouidence," other interpreters would view this encounter as the ultimate corruption of that salvation narrative. In his famous indictment of Spanish atrocities in the New World, Bartolomé de las Casas rests his argument by affirming the congruence of the Spanish conquest with earlier instances of tyranny. Feeling that "Gods prouidence hath appointed me," las Casas states that the purpose of his treatise is to "detect and vnfold those mens errours" who affirm that "the right and principalitie of the Kinges of *Castile* ouer the Indians is, or shoulde consist of armes and great force." To drive home the point, las Casas immediately states that the Spanish have entered "Vpon them euen as *Nemrod* who was the first hunter and oppressour of mankind did euer, and establishe his principalitie, as the holy scripture testifieth: either as great *Alexander* and the Romans, and all other notable and famous tyrants, doe lay the foundation of their Empires: also as the Turke doth nowe adaies inuade, trouble, and oppresse christendome: and yet haue not any of them once approched the spanish tyrannies."[18] In this passage three conflicting models of historical process are at work in the discourse of New World discovery and conquest: a providential model in which a divinely inspired individual speaks out against the atrocities of the Spanish conquest; a cyclical model that places that conquest within a recurring pattern of human tyranny; and a degenerative model that sees the tyranny of the present as a further corruption of tyrannies past. Importantly, the providential narrative of Eden's imagination is destabilized by a fallen nation acting within history. Las Casas sees in the Spanish atrocities a missed opportunity, describing the New World as a place in which the Spanish "might haue liued as in an earthly Paradise, if so bee they had not made themselves vnworthie, because of their exceeding couetousnesse, harde heartednes, and heynous offences: as also vnworthie they were of other moe blessings a great many, which God had set open in these Indies."[19] We are back, then, in de Bry's colonial garden of Eden, and there was a very real question as to whether the European colonists belonged there. It is a scene played out almost verbatim in the English colony of Virginia. De Bry's engravings were based on the American watercolors of John White, who had traveled with Hariot on Sir Walter Raleigh's 1585 expedition under Ralph Lane.[20] The colony was forced to abandon Roanoke with Francis Drake amid stormy weather in July 1586.[21] While Hariot could shrug off the English misdeeds in the New World by merely saying, "although some of our companie...shewed themselves too fierce, in slaying some of the people,...it was on their part iustly deserued," other members of his "companie" would offer a far harsher interpretation.[22] As one member of the expedition reported, "a great storm arose,...and for fear they [the colonists] should be left behind they left all things confusedly, as if they had been chased from thence by a mighty army: and no doubt so they were; for the hand of God came upon them for the cruelty and outrages committed by some of them against the native inhabitants of that country."[23] The English, like the Spanish before them, had been ejected "out of this paradise of the world," finding themselves, like las Casas's conquistadors, the "enemie[s] of God."[24] In both of these instances, we find rather profound examples of what Simon During calls, in a rather different context, "self-othering," placing the self at a temporal and ontological remove from the moral authority of origins and the innocence of the primal condition.[25] The moment of fracture in Eden's providential narrative is also a moment of parallel with a biblical past. The colonists had, in a sense, relived the Fall in the New World, had themselves become the "defining other" to the godly prerogative in a cyclical expulsion from the earthly paradise.[26]

It is into this controversy over the narrative of American colonialism that Milton's Indians emerge, and interpreting the significance of that emergence in some ways depends on how we characterize the shape of Miltonic time in the epic. David Loewenstein argues that the poem's "competing historical configurations — degenerative, cyclical, apocalyptic, typological — represent a series of contesting and unresolved imaginative responses."[27] As we have seen, these same tensions between "historical configurations" were present in the competing narratives of the colonial encounter in the Americas, and Milton seems to engage with the interrelations between historical process and New World discovery by placing his American imagery at the very beginning of the fallen temporal process. I would like to invoke here the historical model forwarded by Marshall Grossman, who argues that God's identification of Adam and Eve as "Authors to themselves" (*PL* 3.122) "reflects a conception of history as a progress of second causes inscribed within a providential design." For Grossman, it is a reading of history as patterned process that "provides a context for moral action, for the judgments and choices through which Milton's Christians are to author themselves."[28] Grossman's framework has the advantage of deemphasizing the large-scale structures of history and replacing the impetus on the actors and interactions *within* history. It is from this active interpretation of history that informs actions in history, I believe, that the ambiguous appearance of Milton's Native Americans derives its transformative energy and its interactional rationale.

Maureen Quilligan recognizes that our encounter with the Native Americans immediately after the Fall is not so much an instance of "first contact" as it is a recurrence of an encounter with ontological and temporal difference that we have already experienced earlier in the poem. Detecting a brief moment of suspension in the simile during which the reader assumes "that the American is indeed unfallen," Quilligan remarks, "In this understanding it is then Columbus…who inhabits the quintessential fallen perspective, and who stands confronting the American as if the discoverer were himself a Satanic character—just as we first see Adam and Eve's nakedness through Satan's eyes."[29] While Neil Forsyth doubts that the ambiguity exists, we need not insist on the reading to note parallels here with the Edenic encounter.[30] As critics have noted, Satan's initial encounter with Eden brings immediately to mind his own history of rebellion, the "remembrance from what state / I fell" (*PL* 4.38–39).[31] But even if, at a rare unguarded moment, Satan is able to acknowledge that "Pride and worse Ambition threw me down / Warring in Heav'n against Heav'ns matchless King" (40–41), he is not able to draw the obvious lessons from that personal history that would influence his behavior toward the difference-in-sameness he encounters in Eden because of his fall. Forsyth notes that, in recognizing his own difference, for Satan "everything and everyone he sees…must become other."[32] But Satan's reaction to otherness is also a repetition, a further round of cyclical disobedience to the divine, and the terms in which he expresses that disobedience are highly significant to how we read the nature of Miltonic history later in the poem. Grappling still with the difference he encounters in Eden, Satan remarks:

> And should I at your harmless innocence
> Melt, as I doe, yet public reason just,
> Honour and Empire with revenge enlarg'd,
> By conquering this new World, compels me now
> To do what else though damnd I should abhorre.   (4.388–92)

Quint emphasizes the cyclical nature of Satan's career throughout the epic. Satan ends as he began, "on his Belly prone" (10.514) after initially being "Prone on the Flood" (1.195), and his punishment is likewise an "annual humbling" that repeats the events of the Fall (10.576).[33] My point is that his initial repetition of rebellion occurs in an encounter with ontological (they are innocent, I am not) and temporal (they are as I was but am no longer) difference, and that it takes the form of an imperial act, a conquest of a "new World" that will again emerge at the outset of fallen history initiated by

Satan's repetitive decision as a kind of replay of the Edenic confrontation. Appropriately enough, he repeats these same sentiments just before the temptation of Eve. Satan says,

> With what delight could I have walkt thee [Eden] round,
> If I could joy in aught, sweet interchange
> Of Hill, and Vallie, Rivers, Woods and Plaines
>
> . . . .
>   but I in none of these
> Find place or refuge.   (9.114–19)

What Satan registers is the feeling of wonder, but it is a wonder tempered by the absolute knowledge that the state of innocence he finds is entirely lost to him, that he must be forever other to whatever charms and joy the New World may hold. We might think of Milton's depiction of Satan here as a kind of internal portrait of las Casas's conquistadors, who likewise enter an "earthly Paradise" they are morally unfit to inhabit, which leads to its ultimate destruction. Eden represents a past to which neither Satan nor his imperial descendants can return. In his detachment from the origin it is "onely in destroying" that Satan "find[s] ease" (9.129), a manifestation of loss he will now release upon the New World of Eden. "Honour and Empire" have significantly given way to destruction, and with the painful birth of history caused by Satan's confrontation with otherness it is the impulse to destroy, clothed in the language of epic heroism, that determines the cycles of fallen history.

Satan as a figure for repetition and historical cycles seems to be a consistent aspect of his characterization throughout Milton's two epics. Achsah Guibbory argues that in *Paradise Regained* "Satan's temptations seek to persuade Christ to repeat the actions of his predecessors, to perpetuate the cyclical pattern of history."[34] Nowhere does this temptation to repetition manifest itself more poignantly than in the discourse of empire. Satan suggests that to be the "true Successour" to "*David's* royal seat" (3.373), the Son must have "the *Parthian* at dispose" either "by conquest or by league" (3.369–70). Moving his sights this time to Rome (his repetition can become tiresome), Satan again advises the Son to

> Aim therefore at no less then all the world,
> Aim at the highest, without the highest attain'd

> Will be for thee no sitting, or not long
> On *David's* Throne, be propheci'd what will.   (4.105–08)

Satan's temptation here is predicated on a gross misunderstanding of the same prophesies he invokes. As Guibbory explains, Satan assumes a necessary likeness between the Son and his progenitor David, who won his kingdom by military force, thereby failing to "recognize the necessary progress from physical to spiritual, from type to antitype."[35] Satan, unable to read the progressive trajectory of historical process, thus assumes a cyclical pattern that manifests itself in a will to conquest, which he perceives as the defining dynamic of human history.

The cyclical pattern of history seems to have concerned Milton profoundly, especially considering his involvement in the revolutionary republican project that explicitly sought to break with the monarchical past.[36] Loewenstein describes Milton's attitude toward the past in the revolutionary prose as an "urge to break through — even obliterate — the bleak, cyclical patterns of tragic history and to reshape fundamentally its configuration."[37] And yet when Milton looks back into the history of his own country, what he found could not have been encouraging. In his *History of Britain*, considering the "Vices" that caused the people to give "*William* thir Conqueror so easie a Conquest," Milton closes by drawing the lessons from the history he has just told and with a warning to his peers: "If these were the Causes of such misery and thraldom to those our Ancestors, with what better close can be concluded, then here in fit season to remember this Age in the midst of her security, to fear from like Vices without amendment the Revolution of like Calamities."[38] In the same way that the Son must "reject [the] cyclical view of history" in order to fulfill his purpose in the providential plan, the reader of history must recognize the patterns in former ages in order to avoid them in their own.[39] Milton, with some doubt, it seems, suggests too the "amendment" of old historical narratives in the present, and that same sentiment (and that same doubt) is apparent in the fallen history of his great epic.

That brings us, then, back to the fallen history of *Paradise Lost*. At the origins of that history we are, like Satan, confronted with our own fallen past, and we confront there also a world and beings strange and yet somehow familiar. While this has been characterized as the nadir of human moral development, it is also the beginning of a process the end of which becomes even more familiar to the poem's historical present. As Balachandra Rajan notes, in the American imagery we find a primitive society that is "closer to the source," and the further from that source we go the closer we get to the satanic.[40] If history is a potentially degenerative process in *Paradise Lost*, a "latter" world that will, "as the former World, / ... tend from bad to worse" (*PL* 12.105–06), and if the natives of the New World stand at its beginning, then the same impulse to "Honour and Empire" that opposed innocence in the Edenic context stands at history's end. In the penultimate vision before the Flood, Adam

> saw wide Territorie spred
> Before him, Towns, and rural works between,
> Cities of Men with lofty Gates and Towrs,
> Concours in Arms, fierce Faces threatning Warr.   (11.638–41)

From here, an army on "Both Horse and Foot"

> drives
> A herd of Beeves, faire Oxen and faire Kine
> From a fat Meddow ground; or fleecy Flock,
> Ewes and their bleating Lambs over the Plaine,
> Thir Bootie; scarce with Life the Shepherds flye,
> But call in aide, which makes a bloody Fray.   (645–51)

Here the conquest emerges in a dialectical opposition between the warlike "Cities of Men" and the "rural works" of the pastoral landscape, and it participates in a recurrent pattern of imagery that defines the nature of imperial conquest throughout the epic. Pandaemonium is figured as "the high Capital" (1.756), the "Metropolis" from which the "great adventurer" set out on the "search / Of Forrein Worlds" (10.439–41). As Satan enters Eden, he might have been "a prowling Wolfe, / Whom hunger drives to seek new haunt for prey, / Watching where Shepherds pen thir Flocks at eeve / In hurdl'd Cotes amid the field secure" (4.183–86).[41] Just before the Columbus passage in book 9, we find the "*Indian* Herdsman" (9.1108) balancing the implied conquest of the lands "*Columbus* found." And, as with the conqueror Satan, the final antediluvian age is one in which

> Might onely shall be admir'd,
> And Valour and Heroic Vertu call'd;
> To overcome in Battle, and subdue
> Nations, and bring home spoils with infinite
> Man-slaughter, shall be held the highest pitch
> Of human Glorie, and for Glorie done
> Of triumph, to be styl'd great Conquerours,
> Patrons of Mankind, Gods, and Sons of Gods,
> Destroyers rightlier call'd and Plagues of men.   (11.689–97)

As in the Edenic conquest, the satanic values of "Valour and Heroic Vertu" stand diametrically opposed to the relative innocence of an earlier state, in this case the pastoral counterparts of the "*Indian* Herdsman" who stands with Adam and Eve at the origins of history. Here again we find a confrontation between the satanic "Conquerours" and the relative innocence of an earlier age, and Adam reads the patterns to be discerned from these encounters as Milton might want us to read them. As Adam notes in reference to Cain's murder of Abel, these "Conquerours" "multiply / Ten thousandfould the sin of him who slew / His Brother" (11.677–79), and the sense of multiplying sin with the progress of time reemphasizes that fallen humanity is increasingly "unlike / To that first naked Glorie."

But the antediluvian vision is prefigured by a more immediate reference to the reader's present. After Adam ascends "a Hill / Of Paradise the highest" (*PL* 11.377–78), the archangel Michael reveals to "him all Earths Kingdomes and thir Glory" (384). Adam sees the kingdoms of Africa and Asia followed by those of Europe, "where *Rome* was to sway / The World," and

> in Spirit perhaps he also saw
> Rich *Mexico* the seat of *Motezume,*
> And *Cusco* in *Peru,* the richer seat
> Of *Atabalipa,* and yet unspoil'd
> *Guiana,* whose great Citie *Geryons* Sons
> Call *El Dorado.*   (405–11)

Reading this passage in the context of seventeenth century chronologies, Kenneth Knoespel suggests that Milton here "orients the study of history," seeking to display before the reader "a pattern operative in all history" that encourages comparison between the biblical events to be revealed by Michael and the poem's own historical moment.[42] But the patterns again seem rather bleak. The vision of the New World conquest both prefigures the "Conquerours" of the antediluvian world and situates these latter conquests in a direct cyclical relationship with the poem's present. The Edenic cycle of innocence-conquest-corruption is repeated as we move from the origins of history, which degenerates to the flood, and the suggestion is that the process of history has come full circle once again in the reader's present. If the Indians represent a type of innocence in the fallen world, then the sons of Geryon, Dante's monster of Fraud in the *Inferno* and the obvious counterpart of Satan's "deceit [and] guile," are there again to corrupt another "new World." But at the same time, the pattern remains incomplete. The final vision Adam (perhaps) is shown seems to problematize the patterned course of history. Adam sees the New World vision only "in Spirit perhaps," and while the "pattern operative in all history" is certainly suggested, that same pattern is also momentarily destabilized, situating the ongoing narrative of the New World in a potential relationship with a time when "*Rome was to sway* / The World," but leaving that temporal connection uncertain as the encounter with the new plays itself out on the stage of contemporary history. The New World lies on the margins of the historical vision.

This brief moment of slippage is especially interesting considering where Milton places it. As in the appearance of "th' *American*" after the Fall, this is one of the very rare instances in the epic where Milton explicitly engages with his own contemporary moment. The poet here peers out to the edges of the patterned historical process and what he finds there is an "vnwritten" continent awaiting the inscription of historical agents. While we can be assured that Milton's readers would have known the fate of "*Mexico*" and "*Peru*," there is still "yet unspoil'd / *Guiana*," a locale that remains uninscribed by the narrative of European colonialism and, significantly, the only unsullied terrestrial region in an epic about the spoliation of everything. What is interesting is that Milton does not locate the "unspoil'd" spaces in existing English colonies, that is, Virginia and New England, but instead in the English colony that most famously was not to be. Raleigh's failure to find the rich city of El Dorado in Guiana left it without a mythic referent, a blank space that had yet to be written over with the enabling mythologies of Western expansion. Knoespel has observed how the "blanks" in early modern chronologies between "one year and the next" suggest new relationships "within or among the accounts of various nations," becoming thereby "a means to elaborate additional narrative structures."[43] While Milton seems to have located the enabling space between the chronological patterns of human history in the New World, what he seems unable to do is to fully articulate a narrative alternative to the providential imperialism of a procolonialist like Richard Eden. Adam explicitly rejects the model of necessary domination proposed by Morton, where one nation must "infallibly...rule" another, gleaning from his historical lesson that "Man over men / [God] made not Lord; such title to himself / Reserving, human left from human free" (12.69–71). However, as Rajan points out, Milton could not find a definitive solution to the problem of dominance in fallen history. As Michael tells Adam, "Tyrannie must be," and the admission amounts to both a "de facto acquiescence to tyranny" and at least a passive acceptance of the overarching structures of cyclical historical process.[44] Nevertheless, Milton shows us the process of time at large and the slippages within it that would allow for alternative narratives. The temporal irresolution in the poem is itself anti-imperial in the sense that it challenges the providential temporality undergirding so much of the imperial propaganda of the period. Milton shows us the moments of individual choice between a "harmless innocence" that can only tenuously exist in a fallen world and the will to "Honour and Empire" that both initiated and came to define the structures of fallen history. As is so often the case in Milton, we are left to choose, to author the next phase of fallen history in the unwritten spaces of a New World.

NOTES

---※---

Notes to Introduction

1. Stanley Fish, *Surprised by Sin: The Reader in "Paradise Lost,"* 2nd ed. (Cambridge, MA: Harvard University Press, 1998), and especially the introduction to *How Milton Works* (Cambridge, MA: Harvard University Press, 2001).

2. See especially Peter C. Herman, *Destabilizing Milton: "Paradise Lost" and the Poetics of Incertitude* (New York: Palgrave Macmillan, 2005); the introduction to Peter C. Herman and Elizabeth Sauer, eds., *The New Milton Criticism* (Cambridge: Cambridge University Press, 2012); as well as some of the authors who appear in that collection.

3. William Kerrigan, "Milton's Place in Intellectual History," in *The Cambridge Companion to Milton,* 2nd ed., edited by Dennis Danielson, 253–67 (Cambridge: Cambridge University Press, 1999), 263–64, 266.

4. Gordon Teskey, *Delirious Milton: The Fate of the Poet in Modernity* (Cambridge, MA: Harvard University Press, 2006), 5.

5. See W. Gardner Campbell, "Hierarchy, Alterity, and Freedom in *Paradise Lost,*" in *Milton's Legacy,* ed. Kristin A. Pruitt and Charles W. Durham, 50–69 (Selinsgrove, PA: Susquehanna University Press, 2005); Marshall Grossman, *Authors to Themselves: Milton and the Revelation of History* (Cambridge: Cambridge University Press, 1987); John Rumrich, *Milton Unbound: Controversy and Reinterpretation* (Cambridge: Cambridge University Press, 1996); William Kolbrener, *Milton's Warring Angels: A Study of Critical Engagements* (Cambridge: Cambridge University Press, 1997); R. A. Shoaf, *Milton, Poet of Duality: A Study of Semiosis in the Poetry and the Prose* (New Haven, CT: Yale University Press, 1985); and two collections from which we take particular inspiration: *Milton Studies,* vol. 28, *Riven Unities: Authority and Experience, Self and Other in Milton's Poetry,* edited by Wendy Furman, Christopher Grose, and William Shullenberger (Pittsburgh: University of Pittsburgh Press, 1992), and *Milton's Rival Hermeneutics: "Reason Is But Choosing,"* edited by Richard DuRocher and Margaret Olofson Thickstun (Pittsburgh: Duquesne University Press, 2012).

6. *The Collected Works of Samuel Taylor Coleridge,* vol. 7, *Biographia literaria,* edited by James Engell and W. Jackson Bate (Princeton, NJ: Princeton University Press, 1983), 14.

Notes to Chapter 1 / Garganigo

1. For the ancient constitution, see J. G. A. Pocock, *The Ancient Constitution and Feudal Law*, 2nd ed. (Cambridge: Cambridge University Press, 1987). For the relevance of ancient constitutionalism to Milton, see Peter Herman, *Destabilizing Milton: "Paradise Lost" and the Poetics of Incertitude* (New York: Palgrave Macmillan, 2005), 61–81.

2. Qtd. in *The Trial of Charles I: A Documentary History*, ed. David Lagomarsino and Charles T. Wood (Hanover, NH: University Press of New England, 1989), 61. Unless otherwise indicated, all emphases are mine.

3. Qtd. in ibid., 65, 66.

4. Qtd. in ibid., 124; see also 120, 123.

5. For speech-acts such as creation and naming in *Paradise Lost*, see Angela Esterhammer, *Creating States: Studies in the Performative Language of John Milton and William Blake* (Toronto: University of Toronto Press, 1994), 88–110. For speech-acts more generally and some sketchy remarks on swearing, see J. L. Austin, *How to Do Things with Words*, 2nd ed., ed. J. O. Urmson and Marina Sbisà (Cambridge, MA: Harvard University Press, 1975), 6, 9, 105, 122, 148, 158–59, 162. For more systematic accounts of swearing, promissory and assertory, see John R. Searle and Daniel Vanderveken, *Foundations of Illocutionary Logic* (Cambridge: Cambridge University Press, 1985), 188, 194; Ashley Montagu, *The Anatomy of Swearing* (London: Rapp and Whiting, 1967); Geoffrey Hughes, *Swearing: A Social History* (London: Penguin, 1991); Timothy Jay, *Why We Curse: A Neuro-Psycho-Social Theory of Speech* (Philadelphia: John Benjamins, 2000). Milton treats oaths in *De doctrina Christiana*, in *Complete Prose Works of John Milton*, 8 vols., ed. Don M. Wolfe et al. (New Haven, CT: Yale University Press, 1973), 6:684–90; hereafter cited as YP.

6. John Milton, *Paradise Lost*, ed. Alastair Fowler, 2nd ed. (London: Longman, 1998), 5.602–08; emphasis mine. All subsequent references are to this edition and appear in the text.

7. See, for example, William Empson, *Milton's God* (London: Chatto and Windus, 1961), 27, 71, 98–104; Michael Bryson, *The Tyranny of Heaven: Milton's Rejection of God as King* (Newark: University of Delaware Press, 2004), 27, 83, 92–96; Herman, *Destabilizing Milton*, 54–57, 85, 99–104. Of the three, Herman's reading comes closest to my own in emphasizing the troubling absolutism of the speech. However, I pull back slightly toward something closer to the positions of Stevie Davies and David Norbrook, which are by no means identical: see Davies, *Images of Kingship in "Paradise Lost"* (Columbia: University of Missouri Press, 1983), 148, 143; Norbrook, *Writing the English Republic* (Cambridge: Cambridge University Press, 1998), 480.

8. Philo, *Allegories of the Sacred Law* and *On the Sacrifice of Cain and Abel*, trans. C. D. Yonge, in vol. 1 of *The Works of Philo Judaeus* (London: George Bell and Sons, 1890), 161–63, 228–30, 218–19; George Lawson, *Theo-Politica* (London, 1659), 172–73.

9. William Ames, *The Marrow of Sacred Divinity* (London, 1642), 290–91.

10. On such state oaths, see John Spurr, "Perjury, Profanity, and Politics," *Seventeenth Century* 8, no. 1 (1993): 29–50; Spurr, "A Profane History of Early Modern Oaths,"

Transactions of the Royal Historical Society 11 (2001): 37–63; Spurr, "'The Strongest Bond of Conscience': Oaths and the Limits of Tolerance in Early Modern England," in *Contexts of Conscience in Europe, 1500–1700*, ed. Harald E. Braun and Edward Vallance (New York: Palgrave, 2004), 151–65; Christopher Hill, *Society and Puritanism in Pre-Revolutionary England* (1958; repr., New York: St. Martin's Press, 1997), 328–61; Susan Staves, *Players' Sceptres: Fictions of Authority in the Restoration* (Lincoln: University of Nebraska Press, 1979), 191–251; Edward Vallance, *Revolutionary England and the National Covenant: State Oaths, Protestantism and the Political Nation, 1553–1682* (Woodbridge, UK: Boydell and Brewer, 2005); David Martin Jones, *Conscience and Allegiance in Seventeenth Century England: The Political Significance of Oaths and Engagements* (Rochester, NY: University of Rochester Press, 1999); Conal Condren, *Argument and Authority in Early Modern England* (Cambridge: Cambridge University Press, 2006). In "Samson's Cords: Imposing Oaths in *Samson Agonistes*," in *Milton Studies*, vol. 50, ed. Albert C. Labriola (Pittsburgh: University of Pittsburgh Press, 2009), 125–49, I read the protagonist's Nazarite vow in the light of such state oaths.

    11. E.g., Richard Cosin, *An Apologie for Svndrie Proceedings by Iurisdiction Ecclesiasticall* (London, 1593), 3.8–9; William Perkins, *The Whole Treatise of the Cases of Conscience*, 2nd ed., ed. T. Pickering (Cambridge, 1606), 382, 384; Lancelot Andrewes, *XCVI. Sermons* (London, 1629), 2.40; Johannes Wolleb, *The Abridgment of Christian Divinitie*, 3rd ed. (London, 1660), 359; Robert Sanderson, *De juramento* (London, 1655), 19–20; Hugo Grotius, *Of the Law of Warre and Peace* (London, 1655), 224; John Tombes, *A Serious Consideration of the Oath of the Kings Supremacy* (London, 1660), 13; John Gauden, *A Discourse concerning Publick Oaths* (London, 1662), 21, 37.

    12. *The Holy Bible…Authorized King James Version*, vol. 2 (New York: Meridian, 1974). Unless otherwise specified, all subsequent quotations are from this edition.

    13. Ames, *Marrow of Sacred Divinity*, 290–91.

    14. Anna Keay, *The Magnificent Monarch: Charles II and the Ceremonies of Power* (London: Continuum, 2008), 4–8 (quotation on 7). Unless otherwise noted, details of the coronation as presented in this paragraph are from the following: Elias Ashmole and Francis Sandford, eds., *The Entire Ceremonies of the Coronations of His Majesty King Charles II and of Her Majesty Queen Mary, Consort to James II* (London, 1761), 4–7, 12–28; Edward Walker, *A Circumstantial Account of the Preparations for the Coronation of His Majesty King Charles the Second, and a Minute Detail of that Splendid Ceremony* (London, 1820), 83–121; John Ogilby, *The Entertainment of His Most Excellent Majestie Charles II, in His Passage through the City of London to His Coronation…A Brief Narrative of His Majestie's Solemn Coronation* (London, 1662), 169–86.

    15. Walker, *Account*, 92–93; Ashmole and Sandford, *Ceremonies*, 8; Ogilby, *Entertainment*, 173.

    16. James Heath, *The Glories and Magnificent Triumphs of the Blessed Restitution of His Sacred Majesty K. Charles II* (London, 1662), 199; Kevin Sharpe, *Rebranding Rule: The Restoration and Revolution Monarchy, 1660–1714* (New Haven, CT: Yale University Press, 2013), 162.

    17. Ashmole and Sandford, *Ceremonies*, 12, 15, 16, 19; emphases in original Walker, *Account*, 95, 98–103; Ogilby, *Entertainment*, 176–81.

18. Ashmole and Sandford, *Ceremonies*, 22–23, 28; Walker, *Account*, 105–21; Ogilby, *Entertainment*, 182–86; *The Diary of Samuel Pepys*, 11 vols., ed. Robert Latham and William Matthews (Berkeley: University of California Press, 2000), 2:88 (Apr. 23, 1661); *The Diary of John Evelyn*, 6 vols., ed. E. S. De Beer (Oxford: Clarendon Press, 1955), 5:278–84; Heath, *Glories and Magnificent Triumphs*, 197 (misnumbered 183); Edmund Ludlow, *A Voyce from the Watch Tower, Part Five: 1660–1662*, ed. A. B. Worden (London: Royal Historical Society, 1978), 286.

19. Andrew Marvell, "On Mr. Milton's *Paradise Lost*," l. 3, in *The Poems of Andrew Marvell*, ed. Nigel Smith (London: Pearson Longman, 2003), 182.

20. Davies, *Images of Kingship*, 127–63. See also Robert Thomas Fallon, *Divided Empire: Milton's Political Imagery* (University Park: Pennsylvania State University Press, 1995), 50; Thomas Corns, *Regaining "Paradise Lost"* (London: Pearson Longman, 2003), 182; Condren, *Argument and Authority*, 159–62. There is a whiff of this line of argument in Empson, *Milton's God*, 101.

21. Norbrook, *Writing the English Republic*, 433–91, esp. 445–46, 474–80.

22. On the notion of reciprocity and reciprocal oaths, see Percy Schramm, *A History of the English Coronation*, trans. L. G. W. Legg (Oxford: Clarendon Press, 1937), 182–83. See also Davies, *Images of Kingship*, 135–36.

23. *Brief Notes upon a Late Sermon*, YP 7:484.

24. *Readie and Easie Way*, YP 7:356–57, 409–20, esp. 409, 411.

25. Ibid., 409.

26. *Commonplace Book*, YP 1:447, 427–28, 435–36; *Tenure of Kings and Magistrates*, 287; *First Defence*, in *Milton: Political Writings*, ed. Martin Dzelzainis (Cambridge: Cambridge University Press, 1991), 212.

27. Blair Worden, "Milton's Republicanism and the Tyranny of Heaven," in *Machiavelli and Republicanism*, ed. Gisela Bock, Quentin Skinner, and Maurizio Viroli (Cambridge: Cambridge University Press, 1990), 232, finds Milton's interest in the coronation oath in his Commonplace Book "precocious."

28. *Commonplace Book*, YP 1:427–29, 435, 447.

29. *Tenure of Kings and Magistrates* and *First Defence*, qtd. in notes 15–16 of YP 1:447.

30. Jones, *Conscience and Allegiance*, 114. Compare p. 3, where Jones quotes Henry Parker's *Observations upon some of His Majesties Late Answers and Expresses* (1642) with regard to the king's being bound by his coronation oath to protect the people.

31. John Milton, *Eikonoklastes*, in *The Works of John Milton*, 18 vols., ed. Frank Allen Patterson et al. (New York: Columbia University Press, 1931–38), 5:300; hereafter cited as CM. Compare Sharon Achinstein's comments on this passage in "Milton and King Charles," in *The Royal Image: Representations of Charles I*, ed. Thomas N. Corns (Cambridge: Cambridge University Press, 1999), 157.

32. *Eikonoklastes*, CM 5:299.

33. On the body natural versus the body politic, see Ernst Kantorowicz, *The King's Two Bodies* (Princeton, NJ: Princeton University Press, 1957).

34. *Eikonoklastes*, CM 5:234; confirmed by Milton's *First Defence*, CM 7:539 (which mentions the "*quas vulgus elegerit*" clause).

35. See also the *First Defence* for the idea of reciprocal oaths: CM 7:81, as well as *Brief Notes on a Late Sermon*, YP 7:484.

36. *First Defence*, CM 7:411. The present tense *rogat*, which Sumner translates as "asks," after the perfect tense *dedit*, which he renders as the present perfect "has taken" (literally "has given," for "*Postquam enim rex consuetum juramentum dedit*" can be literally translated as "After, in fact, the king has given the customary oath"), makes it clear that Milton is referring to the current coronation rite as a survival of ancient principles.

37. *Eikonoklastes*, CM 5:121; *First Defence*, CM 7:453.

38. *Eikonoklastes*, CM 5:267–68, 181, 179, 172–73.

39. Ibid., CM 5:179, 134–35, 234.

40. *First Defence*, CM 7:535–39.

41. Ibid., CM 7:541–43; *Eikonoklastes*, CM 5.134, 300; *Tenure*, 293, 291, 296, 281, 283, 305, and throughout.

42. Milton, *Letters Patent*, YP 8:451–53.

43. Compare Condren's remarks on the coronation oath in *Argument and Authority*, 254–68; John Reeves, *Considerations on the Coronation Oath* (London: J. Wright, 1801), 52–53; and Catherine Bell's discussion of the coronation as ritual in *Ritual: Perspectives and Dimensions* (Oxford: Oxford University Press, 1997), 83–88.

44. Roy Strong, *Coronation from the 8th to the 21st Century* (London: Harper Perennial, 2005), 299–309, and throughout. The classic study of the British coronation as collective ritual is Edward Shils and Michael Young, "The Meaning of the Coronation," *Sociological Review* n.s. 11, no. 2 (1953): 63–81.

45. See also Schramm, *Coronation*, 214, 229; Randolph S. Churchill, *The Story of the Coronation* (London: Derek Verschoyle, 1953), 73.

46. Strong, *Coronation*, 25–26.

47. Ibid., 25–26, 28–30, 5, 17, 22, 44–45, 84–88, 379–81, 489–90. See also Alice Hunt, *The Drama of Coronation: Medieval Ceremony in Early Modern England* (Cambridge: Cambridge University Press, 2008), 26. For the opposite view, see Richard Heyrick, *A Sermon…on…the Coronation-Day of…Charles II* (London, 1661), 21–23, 29.

48. *The Form and Order of the Coronation of Charles the Second* (Aberdeen, 1651), 67–68; compare 3–4, 69–70.

49. *Severall Proceedings of State Affaires* [15–22 Dec. 1653] (London, 1653), 3499 (misnumbered 3498); David Hilliam, *Crown, Orb and Sceptre: The True Stories of English Coronations* (Phoenix Mill, UK: Sutton, 2002), 131–32. Roy Sherwood, *Oliver Cromwell: King in All but Name, 1653–1658* (Phoenix Mill, UK: Sutton, 1997), 7–12, however, insists that it retained regal elements.

50. *Oliver Cromwell's Letters and Speeches*, 3rd ed., 4 vols., ed. Thomas Carlyle (London: Chapman and Hall, 1850), 3:373–74, 383–84, 386, 388, 400–01.

51. *Mercurius Politicus* 369 (25 June–2 July 1657): 7882–83; John Prestwich, *Respublica; or, A Display of the Honours, Ceremonies and Ensigns of the Common-Wealth, under the Protectorship of Oliver Cromwell* (London, 1787), 17–19; Roy Sherwood, *The Court of Oliver Cromwell* (Cambridge: Willingham Press, 1989), 160–62, and Sherwood, *King in All but Name*, 95–104.

52. Carlyle, *Cromwell's Letters and Speeches*, 4:360–61.

53. *Mercurius Politicus* 432 (2–9 Sept. 1658): 803–08 (quotation on 806, my emphases).

54. Gordon Campbell and Thomas N. Corns, *John Milton: Life, Work, and Thought* (Oxford: Oxford University Press, 2010), 345.

55. Strong, *Coronation*, 26. This is Strong's summary of the three promises, rather than their exact wording.

56. Robert S. Hoyt, "The Coronation Oath of 1308," *English Historical Review* 71, no. 280 (1956): 355–56; *Liber regalis* (London, 1871), 6–7 (I translate this source's original Latin, as I do in table 2).

57. Hoyt, "Coronation Oath of 1308," 356; *Liber regalis*, 7–8; Strong, *Coronation*, 92; Condren, *Argument and Authority*, 260–63; Hunt, *Drama of Coronation*, 94, 156.

58. Strong, *Coronation*, 240.

59. CM 5:234, 7:539. Compare Zachary Crofton's similar interpretation of *quas vulgus elegerit* as "shall choose," indicating the monarch's being bound to the laws: *Analepsis Anelephthe* (London, 1660), 99–100, 121.

60. Strong, *Coronation*, 185–86, 238–39.

61. Schramm, *Coronation*, 219; *First Defence*, CM 7:535–39.

62. *Form and Order*, 67–68: "I, for my self and my Successors, shall consent and agree, to all Acts of Parliament enjoying the National Covenant, and the Solemn League and Covenant, and fully establishing Presbyterial Government, the Directory of Worship, Confession of Faith, and Catechisms in the Kingdom of Scotland, as they are approven by the General Assembly of this Kirk and Parliament of this Kingdom; And that I shall give [my] Royal Assent, to Acts and Ordinances of Parliament passed, or to be passed, enjoying the same in my other Dominions: And that I shall observe in my own Practise and Family, and shall never make Opposition to any of these, or endeavour any change thereof." See also 3–4, 69–70.

63. *The Government of the Commonwealth…As It Was Publickly Declared at Westminster, the 16. Day of December, 1653* (London, 1654), 19–20.

64. *Mercurius Politicus* 369 (June 25–July 2, 1657): 7882–83, 432 (Sept. 2–9, 1658): 808.

65. Ashmole and Sandford, *Ceremonies*, 12–13; E. Walker, *Account*, 95–98; Ogilby, *Entertainment*, 176.

66. "An Act for Establishing the Coronation Oath" (1689), in *Statutes of the Realm*, 11 vols., ed. John Raithby (London, 1819), 6:56.

67. Strong, *Coronation*, 278.

68. "Act for Establishing," 6:56; Strong, *Coronation*, 286; Howard Nenner, "Loyalty and the Law: The Meaning of Trust and the Right of Resistance in Seventeenth-Century England," *Journal of British Studies* 48, no. 4 (2009): 865–66.

69. Hilliam, *Crown, Orb and Sceptre*, 153–54 (quotation on 154); Strong, *Coronation*, 286–87.

70. Blair Worden, "Republicanism, Regicide and Republic: The English Experience," in *Republicanism: A Shared European Heritage*, 2 vols., ed. Martin van Gelderen and Quentin Skinner (Cambridge: Cambridge University Press, 2002), 1:314, and Worden,

Literature and Politics in Cromwellian England (Oxford: Oxford University Press), 227–33 (esp. 231); Nigel Smith, *Literature and Revolution in England, 1640–1660* (New Haven, CT: Yale University Press, 1994), 181.

71. Condren, *Argument and Authority,* 149–52; William Walker, "*Paradise Lost* and the Forms of Government," *History of Political Thought* 22, no. 2 (2001): 270–99, esp. 283, 286, 288–90; Paul Rahe, "The Classical Republicanism of John Milton," *History of Political Thought* 25, no. 2 (2004): 243–75, esp. 251–52, 256–57, 268. For the idea of "deradicalization," see Thomas Corns, "Milton and the Characteristics of a Free Commonwealth," in *Milton and Republicanism,* ed. David Armitage, Armand Himy, and Quentin Skinner (Cambridge: Cambridge University Press, 1995), 42.

72. Algernon Sidney, *Discourses concerning Government* (London, 1698), 248, 297–98, 311, 322–29 (esp. 327–29), 338, 341, 363, 375, 391, 414–16, 444, 459, 461, and *The Very Copy of a Paper Delivered to the Sheriffs upon the Scaffold on Tower-Hill, on Friday Decemb. 7, 1683 by Algernon Sidney, Esq., before his Execution* (London, 1683), 2; *The Tryal of Sir Henry Vane…also his Speech and Prayer, &c. on the Scaffold* (London, 1662), 8 ("Preface to Reader"), 13–15, 100, 107–08; Henry Neville, *Plato Redivivus* (London, 1681), 128–30, 227–28; Marchamont Nedham, *The Excellencie of a Free State,* 2nd ed. (London, 1656), 13–14, 162. For the general importance of oaths to English republicans, see Blair Worden, "English Republicanism," in *The Cambridge History of Political Thought, 1450–1700,* ed. J. H. Burns and Mark Goldie (Cambridge: Cambridge University Press, 1991), 468.

73. *Readie and Easie Way,* YP 7:424, 449–50. Compare *First Defence,* in Dzelzainis, *Milton: Political Writings,* 80–81, 83, 85, 88–90, 92, 101–02.

74. Worden, "Milton's Republicanism," 228; Martin Dzelzainis, "Milton's Classical Republicanism" and "Milton and the Protectorate in 1658" and Corns, "Milton and the Characteristics," all in Armitage, Himy, and Skinner, *Milton and Republicanism,* 19, 205, 31, 33, 35; Frank Lovett, "Milton's Case for a Free Commonwealth," *American Journal of Political Science* 49, no. 3 (2005): 466, 469, as well as the arguments in note 104 below.

75. *Readie and Easie Way; Brief Notes,* YP 7:482: for "the space of a raign or two we may chance to live happily anough, or tolerably" under kings—but *only* for a reign or two, not permanently.

76. *Brief Notes,* YP 7:469, 475–76, 481–82, 484; *First Defence,* in Dzelzainis, *Milton: Political Writings,* 99, 153, 94.

77. See the virtual repetition of the Engagement's formula ("the Commonwealth… without a King") in YP 7:330–31, 337–38, 368, 392–93, 431–32.

78. Shakespeare, *Romeo and Juliet,* 2.1.155 ("swear by thy gracious self"), and *The Merchant of Venice,* 5.1.243–47 ("Swear by your double self"; "by my soul I swear / I never more will break an oath with thee"), in *The Norton Shakespeare,* 2nd ed., ed. Stephen Greenblatt et al. (New York: Norton, 2008), 926, 1174; John Donne, "A Hymn to God the Father," 15–16, in *The Oxford Authors: John Donne,* ed. John Carey (New York: Oxford University Press, 1992), 333. Compare William W. E. Slights, "'Swear by Thy Gracious Self': Self-Referential Oaths in Shakespeare," *English Studies in Canada* 13, no. 2 (1987): 147–60.

79. Raithby, *Statutes of the Realm*, 5.322, 366, 446–47 (my italics). The Corporation Oath omits the final clause ("to endeavour... State").

80. Fowler's note on *Paradise Lost* 5.607–08 neglects the passages from Psalms and Romans, as well as those from Shakespeare and Donne.

81. For Milton's Arianism, see, among others, Empson, *Milton's God*, 12, 16–17, 244; Michael Bauman, *Milton's Arianism* (Frankfurt: Peter Lang, 1987); John Rumrich, *Milton Unbound* (Cambridge: Cambridge University Press, 1996), 40–48. For doubts about it in the context of the exaltation/coronation scene in *Paradise Lost*, book 5, see Fallon, *Divided Empire*, 43–44, 48–53.

82. *De doctrina*, CM 15:287. My explication of the swearing couplet will parallel William B. Hunter's analysis of the line "This day I have begot" (*PL* 5.603), but with reservations about his views on Milton's Arianism and the timing of the Son's exaltation. See William B. Hunter, "The War in Heaven: The Exaltation of the Son," in *Bright Essence: Studies in Milton's Theology*, ed. Hunter, C. A. Patrides, and J. H. Adamson (Salt Lake City: University of Utah Press, 1973), 115–30.

83. *De doctrina*, CM 14:183; 15:285, 311, 313, 319–22, 331–35.

84. Ibid., 15:13.

85. Ibid., 15:7–9, 11.

86. Ibid., 15:13.

87. Ibid., 14:249. See also 14:277–83, 287–89, 291–95 (esp. 293–95).

88. See the other citations in ibid., 14:249–51.

89. Ibid., 14:293–95.

90. Compare Joseph Wittreich, *Why Milton Matters* (New York: Palgrave Macmillan, 2006), 80, 123, on Milton's presenting flickers of heresy.

91. Gen. 22:16; Exod. 33:1; Num. 14:23, 32:11; Deut. 1:35, 10:11, 31:20–21 and 23, 34:4; Josh. 1:6; Judg. 2:1; 1 Sam. 3:14; Ps. 89:3; 95:11, 110:4, 119:106; Isa. 14:24, 45:23, 54:9, 62:8; Jer. 5:7, 11:5, 44:26, 49:13, 51:14; Ezek. 21:23; Amos 4:2, 6:8, 8:7.

92. Bruce K. Waltke and M. O'Connor, *An Introduction to Biblical Hebrew Syntax* (Winona Lake, IN: Eisenbrauns, 1990), 488; Blane Conklin, *Oath Formulas in Biblical Hebrew* (Winona Lake, IN: Eisenbrauns, 2011), 3, 19–21, 53–54. Waltke and O'Connor refer to it as the "instantaneous perfective tense" (488).

93. It is possible that the rule applied to other performative ritual-acts or speech-acts, so that the anointing and begetting described in lines 603–05 of God's speech ("This day I have begot," "him have anointed"), especially the anointing, describe present actions being performed by God's speech rather than past actions, earlier in the "day," however long it may be.

94. In Hebrew the verb "to swear" is always in the passive voice: "to be sworn," "to be sevened." On this point, see John Trapp, *A Commentary... upon the Four Evangelists and the Acts* (London, 1647), 152 (on Matt. 5:33); Henry Ainsworth, *Annotations upon the Five bookes of Moses, the Booke of the Psalmes, and the Song of Songs* (London, 1627), 82–83 (on Gen. 21:31); Anthony Burgess, *An Expository Comment... upon the Whole First Chapter to the Second Epistle of St. Paul to the Corinthians* (London, 1661), 659 (on 2 Cor. 1:23). So, actually, in saying "*nishbati ki* _____," the speaker asserts, "I have been sworn that _____," "I have been sevened that _____."

95. "*B-i nishbati*" is literally "I have been sworn, by myself"—that is, by referring to myself as the guarantor of my oath. God's self-oath is thus doubly odd because he is not sworn by anybody outside himself, and the usual passive meaning of the verb is rendered useless.

96. Compare Davies, *Images of Kingship*, 137. By "Trinitarian hymns," I mean the Nicene Creed, sung as part of the coronation, and the "Veni Creator Spiritus," both of which feature Trinitarian lines: respectively, "One God in Persons Three" and "Jesus Christ, the only begotten Son of God…begotten, not made, being of one substance with the Father." See Ogilby, *Entertainment*, 176, 184.

97. Carlyle, *Cromwell's Letters and Speeches*, 3:386, 400–01.

98. Compare the narrator's comment about Satan's "preventing all reply" in the council in hell (*PL* 2.467).

99. Compare Davies, *Images of Kingship*, 155. At the time there appears to be no activity involving regalia such as crown, orb, scepter, ceremonial swords, although after the fact Abdiel mentions the Son's being "endued / With regal sceptre" at 5.815–16; see also 3.339. Again, my point is that the coronation as initially described by Raphael at 5.582–615 conspicuously lacks these objects.

100. Davies, *Images of Kingship*, 143, 145.

101. *The New Oxford Study Bible…Revised Standard Version*, ed. Herbert G. May and Bruce M. Metzger (Oxford: Oxford University Press, 1977), 880.

102. Even if one claims that the angels are allowed a voice later in book 5 when they sing and dance their approval of the Son's exaltation (5.618–27), we don't hear its exact words, as the narrator lets us do in book 3, when the angels again praise the Son (3.345–417, esp. 372–415). Nor are the angels' singing and dancing part of the coronation ceremony proper, which ends with God's speech at 5.615. The example of the English coronation ritual, with its ancillary but separate same-day ceremonies of the precoronation procession to Westminster Abbey and postcoronation banquet in Westminster Hall, would suggest to Restoration readers of *Paradise Lost* that the angels' later singing, dancing, and feasting (5.618–41) are separate from the exaltation/coronation rite itself.

103. Compare Norbrook, *Writing the English Republic*, 480; as well as Roger Lejosne, "Milton, Satan, Salmasius, Abdiel," in Armitage, Himy, and Skinner, *Milton and Republicanism*, 106, 116.

104. Condren, *Argument and Authority*, 149–52; W. Walker, "Forms of Government," 270–99, esp. 283, 286, 288–90; Rahe, "Classical Republicanism," 243–75, esp. 251–52, 256–57, 268. The most succinct objection to the argument against Milton's antimonarchism appears in Worden, "English Republicanism," 469.

105. *Readie and Easie Way*, YP 7:444–45.

106. William Blake, *Milton a Poem* (Copy C), in *Milton a Poem and the Final Illuminated Works*, ed. Robert N. Essick and Joseph Viscomi (Princeton, NJ: Princeton University Press for the William Blake Trust, 1993), 138, plate 12.

Notes to Chapter 2 / Prawdzik

1. Aristotle, *Rhetoric*, 1.2; Plato, "Phaedrus," 257a–b; see Erik Gunderson, *Staging Masculinity: The Rhetoric of Performance in the Roman World* (Ann Arbor: Michigan University Press, 2000).

2. See esp. Stephen Fallon, *Milton among the Philosophers: Poetry and Materialism in Seventeenth-Century England* (Ithaca, NY: Cornell University Press, 1991); John Rogers, *The Matter of Revolution: Science, Poetry and Politics in the Age of Milton* (Ithaca, NY: Cornell University Press, 1996); and N. K. Sugimura, *"Matter of Glorious Trial": Spiritual and Material Substance in "Paradise Lost"* (New Haven, CT: Yale University Press, 2009).

3. Stanley Fish, *Surprised by Sin: The Reader in "Paradise Lost"* (1968; repr., Cambridge, MA: Harvard University Press, 1998), lvii.

4. For discussions of the young Milton as aspiring dramatist, see Timothy J. Burbery, *Milton the Dramatist* (Pittsburgh: Duquesne University Press, 2007); and Ann Baynes Coiro, "Anonymous Milton; or, *A Maske* Masked," *ELH* 71 (2004): 609–29. Herbert Berry offers evidence that Milton's father was a shareholder of the Blackfriars playhall in "The Miltons and the Blackfriars Playhouse," *Modern Philology* 89 (1992): 510–14. For a critique of earlier scholars advancing a "myth of Milton's affiliation with contemporary drama and its *locus*, the theater," see T. H. Howard-Hill, "Milton and 'The Rounded Theatre's Pomp,'" in *Of Poetry and Politics: New Essays on Milton and His World*, ed. P. G. Stanwood, 95–120 (Binghamton, NY: Medieval & Renaissance Texts and Studies, 1995); for a critique of the Shakespeare bias in studies of "influence," see John T. Shawcross, *John Milton and Influence* (Pittsburgh: Duquesne University Press, 1991), 5–38.

5. Discussions of theatricality in *Paradise Lost* include John G. Demaray, *Milton's Theatrical Epic: The Invention and Design of "Paradise Lost"* (Cambridge, MA: Harvard University Press, 1980); Michael Lieb, "Milton's 'Dramatick Constitution': The Celestial Dialogue in *Paradise Lost*, Book III," in *Milton Studies*, vol. 23, ed. James D. Simmonds (1987): 215–40; and Elizabeth Bradburn, "Theatrical Wonder, Amazement, and the Construction of Spiritual Agency in *Paradise Lost*," *Comparative Drama* 40 (2006): 77–98.

6. Barbara K. Lewalski, *"Paradise Lost" and the Rhetoric of Literary Forms* (Princeton, NJ: Princeton University Press, 1985), 7; see also John Steadman, *Epic and Tragic Structure in "Paradise Lost"* (Chicago: University of Chicago Press, 1976); John G. Demaray, *Milton and the Masque Tradition* (Cambridge, MA: Harvard University Press, 1968); and Demaray, *Theatrical Epic*. Daniel Shore, *Milton and the Art of Rhetoric* (Cambridge: Cambridge University Press, 2012); Coiro discusses *Paradise Lost* as a "dramatic poem" that stages the author and engages the audience in negotiating its meaning in "Drama in the Epic Style: Narrator, Muse, and Audience in *Paradise Lost*," in *Milton Studies*, vol. 51, ed. Laura L. Knoppers, 63–100 (Pittsburgh: Duquesne University Press, 2010).

7. See, for instance, Andrew Gurr, *Playgoing in Shakespeare's London* (Cambridge: Cambridge University Press, 1987); Stephen Greenblatt, *Shakespearean Negotiations:*

The Circulation of Social Energy in Renaissance England (Berkeley: University of California Press, 1988); Steven Mullaney, *The Place of the Stage: License, Play, and Power in Renaissance England* (Chicago: University of Chicago Press, 1988); Alexander Leggatt, *Jacobean Public Theatre* (London: Routledge, 1992); and Jean E. Howard, *The Stage and Social Struggle in Early Modern England* (London: Routledge, 1994).

8. Stephen Gosson, "Plays Confuted in Five Actions," in *Shakespeare's Theater: A Sourcebook*, ed. Tanya Pollard, 84–114 (Malden: Blackwell, 2004), 107–08.

9. Philip Stubbes, *Anatomy of Abuses*, in Pollard, *Shakespeare's Theater*, 115–23, 121.

10. Milton's English prose, including the notes on tragedy and the Commonplace Book, are from *The Complete Prose Works of John Milton*, 8 vols., ed. Don M. Wolfe et al. (New Haven, CT: Yale University Press, 1953–82), 8:539–96, 1:489–91, 819–20; hereafter cited as YP followed by book and page number, and titles when necessary.

11. Marius D'Assigny, *The Art of Memory* (London: A. Bell, 1699), frontispiece. For the iconography of rhetoric in the Renaissance, see Heinrich F. Plett, *Rhetoric and Renaissance Culture* (Berlin: De Gruyter, 2004), 501–52; and Earnest James Enchelmayer, "Rhetorical Iconography: Representing Rhetoric in the History of the Visual Arts" (PhD diss., Southern Illinois University at Carbondale, 2005).

12. Cf. Milton, *L'Allegro*, CM 1.1:138–44; "Ad eandem [Leonoram]" [ii], CM 1.1:7–8. References to Milton's poetry (including *Samson Agonistes*) refer to *The Works of John Milton*, 18 vols., ed. Frank Allen Patterson et al. (New York: Columbia University Press, 1931–38), cited by volume and (book and) line numbers. References to Milton's Latin prose and "Of that sort of Dramatic Poem which is call'd Tragedy" are also from this edition, abbreviated as CM, followed by volume and page number.

13. John Bulwer, *Chironomia; or, The Art of Manuall Rhetoricke* (London: R. Whitaker, 1644), frontispiece; engraved by William Marshall, who wrought frontispieces for Milton's 1645 *Poems* and the *Eikon Basilike*; *Chironomia*, 118–19; see also Cicero, *Orator*, in *Brutus, Orator*, trans. G. L. Hendrickson and H. M. Hubbell (Cambridge, MA: Harvard University Press, 1939), 55; and *De oratore*, trans. E. W. Sutton and H. Rackham (Cambridge, MA: Harvard University Press, 1942), 3.222; Valerius Maximus, *Factorum et dictorum memorabilium*, in *Practical Ethics for Roman Gentlemen: The Work of Valerius Maximus*, trans. Clive Skidmore, 8.10.2 (Exeter: University of Exeter Press, 1996), reports that the actors Aesopus and Roscius, credited for instructing Cicero in the art of gesture, attended legal proceedings to study Hortensius's gesture and pronunciation.

14. Richard Bernard, *The Faithfull Shepheard* (London: John Bill, 1607), 89–90; Richard Carter, *The Schismatick Stigmatized* (London: Francis Coles, 1641), 7; Samuel Sheppard, *The Joviall Crew; or, The Devill Turn'd Ranter* (London: W. Ley, 1651); Richard Blome, *The Fanatick History; or, An Exact Relation and Account of the Old Anabaptists, and New Quakers* (London: J. Sims, 1660), title page.

15. Maurice Merleau-Ponty, *Le visible et l'invisible: Suivi de notes de travail* (Paris: Gallimard, 1964): "La chair dont nous parlons n'est pas le matière [the flesh of which we speak is not matter]. Elle est l'enroulement du visible sur le corps voyant, du tangible sur le corps touchant" (191); "Le regard...enveloppe, palpe, épouse les choses visibles [the

look envelops, palpates, espouses the visible things]. Comme s'il était avec elles dans un rapport d'harmonie préétablie, comme s'il les savait avant de les savoir [as though it knew them before knowing them]" (175); my translation throughout.

16. See esp. Michael Schoenfeldt, "'Commotion Strange': Passion in *Paradise Lost*," in *Reading the Early Modern Passions: Essays in the Cultural History of Emotion*, ed. Gail Kern Paster, Katherine Rowe, and Mary Floyd-Wilson, 43–67 (Philadelphia: University of Pennsylvania Press, 2004); Richard J. DuRocher, "'Tears such as Angels weep': Passion and Allusion in *Paradise Lost*," in *Their Maker's Image: New Essays on John Milton*, ed. Mary C. Fenton and Louis Schwartz, 23–46 (Selinsgrove, PA: Susquehanna University Press, 2011); and Maggie Kilgour, "Satan's Envy and Poetic Emulation," in ibid., 47–61.

17. *OED Online*, March 2015, s.v. "witness," v.1.d, Oxford University Press, http://www.oed.com/view/Entry/229714?rskey=jE1P7u&result=2&is (accessed May 4, 2015).

18. *OED Online*, March 2012, s.v. "explode," v., Oxford University Press, http://www.oed.com/view/Entry/66640?redirectedFrom=explode (accessed May 21, 2012); see also *Animadversions*, YP 1:662; *Eikonoklastes*, YP 3:348; *History of Britain*, YP 5:3, and *Doctrine and Discipline of Divorce*, YP 2:241, 351; for "barbarous dissonance" as figuring hostile audience response or explosion, see Brendan M. Prawdzik, "'Look on Me': Theater, Gender and Poetic Identity Formation in Milton's *Maske*," *Studies in Philology* 110, no. 3 (Fall 2013): 812–50.

19. "Une dehiscence de l'Etre"; Merleau-Ponty, *Visible et l'invisible*, 375.

20. See also the aqueous "refluxes" in *Reason of Church-Government*, YP 1:817.

21. Originally in Joseph Hall, *An Humble Remonstrance to the High Court of Parliament* (London: Nathaniel Butter, 1641), 37.

22. Jacques Lacan, *Four Fundamental Concepts of Psycho-Analysis*, ed. Jacques-Alain Miller, trans. Alan Sheridan (New York: Norton, 1998), 65–119.

23. René Descartes, *Les passions de l'âme* (Amsterdam: Chez Louys Elzevier, 1650), 61: "Nos passions ne peuvent pas aussi directement être excitées ny ostées par l'action de notre volonté; mais elles peuvent l'estre indirectement par la representation des choses qui ont coustume d'etre jointes avec les passions que nous voulons avoir, & qui sont contraires à celles que nous voulons rejetter."

24. The instructions recall Cicero's and Quintilian's promotion of the actor's skill of internal mimesis to inspire emotion within and perform it rhetorically; see Cicero, *De oratore*, 2.291–94; and *The Institutio Oratorio of Quintilian*, trans. Harold Edgeworth Butler, vol. 4 (Cambridge, MA: Harvard University Press, 1922), 11.3.61–62, 71.

25. Descartes, *Les passions*, 61–62: "Ainsi pour exciter en soy la hardiesse & oster la peur, il ne suffit pas d'en avoir la volonté, mais il faut s'appliquer à considerer les raisons, les objets, ou les exemples, qui persuadent que le peril n'est pas grand; qu'il y a tousjours plus de seureté en la defense qu'en la fuite; qu'on aura de la gloire & de la joye d'avoir vaincu, au lieu qu'on ne peut attendre que du regret & de la honte d'avoir fui."

26. Ibid., 71: "Qu'il n'y a point d'ame si foible, qu'elle ne puisse estant bien conduite acquerir un pouvoir absolu sur les Passions"; see also the closing phrases of article 50: "il est evident…que ceux mesmes qui ont les plus foibles ames, pourroient acquerir

un empire tres-absolu sur toutes leurs passions, si on employoit assez d'industrie à les dresser, & à les conduire" (It is evident that those persons who have the weakest souls could acquire an absolute empire over their passions if they would employ enough industry to tame and guide them [74]).

27. Milton seems to be thinking of the 202nd article of *Passions*, where Descartes describes the worst "species of Anger, in which predominates Hatred and Sadness" as "not so apparent at first, except perhaps in making the face turn pale.... And as it is the most generous souls which have the most gratitude, so it is those who have the most pride and who are the most lowly and weak who let themselves get most carried away by this species of Anger" ("L'autre espece de Colere, en laquelle predomine la Haine & la Tristesse, n'est pas si apparente d'abord, sinon peut estre en ce qu'elle fait palir le visage... Et comme ce sont les ames les plus genereuses qui ont le plus de reconnoissance, ainsi ce sont celles qui ont le plus d'orgueil, & qui sont les plus basses & les plus infirmes, qui se laissent le plus emporter à cette espece de Colere" [258–59]).

28. The text comes to us piecemeal, in the form of Prolusion 6, published in 1674 and containing the text for the opening Latin portions (the oration and prolusion) of *Vacation Exercise* and "At a Vacation Exercise in the College, part Latin, part English," a set of 50 rhyming English couplets published in the 1673 *Poems, &c. upon Several Occasions*. The 1673 edition contains the English poem (58 lines), a pair of stage directions, and 42 lines of what appears to have been a comic interlude. The remainder, which "was in prose" (line 100 and following), has not survived. The rest has been published as one in John K. Hale, *Milton's Cambridge Latin: Performing in the Genres, 1625–1632* (Tempe: Arizona Center for Medieval and Renaissance Studies, 2005). Citations of the prose portions refer to pages of this edition; translations are Hale's.

29. See Alan H. Nelson, ed., *Records of Early English Drama: Cambridge* (Toronto: University of Toronto Press, 1989), 996–1001.

30. "At vero absit porro ab hoc coetu horrendus et tartareus ille sibili sonus, nam si hic audiatur hodie, credam ego Furias et Eumenides inter vos occulte latitare, et angues suos colubrosque pectoribus vestris immisisse, et proinde Athamantaeos Furores vobis inspiravisse" (Hale, *Milton's Cambridge Latin*, 272–73).

31. This description suggests the thought of Galen. Schoenfeldt, *Bodies and Selves in Early Modern England: Physiology and Inwardness in Spenser, Shakespeare, Herbert, and Milton* (Cambridge: Cambridge University Press, 1999), 131–65, situates *Paradise Lost* in the Galenic tradition.

32. Milton is defending himself against his characterization (as the anonymous author of *Animadversions*) in the *Modest Confutation of a Slanderous and Scurrilous Libell* as a licentious playgoer; cf. Cicero, *Orator*, 28, which helps to interpret the phrase "make up the *atticisme*." Exploiting the Confuter's "likening [of] those grave controversies [over church government] to a piece of Stagery," Milton also labels Joseph Hall the "chiefe Player, be it boasting *Thraso*, or *Davus that troubles all things*, or one who can shift into any shape" (YP 1:879).

33. William Shakespeare, *Hamlet*, 3.2.2–9, in *The Norton Shakespeare: Based on the Oxford Edition*, ed. Stephen Greenblatt et al. (New York: Norton, 1997); see also Anonymous, *A Modest Confutation of a Slanderous and Scurrilous Libell* (London[?],

1642), where the anonymous author of *Animadversions* (Milton) is described as "thrust forth upon the Stage," interrupting the "Solemn scenes" ("it were too ominous to say Tragicall") of debate between Joseph Hall and Smectymnuus (1–2).

34. Cf. Milton, "On Shakespear," CM, 1.1:13–16.

35. In the antiprelatical tracts Milton theatricalizes this ethical entropy through a rhetoric of rote memorization and bodily hardening; see esp. *Of Reformation*, YP 1:520–22; *Reason of Church-Government*, YP 1:828, 833; and *Apology*, YP 1:930.

36. Cf. *Paradise Regained*, CM 2:2.401–03.

37. For narcissism premised upon *difference* as regenerative, see Kilgour, "'Thy Perfect Image Viewing': Poetic Creation and Ovid's Narcissus in *Paradise Lost*," *Studies in Philology* 102, no. 3 (2005): 307–39; see also John Guillory, "Milton, Narcissism, Gender: On the Genealogy of Male Self-Esteem," in *Critical Essays on John Milton*, ed. Christopher Kendrick, 194–233 (New York: G. K. Hall, 1995).

38. Schoenfeldt, "Passion," 67.

39. See also Milton, *L'Allegro*, 117–24.

40. Fallon, *Milton's Peculiar Grace: Self-Representation and Authority* (Ithaca, NY: Cornell University Press), 136–45, sees here a "picture of wavering and competing passions" (141), as "the pressure of self-reference leads to a distortion in the [tract's] reasoning" (136); see also Milton's euphoria in the *Defensio secunda* when, imagining himself "encompassed by…countless multitudes" (*circumseptus copiis*) he "behold[s] from on high" (*sublimis perlustrare*) the "countenances strange and numberless" (*vultus innumeros atque ignotos*) of sympathetic nations lauding the early republic (CM 8:12–15); for a discussion of this passage as a "dramatic element," see Michele Valerie Ronnick, "Concerning the Dramatic Elements in Milton's *Defensiones*: Theater without a Stage," *Classical and Modern Literature: A Quarterly* 15 (1995): 271–79.

41. See Quintilian, *Institutio oratoria*, 11.3.7; and Plutarch, "Demosthenes," in *Twelve Lives*, trans. John Dryden (Cleveland: Fine Editions Press, 1950), 359–60; Macrobius, *Saturnalia*, trans. Robert A. Kaster (Cambridge, MA: Harvard University Press, 2011), 3.14.12, cites friendly debates between Cicero and Roscius about the merits of oratorical eloquence and theatrical action, and suggests that Roscius wrote a book comparing these skills.

42. Daniel Shore, *Milton and the Art of Rhetoric* (Cambridge: Cambridge University Press, 2012), presents a more complicated picture of Milton as the rhetorician working down to an audience.

43. Fish, *Surprised by Sin*, 218.

44. See James Grantham Turner, *One Flesh: Paradisal Marriage and Sexual Relations in the Age of Milton* (Oxford: Clarendon, 1993); and Shannon Miller, *Engendering the Fall: John Milton and Seventeenth-Century Women Writers* (Philadelphia: University of Pennsylvania Press, 2008).

45. "Duplicem enim habemus sub evangelio…scripturam; externam verbi scripti, et internam sancti spiritus, quam is…in cordibus credentium…exaravit" (Under the Gospel we possess a double Scripture; one external, of the written word, the other internal, of the Holy Spirit, inscribed upon the hearts of believers) (my translation of CM 16:272); cf. 266–74; and *A Treatise of Civil Power* (1659): "To protestants…whose

common rule and touchstone is the scripture, nothing can with more conscience, more equitie, nothing more protestantly can be permitted then a free and lawful debate at all times by writing, conference or disputation of what opinion soever, disputable by scripture" (YP 7:249).

46. See, for instance, David Loewenstein, *Representing Revolution in Milton and His Contemporaries: Religion, Politics, and Polemics in Radical Puritanism* (Cambridge: Cambridge University Press, 2001), 273–74; and Norman T. Burns, "'Then Stood up Phinehas': Milton's Antinomianism, and Samson's," in *Milton Studies*, vol. 33, ed. James D. Simmonds, 27–46 (Pittsburgh: University of Pittsburgh Press, 1997).

47. Dayton Haskin, *Milton's Burden of Interpretation* (Philadelphia: University of Pennsylvania Press, 1994); and Phillip J. Donnelly, *Milton's Scriptural Reasoning: Narrative and Protestant Toleration* (Cambridge: Cambridge University Press, 2009).

48. Mary Nyquist, "The Genesis of Gendered Subjectivity in the Divorce Tracts and in *Paradise Lost*," in *Re-Membering Milton: Essays on the Texts and Traditions*, ed. Mary Nyquist and Margaret W. Ferguson, 99–127 (London: Methuen, 1987).

49. Influential readings of Samson's destruction of the Philistine temple as a regenerative act include Mary Ann Radzinowicz, *Toward "Samson Agonistes": The Growth of Milton's Mind* (Princeton, NJ: Princeton University Press, 1978); Joan S. Bennett, *Reviving Liberty: Radical Christian Humanism in Milton's Great Poems* (Cambridge, MA: Harvard University Press, 1989), 119–60; and Christopher Hill, *Milton and the English Revolution* (New York: Penguin, 1979), 428–48. Influential critiques of the regenerationist view include Irene Samuel, "*Samson Agonistes* as Tragedy," in *Calm of Mind: Tercentenary Essays of "Paradise Regained" and "Samson Agonistes" in Honor of John S. Diekhoff*, ed. Joseph A. Wittreich, James G. Taaffe, and Jane Cerny, 235–57 (Cleveland: Press of Case Western Reserve University, 1971); and Joseph Wittreich, *Interpreting "Samson Agonistes"* (Princeton, NJ: Princeton University Press, 1986). Fish, "Spectacle and Evidence in *Samson Agonistes*," *Critical Inquiry* 15 (1989): 556–86, asserts that the play's climactic action leaves us "bereft of interpretive resources," polarizing interpretive responses while preventing their verification (586); see also Sharon Achinstein, "*Samson Agonistes* and the Drama of Dissent," in *Milton Studies*, vol. 33, ed. James D. Simmonds, 133–58 (Pittsburgh: University of Pittsburgh Press, 1997); Joseph Wittreich, *Shifting Contexts: Reinterpreting "Samson Agonistes"* (Pittsburgh: Duquesne University Press, 2002); and Gordon Teskey, *Delirious Milton: The Fate of the Poet in Modernity* (Cambridge: Cambridge University Press, 2006).

50. Derek N. C. Wood, *Exiled from Light: Divine Law, Morality, and Violence in Milton's "Samson Agonistes"* (Toronto: University of Toronto Press, 2001).

51. For instance, Blome writes of early Quaker John Gilpin, who confessed in print that his gestures were caused by demonic possession, that "his body and all the members of it were in motion," "in which motions (he saith) he acted not in the least, but was altogether passive" (*Fanatick History*, 74); Joshua Miller, *Antichrist in Man the Quakers Idol* (London: L. Lloyd, 1655), reminds his readers that Satan works "with forcible and strong impulsions on the spirits of men," that "Scripture must try all such strong motions, or else God knows whither such strong powers will lead" (2).

52. Bulwer, *Pathomyotamia; or, A Dissection of the Significative Muscles of the Affections of the Minde* (London: Humphrey Moseley, 1649), title page.

53. See, for instance, Feisal G. Mohamed, *Milton and the Post-Secular Present: Ethics, Politics, Terrorism* (Stanford, CA: Stanford University Press, 2011), 9, 93.

54. Andrew Marvell, "On Mr. Milton's *Paradise Lost*," in *The Poems of Andrew Marvell*, ed. Nigel Smith, 180–84 (Harlow, UK: Pearson Longman, 2007), 1–10.

Notes to Chapter 3 / Rutherford

I would like to extend my thanks to D. Vance Smith and Andrew Cutrofello for their comments on an early draft of this paper. I am also grateful to Louis Schwartz, Mimi Fenton, and Kathy Meyer for their editorial work.

1. John Milton, *Paradise Lost*, rev. 2nd ed., ed. Alastair Fowler (New York: Longman, 2007), 1.24. Subsequent quotations from *Paradise Lost* are from this edition and will appear parenthetically in the text.

2. John Leonard, *Faithful Laborers: A Reception History of "Paradise Lost,"* 2 vols. (Oxford: Oxford University Press, 2013), 2:479.

3. I use the edition and facing translation of Milton's textbook from *The Works of John Milton*, vol. 11, ed. and trans. Allan H. Gilbert (New York: Columbia University Press, 1935). References to this work, hereafter called *The Art of Logic*, are cited parenthetically by page number in the text.

4. There has been extensive work on Milton's logic, especially in recent years. In *The Logic of the Fall* (New York: Peter Lang, 2006), Richard Arnold discusses the ethical implications of Milton's logical theory in a long historical context and provides illuminating comparisons of the logical structure of speeches by a range of characters. Emma Wilson discusses Milton's logic with reference to pedagogical backgrounds, showing how conventions for university disputation affect representations of debate in Milton's poetry in several articles, including "The Art of Reasoning Well: Ramist Logic at Work in *Paradise Lost*," *Review of English Studies* 61, no. 248 (2010): 55–71; "Reading the 'unseemly logomachy,'" in *Ramus, Pedagogy, and the Liberal Arts*, ed. Steven J. Reid and Emma Annette Wilson (Burlington, VT: Ashgate, 2011); and "How Milton's Education at Christ College, Cambridge Influenced Logical Styles in *Paradise Lost*," in *Their Maker's Image: New Essays on John Milton*, ed. Mary C. Fenton and Louis Schwartz (Selinsgrove, PA: Susquehanna University Press, 2011). For insightful examinations of the abuses of logic in speeches leading up to the Fall, see Lee A. Jacobus, *Sudden Apprehension: Aspects of Knowledge in "Paradise Lost"* (The Hague: Mouton, 1976); Kathleen Swaim, *Before and After the Fall: Contrasting Modes in "Paradise Lost"* (Amherst: University of Massachusetts Press, 1986). In "The Logical Poetics of *Paradise Regained*," *Huntington Library Quarterly* 76, no. 1 (2013): 35–58, Elizabeth Skerpan-Wheeler provides useful information about Milton's logic in its postpublication context, arguing with reference to *Paradise Regained* that Milton's logic is oriented less to debate than to self–discovery. Finally, for an overview of recent work on Milton's logic, see Phillip J. Donnelly, "Logic," in *Milton in Context*, ed. Stephen Dobranski (Cambridge: Cambridge University Press, 2010).

5. For an overview of Ramism in Puritan contexts, see Perry Miller, *The New England Mind: The Seventeenth Century* (Cambridge, MA: Harvard University Press, 1954).

6. "The Life of Petrus Ramus" is Milton's abridgement of a biography composed by Thomas Freigius. In "Milton Edits Freigius' 'Life of Ramus,'" *Renaissance and Reformation* 8, no. 3 (1972): 112–14, Leo Miller notes Milton's sympathy for Ramus, suggesting that perhaps Milton made his abridgement in the early 1640s rather than at a later date because it seems unlikely that he would have removed mention of Ramus's failed eyesight.

7. For discussion of the negative reception of Ramism in England, see Mordechai Feingold, "English Ramism: A Reinterpretation," in *The Influence of Petrus Ramus: Studies in Sixteenth Century Philosophy and Science*, ed. Mordechai Feingold, Joseph S. Freedman, and Wolfgang Rotter (Basel: Schwabe, 2001).

8. Under the heading "Logic," *An Index to the Columbia Edition of the Works of John Milton* provides a useful, though incomplete, catalogue of instances of logic use in Milton's prose works. For information regarding the Ramist compositional principles of Milton's systematic theology, see Gordon Campbell, Thomas Corns, John Hales, and Fiona Tweedie, *Milton and the Manuscript of "De Doctrina"* (Oxford: Oxford University Press, 2007); John Milton, *De doctrina Christiana*, in *The Complete Works of John Milton*, vol. 8, ed. John K. Hale and J. Donald Cullington (Oxford: Oxford University Press, 2012), lv–lxxiii.

9. For a useful situation of Ramist logic within the development of early modern rhetoric, see Peter Mack, *A History of Rhetoric, 1380–1620* (Oxford: Oxford University Press, 2011).

10. See Walter Ong's introduction to *The Art of Logic*, in *The Complete Prose Works of John Milton*, 8 vols., ed. Don M. Wolfe et al. (New Haven, CT: Yale University Press, 1953–82), 8:161; hereafter cited as YP. For similar observations about early modern logic with reference to Milton, see Jacobus, *Sudden Apprehension*, 28; Swaim, *Before and After*, 142.

11. Richard Strier, "Milton's Fetters, or, why Eden Is Better than Heaven," in *The New Milton Criticism*, ed. Peter C. Herman and Elizabeth Sauer (Cambridge: Cambridge University Press, 2012), 26.

12. It is probably also significant that the first sentence after the invocation asks what "cause" moved our grandparents to fall off from their creator (*PL* 1.26–32). Following the general outline of Ramist logic, Milton proceeds to mention the subject of the first chapters of the book of invention, the different kinds of causation. For further information about the logical background of the conception of cause in *Paradise Lost*, see Leon Howard, "'The Invention' of Milton's 'Great Argument': A Study of the Logic of 'God's Ways to Men,'" *Huntington Library Quarterly* 9, no. 2 (1946): 149–73; John M. Steadman, "'Man's First Disobedience': The Causal Structure of the Fall," *Journal of the History of Ideas* 21, no. 2 (1960): 180–97.

13. Samuel Butler [attributed to Richard Leigh], *The Transproser Rehears'd* (London, 1673), 41.

14. Niels Hemmingsen, *The preacher; or, Methode of preachinge, wrytten in Latine* (1574), 50.

15. Roger Hutchinson, *The Image of God; or, Laie Mans Boke* (London, 1560), front matter ("Another Table"), 158.

16. For the classic account of Gill's thought and influence, see A. E. Barker, "Milton's Schoolmasters," *Modern Language Review* 32, no. 4 (1937): 517–36.

17. Alexander Gill, *A Treatise concerning the Trinity* (London, 1601), 13, 21–22.

18. Nigel Smith discusses Biddle's theology and his possible influence on the style of *Paradise Regained* in "'And if God was one of us': Paul Best, John Biddle, and the Anti-Trinitarian Heresy in Seventeenth-Century England," in *Heresy, Literature, and Politics in Early Modern English Culture*, ed. David Loewenstein and John Marshall (Cambridge: Cambridge University Press, 2006).

19. Thomas White, *Controversy-logicke; or, The methode to come to truth in debates of religion* (London, 1659). For an overview of methods of arguing amid Socinian controversies, see Paul C. H. Lim, *Mystery Unveiled: The Crisis of the Trinity in Early Modern England* (New York: Oxford University Press, 2012).

20. Ibid., 130.

21. Peter C. Herman, "*Paradise Lost*, the Miltonic 'Or,' and the Poetics of Incertitude," in *Destabilizing Milton: "Paradise Lost" and the Poetics of Incertitude* (New York: Palgrave, 2005), 43. The problem is perhaps especially acute when the reader has to wait until the start of a new line to learn that what had gone before was merely a possibility (as happens in lines 2, 7, 26, 43, and 44 of the invocation).

22. For discussions of the sources and meanings of Milton's "holy light," see Estelle Haan, "'Heaven's Purest Light': Milton's *Paradise Lost* 3 and Vida," *Comparative Literature Studies* 30, no. 2 (1993): 115–36; Merritt Hughes, "Milton and the Symbol of Light," *SEL* 4, no. 1 (1964): 1–33; William B. Hunter, "Milton's Arianism Reconsidered," in *Bright Essence: Studies in Milton's Theology*, ed. William B. Hunter, C. A. Patrides, and J. H. Adamson (Salt Lake City: University of Utah Press, 1971); Maurice Kelley, "Milton's Arianism Again Considered," *Harvard Theological Review* 54, no. 3 (1961): 195–205; and Michael Lieb, *Poetics of the Holy: A Reading of "Paradise Lost"* (Chapel Hill: University of North Carolina Press, 1981), 185–210.

23. Andrew Mattison, *Milton's Uncertain Eden: Understanding Place in "Paradise Lost"* (New York: Routledge, 2007), 114.

24. Ibid., 114.

25. Lee M. Johnson, "Milton's Epic Style: The Invocations in *Paradise Lost*," in *The Cambridge Companion to Milton*, ed. Dennis Danielson (Cambridge: Cambridge University Press, 1989), 74.

26. Stuart Curran, "God," in *The Oxford Handbook of Milton*, ed. Nigel Smith and Nicholas McDowell (Oxford: Oxford University Press, 2010), 526; William Empson, *Milton's God* (Cambridge: Cambridge University Press, 1981), 117; Victoria Silver, "The Problem of God," in *The Cambridge Companion to Milton*, ed. Louis Schwartz (Cambridge: Cambridge University Press, 2014), 44–45; Stanley Fish, *Surprised by Sin*, 2nd ed. (Cambridge, MA: Harvard University Press, 1998), esp. 86.

27. Thomas Festa, "God as Geometer and Architect in *Paradise Lost*," in Fenton and Schwartz, *Their Maker's Image*, 109. For more general discussions of the hermeneutic circle in Milton's work, see Festa's *The End of Learning: Milton and Education* (New

York: Routledge, 2006); and James Dougal Fleming, *Milton's Secrecy* (Burlington, VT: Ashgate, 2008).

28. In *Ramus, Method, and the Decay of Dialogue* (Chicago: University of Chicago Press, 2004), Walter Ong describes the method:

> The procedure in interpretation is simple and invariable: faced with the text, one asks, What is the question? and, the question determined, What is the argument? and so on from start to finish of the discourse in hand. In doing so, one discovers that the great vice of all discourse is ambiguity. One also discovers the real value of the syllogism; in protracted discourse, the thread on which the arguments are strung gets tangled, and the syllogism serves the excellent purpose of enabling one to disentangle or "unweave" (*retexere*) the thread.... Properly unwound, any discourse is delightfully simple. Cicero's oration *For Milo* is found to amount to no more than one "dialectical ratiocination": "It is permissible to kill a criminal." We might say today that this is the "meaning" of the oration *For Milo*, for everything beyond such summary statement, according to Ramus, is ornament. (191)

29. See *The Advancement of Learning*, in *Francis Bacon: The Major Works*, ed. Brian Vickers (New York: Oxford University Press, 1996), 299.

30. Dennis Burden, *The Logical Epic* (Cambridge, MA: Harvard University Press, 1967), 25–26.

31. Dennis Danielson, *Milton's Good God: A Study in Literary Theodicy* (Cambridge: Cambridge University Press, 1982), 150.

32. Such an analogy is appropriate to Milton's cultural context. In *Trinity*, Gill provides a much more complicated discussion of how God the Father, God the Son, and discourse can function as "three Termes, as I will a while call them: the Terme from whence: the Terme whereto, or wherein: and the middle Terme betweene them" (18–24).

33. The Latin text is from *The Art of Logic*, 490. The translation is from *Virgil*, vol. 2, trans. H. Rushton Fairclough, rev. G. P. Goold, Loeb Classical Library (Cambridge, MA: Harvard University Press), 145.

34. For a discussion of the relation of this passage to Milton's theory of atonement, see Gregory Chaplin, "Beyond Sacrifice: Milton and the Atonement," *PMLA* 125, no. 2 (2010): 354–69. For an analysis of Milton's use of other aspects of the story of Nisus and Euryalus as it appears in the *Aeneid*, see Leah Whittington, "Vergil's Nisus and the Language of Self–Sacrifice in *Paradise Lost*," *Modern Philology* 107, no. 4 (2010): 588–606; and David J. Bradshaw, "Self–Sacrifice and Heroic Martyrdom in the *Aeneid* and *Paradise Lost*," in Fenton and Schwartz, *Their Maker's Image*, 81–92.

35. Milton draws on the same argument from efficient causation in chapter 4 of *De doctrina Christiana*, "Of Predestination," YP 6:188.

36. Zachary Coke, *The art of logick; or, The entire body of logick in English. Unfolding to the meanest capacity the way to dispute well, and to refute all fallacies whatsoever. The second edition, corrected and amended* (London, 1657), 52. Richard Serjeantson notes that Coke's text is an abridged translation of Bartholomäus Keckermann's *Systema logicae* in "Testimony and Proof in Early-Modern England," *Studies in History and Philosophy of Science* 30, no. 2 (1999): 207.

37. This phrase is taken from *Apology against a Pamphlet*, YP 1:927.

38. For a more general discussion of such conceptual circularities, see Richard Popkin's classic study, *The History of Skepticism from Erasmus to Descartes*, rev. ed. (Assen, Netherlands: Van Gorcum, 1964).

39. Matthew Poole, *The nullity of the Romish faith; or, A blow at the root of the Romish Church* (London, 1666).

Notes to Chapter 4 / Kilgour

1. Julius Caesar Scaliger, quoted in David Scott Wilson-Okamura, *Virgil in the Renaissance* (Cambridge: Cambridge University Press, 2010), 47.

2. K. W. Gransden, "The *Aeneid* and *Paradise Lost*," in *Virgil and His Influence: Bimillennial Studies*, ed. Charles Martindale (Bristol, UK: Bristol Classical Press, 1984), 106. For a counterargument that minimizes Virgil's influence in terms of style, see Charles Martindale, *John Milton and the Transformation of Ancient Epic* (London: Croom Helm, 1986).

3. C. S. Lewis, *A Preface to "Paradise Lost"* (1942; repr., Oxford: Oxford University Press, 1959), 35–36.

4. See Joseph Farrell, "Greek Lives and Roman Careers in the Classical *Vita* Tradition," in *European Literary Careers: The Author from Antiquity to the Renaissance*, ed. Patrick Cheney and Frederick A. de Armas (Toronto: University of Toronto Press, 2002), 24–46, esp. 27–31.

5. On the Virgilian *rota* and its influence, see E. R. Curtius, *European Literature and the Latin Middle Ages* (London: Routledge and Kegan Paul, 1953), 231–32; Lawrence Lipking, *The Life of the Poet: Beginning and Ending Poetic Careers* (Chicago: University of Chicago Press, 1981), 76–93; John Coolidge, "Great Things and Small: The Virgilian Progression," *Comparative Literature* 17, no. 1 (1965): 1–23; Richard Neuse, "Milton and Spenser: The Virgilian Triad Revisited," *English Literary History* 45, no. 4 (1978): 606–39; Patrick Cheney, *Spenser's Famous Flight: A Renaissance Idea of a Literary Career* (Toronto: University of Toronto Press, 1993), 51–52; Wilson-Okamura, *Virgil in the Renaissance*, 87–91. However, as Colin Burrow cautions in "English Renaissance Readers and the *Appendix Vergiliana*," *Proceedings of the Virgil Society* 26 (2008): 1–16, the assumption that the poems in the spurious *Appendix Vergiliana* were Virgil's early work means that the Virgilian career model may have appeared less linear and distinct to Renaissance readers than we often assume.

6. Fabius Planciades Fulgentius, *Expositio Vergilianae*, in *Fabii Planciadis Fulgentii V. C. Opera*, ed. R. Helm (Leipzig: Teubner, 1898), 95. Translations are from Fabius Planciades Fulgentius, *Fulgentius the Mythographer*, ed. and trans. Leslie George Whitbread (Columbus: Ohio State University Press, 1971), 128.

7. *Expositio Vergilianae* 105; *Fulgentius the Mythographer*, 134. There were variations in interpretation — Landino read Dido as the lure of the active life — but the general pattern of growth through the rejection of temptation is fairly constant. The mode of reading here itself grows out of an allegorical tradition that had turned the *Odyssey*

into the story of the soul's return home through the resistance of earthly temptations such as the Sirens, Calypso, and Circe; see Robert Lamberton, *Homer the Theologian: Neoplatonist Allegorical Reading and the Growth of the Epic Tradition* (Berkeley: University of California Press, 1986). A crucial difference, of course, is that Odysseus is trying to get back to his original home. His *nostoi* is thus a model for nostalgia; moving forward to a new home, Aeneas can represent progress to a new state.

8. For Aeneas as model for ruler, see Craig Kallendorf, *In Praise of Aeneas: Virgil and Epideictic Rhetoric in the Early Italian Renaissance* (Hanover, NH: University Press of New England, 1989). On the role of Virgil in Renaissance pedagogy generally, see Andrew Wallace, *Virgil's Schoolboys: The Poetics of Pedagogy in Renaissance England* (Oxford: Oxford University Press, 2010). Mantuan's 1498 series of eclogues called *Adulescentia* were standard texts in schools until the seventeenth century; Wallace also reminds us that Mantuan's "Ninth Eclogue" has long been recognized as a source for *Lycidas* (40, 118). Walter Ong first argued in "Latin Language Study as a Renaissance Puberty Rite," *Studies in Philology* 56, no. 2 (1959): 103–24, that the study of Latin in general served to initiate Renaissance boys into adulthood.

9. Thomas Elyot, *The boke named the Gouernour, devysed by syr Thomas Elyot knight* [London: Thomas Berthelet regius impressor excudebat, 1537], 29ʳ–30ᵛ, http://eebo. chadwyck.com (accessed May 1, 2015).

10. Charles Martindale, "Horace, Ovid, and Others," in *The Legacy of Rome: A New Appraisal*, ed. Richard Jenkyns (Oxford: Oxford University Press, 1992), 182.

11. John Watkins, *The Specter of Dido: Spenser and Virgilian Epic* (New Haven, CT: Yale University Press, 1995), 34–38. See also Sabine MacCormack, *The Shadows of Poetry: Vergil in the Mind of Augustine* (Berkeley: University of California Press, 1998).

12. *Virgil*, rev. ed., 2 vols., ed. G. P. Goold, trans. H. Rushton Fairclough (Cambridge, MA: Harvard University Press, 1999). All Latin quotations and English translations from Virgil's works (with some modifications) come from this edition and are hereafter cited in the text. On the influence of Virgil on Freud, see David Damrosch, "The Politics of Ethics: Freud and Rome," in *Pragmatism's Freud: The Moral Disposition of Psychoanalysis*, ed. J. H. Smith and W. Kerrigan (Baltimore: Johns Hopkins University Press, 1986), 102–25; Elizabeth Jane Bellamy, *Translations of Power: Narcissism and the Unconscious in Epic History* (Ithaca, NY: Cornell University Press, 1992), 38–81. Ellen Oliensis, *Freud's Rome: Psychoanalysis and Latin Poetry* (Cambridge: Cambridge University Press, 2009), compares the *Aeneid* especially to *Civilization and Its Discontents*, with "their shared preoccupation with the costs of civilization" (132).

13. Neuse notes "the peculiar Virgilian ambivalence: joy at moving forward balanced by a longing to go back" ("Milton and Spenser," 609); see also Elena Theodorakapoulos, "Closure: The Book of Virgil," in *The Cambridge Companion to Virgil*, ed. Charles Martindale (Cambridge: Cambridge University Press, 1997), 155–65, esp. 157. Odyssean nostalgia is not completely left behind after all.

14. See esp. Mihoko Suzuki, *The Metamorphoses of Helen* (Ithaca, NY: Cornell University Press, 1989). The founding of Rome in particular involves the repeated sacrifice of the one for the many. The pattern begins with the false story told by Sinon in the *Aeneid*, book 2, in which he claims that the Greeks had to sacrifice someone to

begin and end the Trojan War, and is most clearly illustrated when Neptune requires that Pallinurus must die: "*unum pro multis*" (one for many; 5.815). If Turnus is the final sacrificial victim, however, he also suggests how Aeneas, like Palinurus, must sacrifice himself for the nation.

15. Fulgentius makes the connection partly on the basis of etymology: "Turnus enim Grece quasi turosnus dicitur" (*Expositio Vergilianae* 105) (Turnus is pronounced like the Greek *turosnus* [furious rage] [*Fulgentius the Mythographer*, 134]).

16. Lactantius, *Divinae institutiones*, 5.10.8–9, in *Patrologiae cursus completus*, ed. Jacques-Paul Migne, vol. 6, *Lactantii: Opera omnia* (Paris: [Imprimerie Catholique], 1844). The translation is taken from Wilson-Okamura, *Virgil in the Renaissance*, 200, who gives other suspicious readings of the final scene (191–203).

17. See esp. D. C. Feeney, "History and Revelation in Vergil's Underworld," *Proceedings of the Cambridge Philological Society* 32 (1986): 1–24; Philip Hardie, *The Epic Successors of Virgil: A Study in the Dynamics of a Tradition* (Cambridge: Cambridge University Press, 1993), 92–93.

18. Richard F. Thomas lays out the history of this interpretation in later writers (though he does not find it in Milton) in *Virgil and the Augustan Reception* (Cambridge: Cambridge University Press, 2001).

19. Wilson-Okamura, *Virgil in the Renaissance*, thus notes how both readings were available in the Renaissance but argues that "they did not carry equal weight in the scholarship" (201).

20. Louis Martz, *Poet of Exile: A Study of Milton's Poetry* (New Haven, CT: Yale University Press, 1980), 59.

21. Ibid., 43. For Martz, the progression from *L'Allegro* to *Il Penseroso* epitomizes this, as "the two poems move from youth to age" (50). At the same time, the sequence of languages, from the vernacular to ancient tongues, creates a countering undertow so that the volume goes backward even as it goes forward (a double motion also evident in the structure of Milton's last published poems, *Paradise Regained...To Which Is Added Samson Agonistes*).

22. The motto is taken from *Eclogue* 7.27–28: "*baccare frontem / cingite, ne vati noceat mala lingua futuro*" (wreathe my brow with foxglove, lest his evil tongue harm the bard that is to be). On the role of Virgil in the volume, see also Martz, *Poet of Exile*, 36–38; Stella Revard, *Milton and the Tangles of Neaera's Hair* (Columbia: University of Missouri Press, 1997), 162–64; John Hale, "Milton's Self-Presentation of *Poems...1645*," *Milton Quarterly* 25, no. 2 (1991): 39; Neuse, "Milton and Spenser," 606–39; James Holly Hanford, "The Youth of Milton: An Interpretation of His Early Literary Development," in *Studies in Shakespeare, Milton and Donne*, ed. Eugene S. McCartney (London: Macmillan, 1925), 126; Douglas Bush, *A Variorum Commentary on the Poems of John Milton*, vol. 1, *The Latin and Greek Poems* (New York: Columbia University Press, 1970), 285. On the possible influence of Virgil's renowned chastity, see Gordon Campbell, "Milton and the Lives of the Ancients," *Journal of the Warburg and Courtauld Institutes* 47 (1984): 234–38, and "Imitation in *Epitaphium Damonis*," in *Milton Studies*, vol. 19, *Urbane Milton: The Latin Poetry*, ed. James Freeman (Pittsburgh: University of Pittsburgh Press, 1984), 174. For Renaissance critics, Virgil's chastity

extended to his style, which was often characterized by its *castitatas* and *frugalitas*; see Margaret Tudeau-Clayton, *Jonson, Shakespeare and Early Modern Virgil* (Cambridge: Cambridge University Press, 1998), 42–43; Wilson-Okamura, *Virgil in the Renaissance*, 106–08.

23. Northrop Frye, "Literature as Context: Milton's 'Lycidas,'" in *Milton's "Lycidas": The Tradition and the Poem*, rev. ed., ed. C. A. Patrides (Columbia: University of Missouri Press, 1983), 210.

24. Citations from the early works are from *Complete Shorter Poems*, ed. Stella Purce Revard (Malden, MA: Wiley-Blackwell, 2009); those from the epic are from *Paradise Lost*, ed. Barbara Kiefer Lewalski (Malden, MA: Blackwell, 2007), and are hereafter cited in the text.

25. Albert Labriola, "Portraits of an Artist: Milton's Changing Self-Image," in Freeman, *Urbane Milton*, thus sees Milton's fate as starkly juxtaposed with Diodati: "The granting of life to which Milton refers may be contrasted with the death of Diodati" (186).

26. William Shullenberger, *Lady in the Labyrinth: Milton's "Comus" as Initiation* (Teaneck, NJ: Fairleigh Dickinson University Press, 2008).

27. On the political subtext, and in particular the relation between England and Wales at this time, see Michael Wilding, "Milton's 'A Masque Presented at Ludlow Castle, 1634': Theatre and Politics on the Border," *Milton Quarterly* 21, no. 4 (1987): 35–51.

28. See Milton's discussion in *The History of Britain*, in *The Complete Prose Works of John Milton*, 8 vols., ed. Don M. Wolfe et al. (New Haven, CT: Yale University Press, 1953–1982), 5:8–18.

29. Citations to the *Faerie Queene* are taken from *The Faerie Queene*, ed. A. C. Hamilton (London: Longman, 1977).

30. Richard McCabe, *The Pillars of Eternity: Time and Providence in "The Faerie Queene"* (Blackrock: Irish Academic Press, 1989), connects her also to an underlying pattern of generational conflict in which "children turn against parents and parents against children" (106).

31. Milton's account of "Sabra" follows that of Spenser; see *History of Britain*, 18. See also his presentation of Cordelia (22–25) and Boadicea (79–81). Where Spenser admires the latter, Milton does not, presenting her in many ways as a version of the Cleopatra of book 8 of the *Aeneid*: a figure associated with chaos, and a bestialized humanity.

32. Mary Zimmerman's inclusion of Apuleius's myth in her recent stage adaptation of *Metamorphoses* (Evanston, IL: Northwestern University Press, 2002), draws on some of the relations between the two works, but also notes the crucial difference: "Almost none of these stories have completely happy endings. | This is different" (76).

33. As E. J. Kenney notes, the story was commonly read as showing the inadequacy of human action without the intervention of divine grace. Apuleius, *Cupid and Psyche*, ed. E. J. Kenney (Cambridge: Cambridge University Press, 1990), 19. I'm grateful to one of the anonymous readers of this collection who gently nudged me to look at Carol Gilligan's illuminating reading of the myth, *The Birth of Pleasure* (New York: Random

House, 2002). Gilligan uses it as a model for the metamorphosis of destructive models of desire to create a "lawful and equal relationship between a woman and a man" (20) — a subject, of course, of much interest to Milton.

34. On the similarities between Rome and both Eden and the fallen world, see also Gransden, "*Aeneid* and *Paradise Lost*," 95–96, 105–06.

35. On the importance of Virgil's poem at this time, see Anthony Low, *The Georgic Revolution* (Princeton, NJ: Princeton University Press, 1985); its importance is nevertheless qualified by Wilson-Okamura, *Virgil in the Renaissance*, 77–87.

36. Vegio's remarkably adept if gloriously misguided book was, of course, very influential on Virgil's reception; see Wilson-Okamura, *Virgil in the Renaissance*, 239–49.

37. See also Watkins, *Specter of Dido*.

38. Guillaume de Saluste Du Bartas, *The Divine Weeks and Works of Guillaume de Saluste, Sieur Du Bartas*, 2 vols., ed. Susan Snyder, trans. Joshua Sylvester (Oxford: Clarendon Press, 1979), 6.1034–36. See also Mandy Green, *Milton's Ovidian Eve* (Farnham, UK: Ashgate, 2009), 24–26. Du Bartas's Adam also sees the newly created Eve as his own image, "his new-come Halfe," "calling her his Life, / His Love, his Stay, his Rest, his Weale, his Wife, / His other-Selfe, his Helpe (him to refresh) / Bone of his Bone, Flesh of his very Flesh" (*Divine Weeks*, 6.1045, 1047–50) — language that Milton's Adam will use in *Paradise Lost* 4.481–88. What is lacking in Du Bartas's account is *Eve's* version of the relation. By giving two perspectives, Milton emphasizes difference and creates a fruitful friction between the characters.

39. Karen Edwards, "Gender, Sex, and Marriage in Paradise," in *A Concise Companion to Milton*, ed. Angelica Duran (Malden, MA: Blackwell, 2007), 149.

40. On the significance of the analogy between the growing garden and Adam and Eve, see also Barbara Kiefer Lewalski, "Innocence and Experience in Milton's Eden," in *New Essays on "Paradise Lost*," ed. Thomas Kranidas (Berkeley: University of California Press, 1969), 86–117. I discuss this further in *Milton and the Metamorphosis of Ovid* (Oxford: Oxford University Press, 2012), 165–69, 213–18.

41. On the network of allusions, see Leah Whittington, "Vergil's Nisus and the Language of Self-Sacrifice in *Paradise Lost*," *Modern Philology* 107, no. 4 (2010): 588–606; David Bradshaw, "Self-Sacrifice and Heroic Martyrdom," in *Their Maker's Image: New Essays on John Milton*, ed. Mary C. Fenton and Louis Schwartz (Selinsgrove, PA: Susquehanna University Press, 2011), 81–92.

42. See also Eclogue 10.75–76: "solet esse gravis cantantibus umbra, / iuniperi gravis umbra; nocent et frugibus umbrae" (The shade is oft perilous to the singer — perilous the juniper's shade, hurtful the shade even to the crops).

Notes to Chapter 5 / St. Hilaire

Some of the readings of specific passages from the poem in this essay have been adapted from Danielle A. St. Hilaire, *Satan's Poetry: Fallenness and Poetic Tradition in "Paradise Lost"* (Pittsburgh: Duquesne University Press, 2012), esp. 177–202.

1. Joseph H. Summers, *The Muse's Method: An Introduction to "Paradise Lost*," Medieval and Renaissance Texts and Studies (Binghamton, NY: Center for Medieval

and Early Renaissance Studies, 1981), 176–84. For a brief survey of critical positions on Eve's role in the regeneration, see Mandy Green, *Milton's Ovidian Eve* (Burlington, VT: Ashgate, 2009), 198n44.

2. Georgia B. Christopher, "The Verbal Gate to Paradise: Adam's 'Literary Experience' in Book X of *Paradise Lost*," *PMLA* 90, no. 1 (1975): 69, www.jstor.org/stable/461349 (accessed June 13, 2011).

3. Dennis Danielson, "Milton's Arminianism and *Paradise Lost*," in *Milton Studies*, vol. 12, ed. James D. Simmonds (Pittsburgh: University of Pittsburgh Press, 1978), 68. See also Mary C. Fenton, "Regeneration in Books 11 and 12," in *The Cambridge Companion to "Paradise Lost*," ed. Louis Schwartz (New York: Cambridge University Press, 2014), 179–92, esp. 184.

4. Golda Werman, "Repentance in *Paradise Lost*," in *Milton Studies*, vol. 22, ed. James D. Simmonds (Pittsburgh: University of Pittsburgh Press, 1986), 134; Daniel W. Doerksen, "'Let There Be Peace': Eve as Redemptive Peacemaker in *Paradise Lost*, Book X," *Milton Quarterly* 31, no. 4 (1997): 125; Green, *Milton's Ovidian Eve*, 194.

5. John Milton, *Paradise Lost*, 2nd ed., ed. Alastair Fowler (New York: Longman, 1998), 10.932–36. All subsequent citations from the poem are from this edition and hereafter are cited in the text. Critics who have called Eve "heroic" in this scene include Doerksen ("'Let There be Peace,'" 124–30); Rachel Falconer, *Orpheus Dis(re)membered: Milton and the Myth of the Poet-Hero* (Sheffield, UK: Sheffield Academic Press, 1996), 161–72; and Barbara K. Lewalski, *The Life of Milton: A Critical Biography* (Oxford: Blackwell, 2000), 486.

6. Christopher, "Verbal Gate," 74, 75.

7. Doerksen, "'Let There be Peace,'" 129n4, 129n7.

8. Regina M. Schwartz, *Remembering and Repeating: On Milton's Theology and Poetics* (Chicago: University of Chicago Press, 1993), 106. Readings diverge on the subject of Eve's narcissism, but my point is not to engage such arguments here. Schwartz labels Eve's "mee mee only" "narcissism"; a better term here for my own argument might be "solipsism," to distance this moment in book 10 from her accidental self-love in book 4.

9. Summers, *Muse's Method*, 179.

10. Doerksen argues that Adam's words here differ from Eve's because, despite his desire to die for humankind, "Adam does not *act* on this impulse, and specifically he does not apply it to the human who is present with him, Eve" ("'Let There be Peace,'" 126); Green follows Doerksen in this reading (*Milton's Ovidian Eve*, 193–94). In contrast to their final act of repentance at the end of book 10, where the statement of their intent to act is immediately followed by the act (1086–1104), Adam and Eve in their "offers" of self-sacrifice never actually move to enact that gesture.

11. *OED Online*, 2nd ed. (1988), s.v. "conviction," n., dictionary.oed.com, 1.a, 6.a.

12. God explains that death is a solution to the problems Adam has created: death will clean up the impurities of fallenness (10.629–639). See also Fenton's claim that "Both banishment from Eden and death are merciful gifts" ("Regeneration," 186). That Adam sees the sentence of death as evidence of God's "wrath" at this moment in book 10 signals how far he is as yet from a rehabilitated reason.

13. Mary Ann Nevins Radzinowicz, "Eve and Dalila: Renovation and the Hardening of the Heart," in *Reason and the Imagination: Studies in the History of Ideas, 1600–1800,* ed. J. A. Mazzeo (New York: Columbia University Press, 1962), 171.

14. Lewalski, *Life of Milton,* 486.

15. Falconer, *Orpheus Dis(re)membered,* 161.

16. Benjamin Myers, "Prevenient Grace and Conversion in *Paradise Lost,*" *Milton Quarterly* 40, no. 1 (2006): 26, onlinelibrary.wiley.com.authenticate.library.duq.edu/doi/10.1111/j.1094–348X.2006.00116.x/pdf (accessed Mar. 20, 2011).

17. Compare to *De doctrina Christiana,* in which Milton states that "Supernatural renovation…restores man's natural faculties of faultless understanding and of free will more completely than before" (qtd. in Fenton, "Regeneration," 184).

18. William Walker, "On Reason, Faith, and Freedom in *Paradise Lost,*" *SEL* 47, no. 1 (2007): 158, muse.jhu.edu.authenticate.library.duq.edu/journals/studies_in_english_literature/v047/47.1walker.html (accessed Apr. 23, 2008). Walker situates the poem's depiction of freedom and reason within the rationalist philosophical tradition.

19. *OED Online,* 2nd ed. (1988), s.v. "erect," adj. and n., dictionary.oed.com. *Regere* is the verb that in Latin produces the adjective form *rectus,* which means, among other things, "right."

20. For the legal implications of Satan's hypothesis that an act of grace might return him to God, see Alison A. Chapman, "Satan's Pardon: The Forms of Judicial Mercy in *Paradise Lost,*" in *Milton Studies,* vol. 55, ed. Laura L. Knoppers, 204–42 (Pittsburgh: Duquesne University Press, 2014). Chapman notes further that Satan "is thinking about a strictly individual form of remission. In effect, he is asking, 'Am *I* eligible for pardon?,' and not 'Are *we?*'" (226).

21. Harold Skulsky, *Milton and the Death of Man: Humanism on Trial in "Paradise Lost"* (Newark: University of Delaware Press, 2000), 179.

22. The totalizing, flattening force of Satan's "all" here further demonstrates the loss of his freedom. See Diane Kelsey McColley, "'All in All': The Individuality of Creatures in *Paradise Lost,*" in *"All in All": Unity, Diversity, and the Miltonic Perspective,* ed. Charles W. Durham and Kristin A. Pruitt (Selinsgrove, PA: Susquehanna University Press, 1999), 39–47.

23. For the importance of hope in the Miltonic universe, see Mary C. Fenton, *Milton's Places of Hope: Spiritual and Political Connections of Hope with Land* (Burlington, VT: Ashgate, 2006). She notes that, for Milton, hope was "fundamentally vigorous, creative, and regenerative," and that "the certitude of hope guides one through the present toward the future" (22).

24. Green, *Milton's Ovidian Eve,* 188.

25. If, as Fenton argues, "true hope requires faith in God and in the ways of God," to cut oneself off from hope is to pursue an unfaithful course ("Regeneration," 179).

26. *OED Online,* 2nd ed. (1988), s.v. "proof," n., 7.a, 1.a, dictionary.oed.com. Raphael utilizes this sense in telling Adam and Eve, "for how / Can hearts, not free, be tried whether they serve / Willing or no" (5.531–33).

27. God's emphasis on obedience and service has been a site of critical contention for many Milton scholars. Compare Michael Bryson, *The Tyranny of Heaven: Milton's*

Rejection of God as King (Newark: University of Delaware Press, 2004), to Diane McColley, "Beneficent Hierarchies: Reading Milton Greenly," in *Spokesperson Milton: Voices in Contemporary Criticism*, ed. Charles W. Durham and Kristin Pruitt McColgan (Selinsgrove, PA: Susquehanna University Press, 1994), 231–48. For discussion of the intertwined relationship between love and service in the Renaissance, see David Schalkwyk, *Shakespeare, Love and Service* (Cambridge: Cambridge University Press, 2008).

28. Anthony Low, "'Umpire Conscience': Freedom, Obedience, and the Cartesian Flight from Calvin in *Paradise Lost*," *Studies in Philology* 96, no. 3 (1999): 354. For more on love's relation to will and reason, both in Thomist thought and in Renaissance literature, see Danielle A. St. Hilaire, "Pity and the Failures of Justice in Shakespeare's *King Lear*," *Modern Philology* 113, no. 4 (2016): 482–506. As Low's argument suggests, calling love an "emotion" in Christian thought is somewhat reductive; *caritas*, Christian love, is considered a virtue rather than a passion. That love requires action in the Miltonic universe is further supported by Michael's words to Adam in book 12: "add / Deeds" to the "wisdom" he has gained from Michael (12.581–82, 576). See St. Hilaire, *Satan's Poetry*, 200–02; Fenton, "Regeneration," 183.

29. *OED Online*, 2nd ed. (1988), s.v. "serve," v.¹, 27.c, dictionary.oed.com.

30. Russell M. Hillier, "'The Good Communicated': Milton's Drama of the Fall and the Law of Charity," *Modern Language Review* 103 (2008): 1–21.

31. Diane Kelsey McColley, *Milton's Eve* (Chicago: University of Illinois Press, 1983), 190.

32. For an expansion and elaboration of this point, see St. Hilaire, *Satan's Poetry*, 183–200.

33. Compare to Milton's famous claim in *Areopagitica*, in *Complete Prose Works of John Milton*, 8 vols., ed. Don M. Wolfe et al. (New Haven, CT: Yale University Press, 1959), that he "cannot praise a fugitive and cloister'd virtue, unexercis'd & unbreath'd" (2:515).

34. William Shullenberger, "Sorting the Seeds: The Regeneration of Love in *Paradise Lost*," in *Milton Studies*, vol. 28, ed. Wendy Furman, Christopher Grose, and William Shullenberger (Pittsburgh: University of Pittsburgh Press, 1992), 167.

35. Green, *Milton's Ovidian Eve*, 194. Werman similarly argues that Eve's "intuitive good sense," as opposed to Adam's reason, is the "necessary impetus to their first steps out of despair," only after which Adam's "right reason" can take over ("Repentance in *Paradise Lost*," 134).

36. *OED Online*, 2nd ed. (1988), s.v. "attentive," adj., 1.a, 2, dictionary.oed.com.

Notes to Chapter 6 / Dean

1. All references to Milton's poetry are taken from *The Riverside Milton*, ed. Roy Flannagan (Boston: Houghton Mifflin, 1998). References to Milton's prose are from *The Complete Prose Works of John Milton*, 8 vols., ed. Don M. Wolfe et al. (New Haven, CT: Yale University Press, 1953–1982), hereafter cited in the text as YP. Biblical citations

(except those in Milton's prose) are taken from the Authorized Version of 1611. Mary Beth Rose is the most recent among many Miltonists to discuss Milton's addition of the character of Mary in *Paradise Regained*. See her "Why Is the Virgin Mary in *Paradise Regain'd?,*" in *Visionary Milton: Essays on Prophecy and Violence,* ed. Peter E. Medine, John T. Shawcross, and David V. Urban, 193–213 (Pittsburgh: Duquesne University Press, 2010).

2. Although Rose notes the five references to the Annunciation in *Paradise Regained* and points out the contrast between public and private in the brief epic, I have not yet located any scholar who discusses the five allusions to Jesus's childhood visits to the temple in *Paradise Regained.* I am grateful to Russell Hillier's suggestion that I investigate these allusions. In *Paradise Regained* these allusions to two passages in Luke (2:33–39, 41–51) include 1.209–14, 255–58; 2.87–92, 96–99; and 4.215–21.

3. See Russell Hillier, *Milton's Messiah: The Son of God in the Works of John Milton* (Oxford: Oxford University Press, 2011), 178–227, for a compelling recent discussion of how the temptation on the pinnacle in *Paradise Regained* is both an exaltation and an anticipation of Jesus's temptation on the cross. This essay builds upon his work.

4. Satan's fixation on place in *Paradise Lost* is continued in *Paradise Regained.* For two examples of this fixation in *Paradise Lost,* see 1.242 and 2.26 for Satan's early valuation of place. His suggestions in *Paradise Regained* of the intrinsic value of place seem cynical or self-contradictory in light of his earlier pronouncement that "The mind is its own place, and in it self / Can make a Heav'n of Hell, a Hell of Heav'n" (*PL* 1.254).

5. John's gospel also notes the low status of the village of Nazareth; see John 1:46: "Can there any good thing come out of Nazareth?"

6. See Mark 12:35–37 for Jesus's assertion that the Christ is both David's "son" and his "lord."

7. Satan's assertion of Jesus's relationship to King David through Mary is inaccurate. Mary seems to be a descendant of Aaron. See Matthew 1:1–20 and Luke, chapters 1 and 2. The Jewish monarchy could only pass through the paternal line, not the maternal. As a woman, Mary could not inherit the throne of David, even if she were his descendant. Thus, the Gospels trace Jesus's ancestry through Joseph, his father by law and by adoption.

8. See Shakespeare's *Henry V,* 1.1. 36–98, when the Archbishop of Canterbury cynically urges King Henry to claim the throne of France through his female line of descent in order to deflect Henry's possible support of a bill in Parliament, which would tax and nationalize many church holdings, thus diminishing the Archbishop's temporal empire. Satan's motivations for presenting his proposals (potential loss of dominion) and their content (assume military power with diabolical support for your right) match those of Shakespeare's archbishop.

9. For examples of the biblical phrase "father's house" in the Authorized Version, see 2 Samuel 24:17 for designation of the Davidic dynasty; for Herod's temple, see John 2:16; for this designation for heaven, see John 14:2.

10. See Vanita Neelakanta, "*Paradise Regained* in the Closet: Private Piety and the Brief Epic," in *To Repair the Ruins: Reading Milton,* ed. Mary C. Fenton and Louis Schwartz, 147–72 (Pittsburgh: Duquesne University Press, 2012) for her discussion

of Satan's desire to "figure out the mystery of Jesus' true identity and mission" (167–68).

11. William Perkins, *The Combat Betweene Christ and the Divell displayed* (1606), 25.

12 Bishop Lancelot Andrewes, *Seven Sermons upon the Temptations of Christ* (1642), 28.

13. For a few examples of these seventeenth century commentators' assertions of temple corruption but residual holiness during Jesus's time, see John Udall, *Combate betwixt Christ and the devill* (1588), 14; Perkins, *Combat*, 25–26; Daniel Dyke, *Michael and the Dragon* (1616), 278–79; Thomas Taylor, *Christ's Combate* (1618), 160–65; William Cowper, *Workes of Mr. William Cowper* (1623), 278–79; Andrewes, *Seven Sermons*, 29; John Trapp, *Annotations upon the Old and New Testament* (1647), 63; John (Giovanni) Diodati, *Pious and Learned Annotations upon the Holy Bible* (1648), 7; Samuel Cradock, *Harmony of the Four Evangelists* (1668), 40. More could be cited. My research for this essay included at least 20 such sermons, commentaries, harmonies, and handbooks on the temptation of Christ published in the late sixteenth and throughout the seventeenth centuries. John (Giovanni) Diodati was an acquaintance of Milton's; they may have met in Geneva in 1638. He is the uncle of Milton's friend Charles Diodati.

14. Taylor was a Church of England clergyman and disciple of William Perkins. He frequently clashed with the Laudians, who managed to delay and nearly deny Taylor the doctorate he earned at Cambridge. *The Oxford Dictionary of National Biography*, vol. 53 (2004), s.v. "Taylor, Thomas (1576–1632)," cites contemporaries that describe him as a Calvinist, one who opposed "Popery and Arminianisme" as well as "separatism and antinomianism," who nonetheless upheld the godliness of the established church (986). According to the *DNB*, *Christ's Combat*, among the earliest of his many published works, demonstrates his expertise in typology, for which he later became well known.

15. Taylor, *Christ's Combat*, 165; see also 160.

16. This is Hillier's (*Milton's Messiah*, 178–227) basic argument for Satan's "lifting up of the Son." He does not discuss Anna and Simeon's earlier uplifting of Jesus.

17. See Noam Reisner, "Spiritual Architectonics: Destroying and Rebuilding the Temple in *Paradise Regained*," *Milton Quarterly* 43, no. 3 (Oct. 2009): 166–82; quotations at 166, 167.

18. *Eikonoklastes*, YP 3:405, and Reisner, "Spiritual Architectonics," 175.

19. Reisner, "Spiritual Architectonics," 168; see YP 1:939. The remaining quotations in this paragraph are at 168.

20. See Hillier, *Milton's Messiah*, 223–24. Milton also notes the corruption of Herod's temple. In *De doctrina*, book 2, chapter 4, Milton refers to Herod's "repair" of the temple and comments that Herod was "none other than the enemy of Christ" (YP 6:667).

21. Jesus is "recompens't," like Milton's discussion of the apostles in *Paradise Lost*; he also enjoys "inward consolations" as a result of the patience he has learned during the repeated cycles of humiliation and exaltation to which he has been subject throughout his life and which he anticipates at this stage. Thus, like them, Jesus shares the apostles' ability "to resist / Satan's assaults" and "amaze / Thir proudest persecuters" in *Paradise Lost* 12.491–97.

22. See this discussion in *De doctrina* as translated in YP 6:438–43.

23. *De doctrina Christiana* and Milton's epics differ in their purposes and genres. As suggested by W. B. Hunter, "The War in Heaven: The Exaltation of the Son," in *Bright Essence: Studies in Milton's Theology*, ed. W. B. Hunter, C. A. Patrides, and J. H. Adamson, 115–30 (Salt Lake City: Utah University Press, 1971); Barbara Kiefer Lewalski, *Milton's Brief Epic: The Genre, Meaning, and Art of "Paradise Regained"* (Providence, RI: Brown University Press, 1966), 185; Hillier, *Milton's Messiah*; and especially Albert C. Labriola, "'Thy Humiliation Shall Exalt': The Christology of *Paradise Lost*," in *Milton Studies*, vol. 15, ed. James D. Simmonds, 29–42 (Pittsburgh: University of Pittsburgh Press, 1981), what is laid out in the treatise as strict time sequence, exaltation following humiliation, can be presented as a cycle of exaltations and humiliations and parodies of the same in the poetry.

24. For biblical references to Jesus's exaltation following his baptism, see Matthew 4, Mark 1, Luke 4, and John 1; for references to his transfiguration, see Matthew 17:1–13, Mark 9:2–13, and Luke 9:28–36. For the attesting voice at the end of Jesus's public ministry, see John 12:28. The Son defines exaltation in *Paradise Regained* as

> when God
> Looking on the Earth, with approbation marks
> The just man, and divulges him through Heaven
> To all his Angels, who with true applause
> Recount his praises.   (*PR* 3.60–64)

This occurs during the action of *Paradise Regained* at 1.130–81 and 4.596–635.

25. My focus in this section is the central exaltation of *Paradise Regained*: Jesus's uplifting by Satan in 4.549–61; however, there are at least three other exaltations in the brief epic: the Father's attestation of Jesus at his baptism (1.29–32), the heavenly host's victory hymn (1.168–81), and Jesus's exaltation by angels following Satan's fall (4.581–635).

26. The Son's human susceptibility to temptation, Satan's physical power over the Son, Satan's violence, and the Son's restraint of his divine prerogatives are major points of agreement among many of the commentators on the temptation of Christ. See, for example, John Calvin, *A Harmonie upon the Three Evangelistes*, trans. Eusebius Pagit (London, 1610), 128–34; John Knox, *A Notable and Comfortable Exposition upon the Fourth of Mathew* (London, 1583); John Udall, "Third Sermon," in *The Combate betwixt Christ and the Devill* (London, 1588); Taylor, *Christ's Combat*, 154–278; Thomas Fuller, *A Comment on the Eleven First Verses of the Fourth Chapter of St. Matthew's Gospel* (London, 1652), 65–79; and John Eliot, *The Harmony of the Gospels* (Boston, 1678), 34–65.

27. See Ashraf Rushdy, "Standing Alone on the Pinnacle: Milton in 1752," in *Milton Studies*, vol. 26, ed. James D. Simmonds (Pittsburgh: University of Pittsburgh Press, 1991), 208–09.

28. Satan specifically exploits these avenues of humiliation at several points in *Paradise Regained*. A few instances include poverty (2.412–22), isolation (1.322–25,

3.21–25), and hunger (2.319–21). Examples of Satan's limitations in *Paradise Regained* include 1.377, 411–21; 495–96; 3.251–52; 4.21–24, 394–96.

29. See Labriola, "'Thy Humiliation Shall Exalt,'" for a discussion of the cycles of exaltation and humiliation of the Son in *Paradise Lost*. Also see *De Doctrina* (YP 6:438–52).

30. This moment is in preparation for his final humiliation on the cross and in the grave, followed by his decisive exaltation at the Resurrection and later at Satan's final defeat. Neelakanta, "*Paradise Regained* in the Closet," 156, parallels these references to Jesus's childhood with the exhaustive self-examinations recommended by seventeenth century advocates of the prayer closet. Not only Jesus but also Mary and Satan refer to Jesus's childhood experiences.

31. Although not explicit, Satan probably also alludes to Jesus's Lucan visit to the temple as a 12 year old in *Paradise Regained* 4.552–54.

32. The only recent literary discussion I have located on the topic of Jesus's obedient disobedience at the temple in Luke 2:41–52 is Robert W. Reeder, "'Have I Caught Thee?': Cordelia and the Runaway Jesus," *Early Modern Literary Studies* 15, no. 1 (2009–10), http://purl.oclc.org/emls/15-1/reedcord.htm (accessed Mar. 3, 2010). Reeder's essay focuses on Cordelia's status as Christ figure in *King Lear*, who, like Christ in Luke 2:49, pursues her father's business in "'loving disobedience' or 'questioning obedience'" (paragraph 20).

33. Jesus's return to Nazareth, but not necessarily his mother's home, is suggested in the Synoptics. See Matthew 4:12–13, Mark 1:14, and Luke 4:14–16.

34. See *De doctrina* for Milton's description of the Son's final exaltations, which culminate in his session at God's right hand in heaven (YP 6:444–43). See Neelakanta, "*Paradise Regained* in the Closet," for a discussion of Jesus's "reen[try into] the human world as he had temporarily left it: privately, unspectacularly, and unobserved" (172). Her emphasis upon the interior holiness Milton's Jesus attains through the experience of private prayer nicely coalesces with my emphasis upon Jesus's body as the new temple.

35. Reisner, "Spiritual Architectonics," 171.

36. Hillier, *Milton's Messiah*, 223–24.

37. The Authorized Version translates Malachi 3:1b as: "the Lord, whom ye seek, shall suddenly come to his temple, even the messenger of the covenant." Following Calvin, some exegetes of Milton's time associated this temple with Herod's and with the established church. See Calvin, *Institutes of the Christian Religion*, ed. John T. McNeill, trans. Ford Lewis Battles (Louisville, KY: Westminster, 1960), I, xiii, 10.

38. Neelakanta, "*Paradise Regained* in the Closet," 158.

39. See Ephesians 6:14–18 for a discussion of spiritual weapons. The use of "stand" in Ephesians 6 does not specify a posture for prayer but a "withstanding" of spiritual assault. Similarly, Milton does not prescribe standing as the only posture for prayer either in *Paradise Regained* or *De doctrina*, which cites several possible postures for prayer (YP 6:672–73). For a valuable discussion of private prayer in *Paradise Regained*, see Neelakanta's essay (ibid.); for her discussion of Jesus's rejection of "spectacular devotion…[and] strict policing of his physical presence," see esp. 170. While I share her

concern to place the co-published poems in parallel and opposition, I do not read Milton's Samson as "remain[ing] mired in self-defeating solipsism" (157).

40. Solomon was David's true heir and successor; see 1 Kings 1–2.

41. Solomon, unlike David (2 Sam. 7:11–13, 1 Kings 6:1), was allowed to build the temple.

42. See Lewalski, *Milton's Brief Epic*, 191–92, for a discussion of Jesus's childhood ambitions as prefiguring Satan's temptations.

43. See Revelation 11:2; 21:2, 10, 22; and 22:19 for designations and descriptions of the New Jerusalem as "the holy City" and the only temple within it — "the Lord God Almighty and the Lamb."

44. Mary Beth Rose, "Why Is the Virgin Mary," 206.

45. Rosemond Tuve, *Images and Themes in Five Poems by Milton* (Cambridge, MA: Harvard University Press, 1957), 37.

46. Robert L. Enzminger, *Divine Word: Milton and the Redemption of Language* (Pittsburgh: Duquesne University Press, 1985), 109. See also Hillier, *Milton's Messiah*, 200.

47. Neelakanta, "*Paradise Regained* in the Closet," suggests that Jesus's reemergence from the wilderness and return to Mary's house in Nazareth could be read as that of "the closet devotee who … strengthened and fortified … return[s] to the public world and its obligations" (172). Refer to her essay for a valuable discussion of the relevance of seventeenth century prayer closets to *Paradise Regained*.

48. The Greek word-play inherent in *endemeo* and *ekdemeo* is found only here in 2 Corinthians 5:1–9 in the New Testament. Milton cites the second word in Greek in his discussion of 5:1–20 in *De doctrina* (YP 6:413–14).

49. Milton also cites 2 Corinthians 5:1 in *De doctrina*, book 1, chapter 16 (YP 6:452), where he translates part of verse 1 as, "the *earthly house* of this life and that *eternal home in the heavens*." The context of this passage is Milton's defense of soul-sleep.

50. This is how Milton (in Carey's translation of *De doctrina*) interprets 2 Corinthians 5:1 (YP 6:452).

51. Reisner, "Spiritual Architectonics," reads Jesus's final stand on the pinnacle of the temple as "already encod[ing] the destruction of the structure on which he stands and its eventual edification in Christ's resurrected body" (78). This reading of Herod's temple as prefiguring its own ruin coalesces with Brady's discussion of ruined, formerly sacred sites, which, as ruins, stand as cautionary sites (see Brady's essay in this volume).

52. Jesus, as the Father indicates in *Paradise Lost* 3.309 when the Son offers to become incarnate, is "by Merit more then Birthright Son of God." This "Merit" is demonstrated by the Son's motive for incarnation; the Father explains, "Because thou hast … quitted all to save / A World from utter loss" (*PL* 3.305–08). See the Father's explanation of the Son's status and work in *Paradise Regained* 1.166–67: "This perfect Man, by merit call'd my Son, / [is] To earn Salvation for the Sons of men."

53. The Son himself acknowledges the future completion of his cycle of humiliation and exaltation when he prophesies his "exaltation without change or end" and reminds Satan "my rising is thy fall" (*PR* 3.197, 201). See Hillier, *Milton's Messiah*, 178–227; and Lewalski, *Milton's Brief Epic*, 185.

54. See *De doctrina* (YP 6:232–33) for a discussion of Christ's body/the church as the temple.

55. Jesus's choice of location emphasizes his separate essence from the Father. In *De doctrina*, Milton asserts, "Christ's human nature is in supreme glory, it nevertheless exists in one definite place and not, as some people would like to think, everywhere" (YP 6:442).

56. Not even the garden of Eden is a place of intrinsic sanctity in *Paradise Lost* but, rather, one whose sanctity resides in its residents; when they no longer enjoy holiness and innocence, they must be expelled, "purged…off"; the place itself is later rendered empty and desolate (*PL* 11.48–52, 259–62, 829–835). See also Brady's essay in this volume.

NOTES TO CHAPTER 7 / BRADY

1. All references to *Paradise Lost* are to *The Complete Poetry of John Milton*, rev. ed., ed. John T. Shawcross (New York: Anchor Books, Doubleday, 1971); hereafter cited in the text.

2. See, for example, David Loewenstein, *Milton and the Drama of History: Historical Vision, Iconoclasm, and the Literary Imagination* (Cambridge: Cambridge University Press, 1990), 108–09; John R. Knott, "Milton's Wild Garden," *Studies in Philology* 102, no. 1 (Winter 2005): 81; Mary C. Fenton, *Milton's Places of Hope: Spiritual and Political Connections of Hope with Land* (Aldershot, UK: Ashgate, 2006), 133; and Barbara Lewalski, "Milton's Paradises," in *Renaissance Ecology: Imagining Eden in Milton's England*, ed. Ken Hiltner, 15–30 (Pittsburgh: Duquesne University Press, 2008), 19.

3. For the most part, the links between *Paradise Lost* 11.824–38 and Reformed theology are implicit in the critical commentary. Joseph E. Duncan is one of the few to make explicit connections; see his *Milton's Earthly Paradise: A Historical Study of Eden* (Minneapolis: University of Minnesota Press, 1972), 190–94. Christopher Fitter also ties the passage to Reformed theology; see his "'Native Soil': The Rhetoric of Exile Lament and Exile Consolation in *Paradise Lost*," in *Milton Studies*, vol. 20, ed. James D. Simmonds (Pittsburgh: University of Pittsburgh Press, 1984), 149–50.

4. Of late, a varied and substantial body of work has developed emphasizing the importance of place in *Paradise Lost*. An exhaustive list of such works would be prohibitively long; however, important monographs include Bruce McLeod's *The Geography of Empire in English Literature, 1580–1745* (Cambridge: Cambridge University Press, 1999); Ken Hiltner's *Milton and Ecology* (Cambridge: Cambridge University Press, 2003); Fenton's *Milton's Places of Hope*; and Jeffrey S. Theis's *Writing the Forest in Early Modern England: A Sylvan Pastoral Nation* (Pittsburgh: Duquesne University Press, 2009). Ecological readings of *Paradise Lost* by Diane McColley and Richard DuRocher are seminal to subsequent studies. See DuRocher's "The Wounded Earth in *Paradise Lost*," *Studies in Philology* 93 (Winter 1996): 93–115; and McColley's *A Gust for Paradise: Milton's Eden and the Visual Arts* (Urbana: University of Illinois Press, 1993). For a helpful overview of ecological themes in Milton's work, see Diane McColley, "Milton

and Ecology," in *A Companion to Milton*, ed. Thomas N. Corns, 157–73 (Malden, MA: Blackwell, 2001). I have explored some of the tensions between place and space in *Paradise Lost* in "Space and the Persistence of Place in *Paradise Lost*," *Milton Quarterly* 41 (2007): 167–82, and "Satan and the Power of Place in *Paradise Lost*," in *John Milton: "Reasoning Words*," ed. Kristin A. Pruitt and Charles W. Durham, 115–28 (Selinsgrove, PA: Susquehanna University Press, 2008). John Gillies covers similar terrain and comes to somewhat different conclusions in "Space and Place in *Paradise Lost*," *ELH* 74 (2007): 27–57.

5. Loewenstein links the lingering poignancy of the "destruction" of paradise to the collapse of republican idealism at the Restoration, and to Milton's need to "redefine radically his own sense of 'place'" (*Drama of History*, 109). Gillies suggests a connection to Milton's experience of blindness, which he says may signify "the pathos or primordiality of place…experienced or imagined from a position of absolute exclusion" ("Space and Place," 53). Knott argues that the scene evokes the "loss of a relationship with the natural world that had a degree of intimacy and ease, and a capacity for unselfconscious delight in sensuous pleasure" ("Milton's Wild Garden," 81).

6. Alison A. Chapman, "Milton's *Genii Loci* and the Medieval Saints," in *To Repair the Ruins: Reading Milton*, ed. Mary C. Fenton and Louis Schwartz, 195–216 (Pittsburgh: Duquesne University Press, 2012), 197.

7. Vanita Neelakanta, "*Paradise Regained* in the Closet: Private Piety in the Brief Epic," in Fenton and Schwartz, *To Repair the Ruins*, 153–55.

8. Fenton, *Milton's Places of Hope*, 123–24.

9. Ibid., 163.

10. See Alexandra Walsham, *The Reformation of the Landscape: Religion, Identity, and Memory in Early Modern Britain and Ireland* (Oxford: Oxford University Press, 2012); Andrew Spicer, "'God Will Have a House': Defining Sacred Space and Rites of Consecration in Early Seventeenth Century England," in *Defining the Holy: Sacred Space in Medieval and Early Modern Europe*, ed. Sarah Hamilton and Andrew Spicer (Aldershot, UK: Ashgate, 2005), 207–30; and Spicer, "'What Kinde of House a Kirk Is': Conventicles, Consecrations and the Concept of Sacred Space in Post-Reformation Scotland," in *Sacred Space in Early Modern Europe*, ed. Will Coster and Andrew Spicer, 81–103 (Cambridge: Cambridge University Press, 2005). Walsham and Spicer build upon the seminal work of Robert Scribner, one of the first historians to critique the notion that the Reformation catalyzed the "disenchantment of the world"; see Robert W. Scribner, "The Impact of the Reformation on Daily Life," in *Mensch und Objekt im Mittelalter und in der frühen Neuzeit Leiben, Alltag, Kultur….*, ed. Gerhard Jaritz, 315–43 (Vienna: Verlag der Osterreichischen Akademie der Wissenschaften, 1990); and Scribner, "The Reformation, Popular Magic, and the 'Disenchantment of the World,'" *Journal of Interdisciplinary History* 23 (Winter 1993): 475–94. For a recent overview of the origins of and ongoing debate over the "disenchantment of the world," see Walsham, "The Reformation and 'The Disenchantment of the World,' Reassessed," *Historical Journal* 51, no. 2 (2008): 497–528. Alison A. Chapman makes parallel inroads on the Weberian thesis in her fascinating essay "Marking Time: Astrology, Almanacs, and English Protestantism," *Renaissance Quarterly* 60, no. 4 (2007): 1257–90.

11. Walsham, *Reformation of the Landscape*, 151.

12. On the "destruction" of paradise in *Paradise Lost*, see Lewalski, "Milton's Paradises," 19; Gillies, "Space and Place," 46; and Loewenstein, *Drama of History*, 107–09. John Leonard is one of the few to note the significance of the desert island; his note to *Paradise Lost* 11.834 associates it with the island of Hormuz in book 2. See John Leonard, ed., *Paradise Lost* (London: Penguin, 2000), 443. Karen Edwards also avoids the critical commonplace of the island as an image of obliteration in "The Natural World," in *Milton in Context*, ed. Stephen B. Dobranski (Cambridge: Cambridge University Press, 2010), 415.

13. Joseph E. Duncan, *Milton's Earthly Paradise: A Historical Study of Eden* (Minneapolis: University of Minnesota Press, 1972).

14. Although some writers of late antiquity and the Middle Ages, most notably Philo (d. CE 50) and Origen (d. 252 or 254), propounded figurative interpretations of the Genesis garden of Eden, the majority of commentators from this period argued for the historical reality of earthly paradise: see Jean Delumeau, *History of Paradise: The Garden of Eden in Myth and Tradition*, trans. Matthew O'Connell (Urbana: University of Illinois Press, 2000), 15–21; and Duncan, *Milton's Earthly Paradise*, 38–88. Alessandro Scafi places the early debates over the historical reality of Eden in the context of the exegetical challenges posed by the Genesis text; see his *Mapping Paradise: A History of Heaven on Earth* (Chicago: University of Chicago Press, 2006), 32–43. On medieval postlapsarian geographies of paradise, see Scafi, *Mapping Paradise*, 160–90; and Delumeau, *History of Paradise*, 39–70.

15. Scafi, *Mapping Paradise*, 170. Scafi is particularly attentive to the nuances of medieval commentary. He points out that these efforts to reconcile literal readings of the Bible with Aristotelian physics and geography do not necessarily indicate naïveté on the part of commentators; rather, the presence of insurmountable obstacles setting paradise apart from the earth indicates that, for these writers, "Eden belonged to a different dimension" (ibid., 52).

16. Ibid., 258–61. Both Duncan and Delumeau attribute the decline of the tradition of paradise extant to exegetical practices among Renaissance humanist scholars of the Bible, and to the new geographical discoveries that failed to find evidence of paradise on earth (Duncan, *Milton's Earthly Paradise*, 89–90, 188–89; Delumeau, *History of Paradise*, 149, 152). Scafi agrees that the new exegetical practices were an important cause for the shift but finds the emphasis on the impact of geographical exploration and discovery misplaced since medieval writers had understood paradise to be inaccessible (Scafi, *Mapping Paradise*, 240–42).

17. See Duncan, *Milton's Earthly Paradise*, 188–94, and Delumeau, *History of Paradise*, 152. Scafi points out that the first exegete to argue explicitly that the garden of Eden had disappeared in the flood was Augustinus Steuchus, head of the Vatican Library, in his 1529 work, *Recognitio Veteris Testamenti ad hebraicam veritatem* (Scafi, *Mapping Paradise*, 262–64). The most prominent Catholic defender of the traditional view of paradise extant was Cardinal Bellarmine, who was often named in Protestant refutations of this theory (Duncan, *Milton's Earthly Paradise*, 191–92).

18. Duncan, *Milton's Earthly Paradise*, 192.

19. Scafi, *Mapping Paradise*, 262–68.

20. Martin Luther, *Lectures on Genesis, Chapters 1–5*, in *Luther's Works*, ed. Jaroslav Pelikan, vol. 1 (St. Louis: Concordia, 1958).

21. Ibid.

22. Ibid., 90.

23. For discussions of English writers of the early seventeenth century who held this view, see Scafi, *Mapping Paradise*, 266–77; Delumeau, *History of Paradise*, 153–54; and Duncan, *Milton's Earthly Paradise*, 89–101.

24. George Coffin Taylor, *Milton's Use of Du Bartas* (Cambridge, MA: Harvard University Press, 1934).

25. "Eden," in *The Divine Weeks and Works of Guillaume de Saluste Sieur du Bartas*, vol. 2, ed. Susan Snyder, trans. Josuah Sylvester (Oxford: Oxford University Press, 1979), lines 171–88; hereafter cited in the text by line number.

26. Luther, *Lectures on Genesis*, 88.

27. Lewalski, "Milton's Paradises," 19; Gillies, "Space and Place," 44.

28. DuRocher demonstrates that "the Fall has a palpable effect on nature" ("Wounded Earth," 96). According to Michael Lieb, Eden loses its importance as a holy place after the Son's proffered sacrifice; see Lieb, "'Holy Place': A Reading of *Paradise Lost*," *SEL* 17, no. 1 (Winter 1977): 145. Gillies argues that, after the Fall and the flood, "place is no longer a primary expression of human being-in-the-world" in *Paradise Lost* ("Space and Place," 46). However, I have argued elsewhere that place proves resistant to supersession or assimilation in the poem; see "Persistence of Place" and "Power of Place."

29. Edwards, "The Natural World," 415.

30. Ibid.

31. Walsham, *Reformation of the Landscape*, 147–51.

32. Ibid., 273–79, 151–52.

33. Martin Luther, *Sermons I*, in *Luther's Works*, vol. 51, ed. and trans. John W. Doberstein (Philadelphia: Fortress Press, 1959), 337.

34. Ibid., 337–38.

35. John Calvin, *Institutes of the Christian Religion*, rev. ed., trans. Ford Lewis Battles (Grand Rapids, MI: William B. Eerdmans, 1986), 73.

36. Ibid.

37. "Ad locum orandi quod attinet, omnis est idoneus." John Milton, *De doctrina Christiana*, in *The Works of John Milton*, vol. 17, ed. James Holly Hanford and Waldo Hilary Dunn (New York: Columbia University Press, 1934), 37. All translations from *De doctrina* are mine, with many thanks to Deborah Cromley for her valuable assistance.

38. Ibid., 92–95. "In privatis etiam precibus ubi occultius esse possumus: Matt. vi:6. *introito in conclave tuum*. et xiv:23. *ascendit in montem seorsim ad orandum*. In publico enim privatim orare, hypocriticum est…In sacrario tamen et templo Hierosolymis privatas concipere preces olim licebat."

39. Luther, *Sermons I*, 337. I am indebted to Deborah Cromley for her insight into Milton's concern with privacy in this passage.

40. Calvin, *Institutes*, 73–74.

41. *De doctrina*, 95. "Tempus orandi nullum etiam non est idoneum…Potissimum autem vesperi, mane et meridie."

42. Spicer, "God Will Have a House," 213–16.

43. Ibid., 229; Gordon Campbell and Thomas N. Corns, *John Milton: Life, Work, and Thought* (Oxford: Oxford University Press, 2008), 67–68. Campbell and Corns suggest the Laudian chapel-of-ease as one of Hammersmith's main attractions for John Milton Sr., who may have served as its churchwarden.

44. Spicer, "'What Kinde of House,'" 89–92.

45. Fenton, *Milton's Places of Hope*, 2.

Notes to Chapter 8 / Meyers

1. Benedict Robinson, "Returning to Egypt: 'The Jew,' 'the Turk,' and the English Republic," in *Milton and the Jews*, ed. Douglas Brooks (Cambridge: Cambridge University Press, 2008), 189. Robertson uses the term "orientalist" in his work seemingly incidentally and without engaging in the discussion surrounding its use in reference to early modern English texts.

2. See Norman Daniel, *Heroes and Saracens: An Interpretation of the "Chansons de Geste"* (Edinburgh: Edinburgh University Press, 1984). For a dissenting opinion, see Jo Ann Hoeppner Moran Cruz, who points to examples of the Saracens' cowardliness, trickery, materialism, and willingness to destroy their own idols. Moran Cruz, "Popular Attitudes toward Islam in Medieval Europe," in *Western Views of Islam in Medieval and Early Modern Europe: Perceptions of Other*, ed. David R. Blanks and Michael Frassetto (London: Macmillan, 1999), 56–57.

3. Luis Vaz de Camões, *The Lusíads*, trans. Landeg White (1997; repr., Oxford: Oxford University Press, 2001), 10.138.

4. My explanation follows White's in his introduction to *The Lusíads*; see the introduction to the above edition, ix–x.

5. John E. Wills, *The World from 1450–1700* (Oxford: Oxford University Press, 2009), 140.

6. Through much of the fifteenth and sixteenth century, the Ottoman Empire was at the height of its power, cultural sophistication, and commercial prominence. Its position on the world stage has been the focus of much recent historicist criticism of the early modern period, which has stressed the unsuitability of postcolonialist discourse as a means of understanding the relationship between Europe and the Mediterranean world. For important examples of these studies, see Nabil Matar, *Islam in Britain, 1558–1685* (Cambridge: Cambridge University Press, 1998); Benedict Robinson, *Islam and Early Modern English Literature: The Politics of Romance from Spenser to Milton* (New York: Palgrave Macmillan, 2007); John Michael Archer, *Old Worlds: Egypt, Southwest Asia, India, and Russia in Early Modern English Writing* (Stanford, CA: Stanford University Press, 2001), 1–22; Daniel Vitkus, *Turning Turk: English Theater and the Multicultural Mediterranean, 1570–1630* (New York: Palgrave Macmillan, 2003); and Richmond Barbour, *Before Orientalism: London's Theatre of the East, 1576–1626* (Cambridge: Cambridge University Press, 2003).

7. Leeds Barroll, "Mythologizing the Ottoman: The Jew of Malta and the Battle of Alcazar," in *Remapping the Mediterranean World in Early Modern English Writings*, ed. Goran Stanivukovic (New York: Palgrave, 2007), 119.

8. Nabil Matar and Gerald MacLean, *Britain and the Islamic World, 1558–1713* (Oxford: Oxford University Press, 2011), 6. I am following Matar's and MacLean's detailed explanation of the growth of England's participation in and knowledge about the Mediterranean world through the seventeenth century.

9. Had Milton wished it, it would likely have been possible for him to learn Arabic while at Cambridge. The first Cambridge professor of Arabic, Abraham Wheelock, was not appointed until 1632, the year that Milton left the university; notably, the appointment of a professor of Arabic at Oxford in 1636 was the enthusiastic project of Archbishop Laud, who was Oxford's chancellor at the time and who, although not a scholar of Arabic, collected and donated a large number of Arabic manuscripts to the university. There were, however, some students at Cambridge in the 1620s who managed to acquire skill in the language, whether independently or with the help of private scholars like William Bedwell. On the establishment of Arabic professorships and scholarship at Cambridge and Oxford, see G. J. Toomer, *Eastern Wisedome and Learning: The Study of Arabic in Seventeenth-Century England* (Oxford: Clarendon Press, 1996), 85–115. For information on William Bedwell, the "first Englishman after the Middle Ages to undertake the serious study of Arabic" (56), see 56–64.

10. Rudi Matthee, "The Safavids under Western Eyes: Seventeenth-Century European Travelers to Iran," *Journal of Early Modern History* 13 (2009): 139. Matthee's article offers a helpful overview of a number of European travelers' accounts of Safavid Persia.

11. Vitkus, *Turning Turk*, 8: "In early modern parlance 'the Orient' had a very generalized geographic meaning: it did not refer to a particular imaginary entity with all of the features that post-Renaissance Orientalists would later attribute to that entity . . . [and] no such academic or intellectual cadre existed before the late seventeenth century. From the perspective of an England without Orientalism, Mediterranean and Islamic alterity comprised many divergent identities, and these were defined by an overlapping set of identity categories, including race, religion, somatic difference, sexuality, and political affiliation. But alterity was also manifested in the *behavior* of foreign peoples — in the many specific practices, sexual regimes, religious activities, laws, values, and customs that were observed or made known to English subjects."

12. Shankar Raman, *Framing "India": The Colonial Imaginary in Early Modern Culture* (Stanford, CA: Stanford University Press, 2002), 2.

13. Pompa Banerjee, "Milton's India and *Paradise Lost*," in *Milton Studies*, vol. 37, ed. Albert C. Labriola (Pittsburgh: University of Pittsburgh Press, 1999), 142.

14. For a compelling account of the impact of *sati*, seen as an infamous Indian practice, see Archer, *Old Worlds*, 139–92.

15. My explanation of the effect of early modern trading activity on Southeast Asia follows Wills, *The World*, 85–91.

16. Two notable studies that have emphasized the importance of reevaluating relations between China and Europe are Andre Gunder Frank's *ReOrient: Global Economy in*

the Asian Age (Berkeley: University of California Press, 1998), and Kenneth Pomeranz's *The Great Divergence: Europe, China, and the Making of the Modern World Economy* (Princeton, NJ: Princeton University Press, 2000). Frank insists on the importance of a "holistic global world perspective" (29) rather than one that takes a particular region as its starting point, and he details a web of global interaction, primarily through the flow of currency throughout the world. Pomeranz argues for a reassessment of China's importance to the world through an extensive comparison of particular social, financial, cultural, agricultural, technological, and other factors in China to those of European nations. In particular, for Frank, this reinterpretation of non-European prominence has profound consequences for our contemporary understanding: "The Western interpretation of its own 'Rise of the West' has suffered from a case of 'misplaced concreteness'...'Leadership' of the world system — more than 'hegemony' — has been temporarily 'centered' in one sector or region (or a few) only to shift again to one or more others" (7), a fact as important for our perspective on contemporary Asia as for our understanding of the early modern world.

17. See D. E. Mungello, *The Great Encounter of China and the West, 1500–1800*, 2nd ed. (Oxford: Rowman and Littlefield, 2005), 7–9.

18. Robert Markley, *The Far East and the English Imagination, 1600–1730* (Cambridge: Cambridge University Press, 2006), 71. This book is an important contribution to a tradition of academic study of the world before orientalism that has primarily focused on early modern Europe's relationship with the Middle East.

19. See Frank, *ReOrient*, 143.

20. Markley, *The Far East*, 11–12.

21. Wills, *The World*, 113–14.

22. See Mungello, *Great Encounter*, 6.

23. For a concise explanation of the factors that led to this shift in power in the region, see Charles H. Parker, *Global Interactions in the Early Modern Age, 1400–1800* (Cambridge: Cambridge University Press, 2010), 96–98.

24. Milton, *A Brief History of Moscovia*, in *The Complete Prose Works of John Milton*, vol. 8, ed. Maurice Kelley (New Haven, CT: Yale University Press, 1982), 475, 503, 524.

25. This has particular resonance in *Paradise Lost*, in which, as Markley explains, "'The destin'd Walls / Of *Cambalu*,' for Milton, thus serve a complex double function: they stand synecdochically for the riches that will help Europeans overcome the curses of sin and scarcity and they pose a formidable challenge to Eurocentric visions of history, politics, and theology" (*The Far East*, 71).

26. The image is a confusing one — as with many of Milton's references, it is too easy to collapse the "as" with the person or event being described:

> Here walk'd the Fiend at large in spacious field.
> As when a Vultur on *Imaus* bred,
> Whose snowie ridge the roving Tartar bounds,
> Dislodging from a Region scarce of prey
> To gorge the flesh of Lambs or yeanling Kids

> On Hills where Flocks are fed, flies toward the Springs
> Of *Ganges* or *Hydaspes*, *Indian* streams;
> But in his way lights on the barren Plaines
> Of *Sericana*, where *Chineses* drive
> With Sails and Wind thir canie Waggons light:
> So on this windie Sea of Land, the Fiend
> Walk'd up and down alone bent on his prey.   (*PL* 3.430–41)

The edition to which I refer is *Paradise Lost*, ed. Barbara Lewalski (Malden, MA: Blackwell, 2007). All references to Milton's poem are to this edition and will be cited parenthetically in the text. For an illuminating reading of this passage as an apocalyptic vision of Asia that reduces the region to a decaying corpse being preyed upon by the vulturelike Satan, while simultaneously correlating the wandering Chinese to the Israelites, see Rachel Trubowitz, "'The people of Asia and with them the Jews': Israel, Asia, and England in Milton's Writings," in *Milton and the Jews*, ed. Douglas Brooks (Cambridge: Cambridge University Press, 2008), 163–64.

27. For example, Robinson reads the description of Pandaemonium against passages in *The Readie and Easie Way* and finds that, for Milton, "earthly monarchy is itself a usurpation on the true claims of the one and only king, and so all monarchy is 'oriental,' that is, magnificent and luxurious, but empty" ("Returning to Egypt," 187).

28. Gerald MacLean, "Milton, Islam and the Ottomans," in *Milton and Toleration*, ed. Sharon Achinstein and Elizabeth Sauer (Oxford: Oxford University Press, 2007), 290.

29. Balachandra Rajan, *Under Western Eyes: India from Milton to Macaulay* (Durham, NC: Duke University Press, 1999), 51–52.

30. Robinson, *Islam*, 154.

31. However essential to Milton's argument both theologically and geographically, this is not unproblematic. Rajan, although he is writing specifically about Indian references in *Paradise Lost*, encapsulates the problem nicely: the references can overall "be regarded as collectively proposing the Satanization of the Orient in a way becoming familiar to Milton's time. Milton's contemporaries were not unanimous on this matter. Commercial relations with the East were strengthening, and it was hard to argue that the Devil and his associates were the only possible source of supply for commodities that European nations wanted" (Rajan, *Under Western Eyes*, 50). As Markley discusses, Milton was highly aware of the possibilities as well as the pitfalls of Asian trade. Walter Lim, examining a body of Milton's prose works in addition to *Paradise Lost*, concludes that "in his literary and polemical use of the matter of Asia, Milton reveals that his perception and understanding of the East are really far from monolithic — ideological and cultural binary structures are complicated by the practical recognition that focusing on the English nation's immediate political interests cannot be fully divorced from the pressures of inescapable international contact and encounters. Asia may be the (symbolic) space of the Other, but its existence cannot be repudiated without risking the consequence of being left behind in the energetic European push for economic and political expansionism." Lim, "John Milton, Orientalism, and the Empires of the East,"

in *The English Renaissance, Orientalism, and the Idea of Asia,* ed. Debra Johanyak and Walter Lim (New York: Palgrave, 2010), 231. What is perhaps most striking about the Eastern images in *Paradise Lost* is how little Milton's actual awareness registers as deep engagement with Middle Eastern or Asian images. Instead, he creates an elegant theological universe in which metaphorical Eastern imperialism both draws upon and foreshadows that imperialism's actual entrance into the world. This system seems closed and complete, rather than considering possible individuation among individual Eastern governments, or different potential ways of understanding and interacting with Middle Easterners and Asians.

32. David Quint, *Epic and Empire: Politics and Generic Form* (Princeton, NJ: Princeton University Press, 1993), 253–66; J. Martin Evans, *Milton's Imperial Epic: "Paradise Lost" and the Discourse of Colonialism* (Ithaca, NY: Cornell University Press, 1996); Markley, *The Far East,* 83–84; Su Fang Ng, "Pirating Paradise: Alexander the Great, the Dutch East Indies, and Satanic Empire in *Paradise Lost,*" in *Milton Studies,* vol. 52, ed. Laura L. Knoppers, 59–91 (Pittsburgh: Duquesne University Press, 2011).

33. "The 'Lordly eye': Milton and the Strategic Geography of Empire," in *Milton and the Imperial Vision,* ed. Balachandra Rajan and Elizabeth Sauer (Pittsburgh: Duquesne University Press, 1999), 59.

34. Markley, *The Far East,* 83. Markley's point is that the Dutch, to whom he argues Satan is compared, "have perverted a godly commerce to corrupt and corrupting ends" (ibid.). However, considering seventeenth century concerns about the effects of trade and cultural encounter on Europeans, it may also be relevant that Satan's actions are correlated with the dispersal of Indian and Southeast Asian luxury goods into Europe.

35. Anne Ferry, *Milton's Epic Voice: The Narrator in "Paradise Lost"* (1963; repr., Chicago: University of Chicago Press, 1983), 52.

36. Evans acknowledges Ferry's objection but argues that "at the beginning of Book 4 we finally see the garden of Eden at least partially through the Devil's consciousness" (*Milton's Imperial Epic,* 163n8, 62). For Archer, Satan's "metropolitan and acquisitive vision immediately superposes the future cycle of empires upon the waiting globe. Similarly, our prospect of Paradise itself is soon tainted by Satan's" (*Old Worlds,* 86). Robinson argues that "the delights of Eden, identified in their fullest sensory immediacy with smell, present themselves to Satan as commodities, spices and perfumes readily appropriable as 'balmy spoils'" (*Islam,* 152). This interpretation, however, may elide the narrator's comparison of Satan's reaction to "them who saile / Beyond the *Cape of Hope*" and are "well pleas'd" (*PL* 4.159–64) with the smell wafting off the Arabian islands. The comparison is explicitly only to the pleasure that both parties feel at their respective "odorous sweets" (4.166).

37. Barbara Lewalski, *Dominion Undeserved: Milton and the Perils of Creation* (Ithaca, NY: Cornell University Press, 2013), 48.

38. It is important, however, not to overstate the difference in the minds of early modern English readers between "Classical" and "Asian." Greece was an ambiguous place, functioning as both the seat of Classical knowledge and an exotic, Eastern locale. Moreover, the importance of Egypt to the Classical tradition, its tremendous influence upon Greek culture, was well known to readers through sources like the historians

Herodotus, Diodorus, and Plutarch, and was widely acknowledged. On early modern England's interest in and understanding of ancient Egypt, see Archer, *Old Worlds*, 23–62.

39. Robinson, *Islam*, 153.

40. Ibid., 154.

Notes to Chapter 9 / Wisebaker

1. William Harrison, *An Historicall Description of the Iland of Britaine*, in Raphael Holinshed, *Chronicles* (London, 1587), 1.

2. Richard Eden, *The Decades of the Newe Worlde or West India* (1555), in *The First Three English Books on America*, ed. Edward Arber (New York: Kraus Reprint, 1971), 57.

3. Walter S. H. Lim, *The Arts of Empire: The Poetics of Colonialism from Raleigh to Milton* (Newark: University of Delaware Press, 1998), 195.

4. Francesco Guicciardini, *The History of Italy*, trans. Sidney Alexander (New York: Macmillan, 1969), 182. Tellingly, this passage was suppressed in all editions before 1774, including the sixteenth century translation of Geffray Fenton, *The historie of Guicciardin* (London, 1579).

5. Anthony Pagden, *European Encounters with the New World: From Renaissance to Romanticism* (New Haven, CT: Yale University Press, 1993), 11. See also Pagden, *The Fall of Natural Man: The American Indian and the Origins of Comparative Ethnology* (Cambridge: Cambridge University Press, 1982), 22–23; Karen Ordahl Kupperman, *Settling with the Indians: The Meeting of English and Indian Cultures in America, 1580–1640* (London: J. M. Dent, 1980), 108. For a discussion of this theory with reference to *Paradise Lost*, see J. Martin Evans, *Milton's Imperial Epic: "Paradise Lost" and the Discourse of Colonialism* (Ithaca, NY: Cornell University Press, 1996), 86–87.

6. Evans, *Milton's Imperial Epic*, 147.

7. David Quint, *Epic and Empire: Politics and Generic Form from Virgil to Milton* (Princeton, NJ: Princeton University Press, 1993), 8–9, 282, 303–04. Janel Mueller, in "Dominion as Domesticity: Milton's Imperial God and the Experience of History," in Rajan and Sauer, *Milton and the Imperial Vision*, has taken issue with Quint's reading, suggesting that the poem "proceeds from an imperial to a postimperial construction of the course of human history," which devalues the public heroics of traditional epic and foregrounds the power relations within the domestic setting (25–26).

8. J. H. Elliot, *The Old World and the New: 1492–1650* (Cambridge: Cambridge University Press, 1970), 31. Also see William M. Hamlin, *The Image of America in Montaigne, Spenser, and Shakespeare* (New York: St. Martin's Press, 1995), 6–12.

9. John Milton, *Paradise Lost*, in *The Riverside Milton*, ed. Roy Flannagan (Boston: Houghlin Mifflin, 1998), 9.997, 1016. All references to Milton's poems are from this edition, hereafter cited by book and line number parenthetically in the text.

10. Paul Stevens, "*Paradise Lost* and the Colonial Imperative," in *Milton Studies*, vol. 34, ed. Albert C. Labriola (Pittsburgh: University of Pittsburgh Press, 1996), 15. See also Stevens, "Milton and the New World: Custom, Relativism, and the Discipline of

Shame," in Rajan and Sauer, *Milton and the Imperial Vision*, 109–11; Evans, *Milton's Imperial Epic*, 99–101.

11. Sharon Achinstein, "Imperial Dialectic: Milton and Conquered Peoples," in Rajan and Sauer, *Milton and the Imperial Vision*, 87.

12. Evans, *Milton's Imperial Epic*, 103.

13. Andrew Hadfield, *Literature, Travel, and Colonial Writing in the English Renaissance, 1545–1625* (Oxford: Clarendon, 1998), 116. For further discussion of the Adam and Eve engraving, see John Faupel, *A brief and true Report of the new found Land of Virginia: A Study of the de Bry Engravings* (East Grinstead, UK: Antique Atlas, 1989), 18. For a discussion of de Bry's larger project in the *Voyages*, see Michiel van Groesen, *The Representations of the Overseas World in the De Bry Collection of Voyages (1590–1634)* (Leiden, Netherlands: Brill, 2008).

14. Bernadette Bucher, *Icon and Conquest: A Structural Analysis of de Bry's "Great Voyages*," trans. Basia Miller Gulati (Chicago: University of Chicago Press, 1981), 27. As Bucher further points out, de Bry's companion series to the American voyages, *India Orientalis*, which dealt with colonial voyages to the East, began with an engraving of Noah's ark, arguing that these two biblical allusions comprise a strategy "to inscribe the existence of the Amerindian and the newly discovered lands into the biblical schema of the common origin of man" (53).

15. Andrew Hadfield, "Eden, Richard (c. 1520–1576)," *Oxford Dictionary of National Biography* (Oxford: Oxford University Press, 2004); online ed., Jan. 2008, http://www.oxforddnb.com/view/article/8454 (accessed May 30, 2015).

16. Eden, *Decades*, 50.

17. Ibid., 50, 51.

18. Bartolomé de las Casas, *The Spanish Colonie*, trans. M. M. S. (London, 1583; facs. ed. New York: Da Capo, 1977), sig. Q2r.

19. Ibid., sig. F3v. As critics have noted, Milton would likely have been familiar with las Casas's text by virtue of his nephew John Phillips's 1656 translation entitled *The Tears of the Indians*. See Rodger Martin, "The Colonization of Paradise: Milton's Pandemonium and Montezuma's Tenochtitlan," *Comparative Literature Studies* 35, no. 4 (1998): 323; Evans, *Milton's Imperial Epic*, 10.

20. On this expedition, see Kupperman, *Settling with the Indians*, 14.

21. See Paul Hulton, *America 1585: The Complete Drawings of John White* (Chapel Hill: University of North Carolina Press, 1984), 12.

22. Thomas Hariot, *A Briefe and true report of the New Found Land of Virginia* (Frankfurt, 1590), sig. d1v.

23. Richard Hakluyt, comp., *Voyages and Discoveries*, ed. and abr. Jack Beeching (London: Penguin, 1972), 304.

24. Ibid.; las Casas, *Spanish Colonie*, sig. M1r.

25. Simon During, "Rousseau's Patrimony: Primitivism, Romance, and Becoming Other," in *Colonial Discourse/Postcolonial Theory*, ed. Francis Barker, Peter Hulme, and Margaret Iverson (Manchester: Manchester University Press, 1994), 60. On the dynamics of interaction in the discovery of America, see Tzvetan Todorov, *The Conquest of America: The Question of the Other*, trans. Richard Howard (New York: Harper and Row, 1984).

26. See Achsah Guibbory, *The Map of Time: Seventeenth-Century English Literature and Ideas of Pattern in History* (Urbana: University of Illinois Press, 1986), who argues that "the Fall could be interpreted as occurring throughout history" (7).

27. David Loewenstein, *Milton and the Drama of History: Historical Vision, Iconoclasm, and the Literary Imagination* (Cambridge: Cambridge University Press, 1990), 7. For further discussion of the shape of Miltonic time, see Guibbory, *Map of Time*, chap. 6.

28. Marshall Grossman, *"Authors to themselves": Milton and the Revelation of History* (Cambridge: Cambridge University Press, 1987), vii, 3.

29. Maureen Quilligan, "Freedom, Service, and the Trade in Slaves: The Problem of Labor in *Paradise Lost*," in *Subject and Object in Renaissance Culture*, ed. Margreta de Grazia, Maureen Quilligan, and Peter Stallybrass (Cambridge: Cambridge University Press, 1996), 229.

30. Neil Forsyth, *The Satanic Epic* (Princeton, NJ: Princeton University Press, 2003), 59.

31. Ibid., 58–59; Evans, *Milton's Imperial Epic*, 134.

32. Forsyth, *Satanic Epic*, 59.

33. Quint, *Epic and Empire*, 282.

34. Guibbory, *Map of Time*, 177.

35. Ibid.

36. But see Andrew Barnaby, "'Another Rome in the West?': Milton and the Imperial Republic, 1654–1670," in *Milton Studies*, vol. 30, ed. Albert C. Labriola, 67–84 (Pittsburgh: University of Pittsburgh Press, 1993), who argues that in the *Second Defense* Milton "figures the geographical contours of Roman imperial conquest as a crossing of time and space that marks the return of liberty to history" (76) in the foundation of the English Commonwealth. Barnaby goes on to argue that Milton disparages this same notion of the republican *translatio imperii* in the Roman passage in book 4 of *Paradise Regained*.

37. Loewenstein, *Drama of History*, 94.

38. John Milton, *History of Britain*, in *Complete Prose Works of John Milton*, 8 vols., ed. Don M. Wolfe et al. (New Haven, CT: Yale University Press, 1971), 5.402–03.

39. Guibbory, *Map of Time*, 188.

40. Balachandra Rajan, *Under Western Eyes: India from Milton to Macaulay* (Durham, NC: Duke University Press, 1999), 61. On the superlative value placed on origins in seventeenth century literature, see Alvin Snider, *Origin and Authority in Seventeenth-Century England: Bacon, Milton, Butler* (Toronto: University of Toronto Press, 1994); David Quint, *Origin and Originality in Renaissance Literature: Versions of the Source* (New Haven, CT: Yale University Press, 1983).

41. On the urban/pastoral dichotomy in *Paradise Lost*, see Lim, *Arts of Empire*, 237. On the satanic associations of material culture, see Forsyth, *Satanic Epic*, 56–57.

42. Kenneth J. Knoespel, "Milton and the Hermeneutics of Time: Seventeenth-Century Chronologies and the Science of History," *Studies in the Literary Imagination* 22 (1989): 25–26.

43. Ibid., 21.

44. Rajan, *Under Western Eyes*, 64.

ABOUT THE CONTRIBUTORS

———— ✤ ————

Maura Brady is associate professor of English at Le Moyne College, where from 2011 to 2014 she held the Kevin G. O'Connell Distinguished Professorship in the Humanities. Her work on John Milton has appeared in *Milton Studies*, *Milton Quarterly*, and *John Milton: "Reasoning Words,"* edited by Kristin A. Pruitt and Charles W. Durham. Her essay "Galileo in Action: The 'Telescope' in Paradise Lost," which appeared in *Milton Studies*, vol. 46, was awarded the Schachterle Prize from the Society for Literature, Science, and the Arts.

Margaret Justice Dean, professor emerita of English at Eastern Kentucky University, initiated and directed the writing center and served as resident Miltonist as well as organizer and convener of that university's biennial Milton Marathon. A protégé of the late John Shawcross, she had the privilege of completing her dissertation under his direction as one of his last doctoral students at the University of Kentucky. Her research and publications have emphasized Milton's engagement with Reformation martyrology and opposition to the established church.

Mary C. Fenton is professor of English at Western Carolina University. Her essays on Milton have been published in *SEL*, *Milton Studies*, *Milton Quarterly*, *The Cambridge Companion to "Paradise Lost,"* and in several book chapters. She is author of *Milton's Places of Hope: Spiritual and Political Connections of Hope with Land*, and coeditor with Louis Schwartz of *Their Maker's Image: New Essays on John Milton* and *To Repair the Ruins: Reading Milton*. She served as 2011 president of the Milton Society of America and dean of the Graduate School and Research at WCU from 2012 to 2015.

Alex Garganigo serves as associate professor of English at Austin College. His book on loyalty oaths in Restoration Literature, *Samson Cords: Imposing Oaths in Milton, Marvell, and Butler,* is forthcoming, and his latest project tackles the politics of Lucianism in early modern England.

Maggie Kilgour serves as Molson Professor of English at McGill University. Her publications include *From Communion to Cannibalism: An Anatomy of Metaphors* *of Incorporation; The Rise of the Gothic Novel; Milton and the Metamorphosis of Ovid,* awarded the James Holly Hanford Prize by the Milton Society of America; and a co-edited collection of essays, *Dantean Dialogues.*

Talya Meyers is a lecturer at the University of California, Santa Barbara. Her work currently deals with representations of the Middle East, Africa, and Asia in early modern European epics. She has published in *Spenser Studies* and *The Princeton Encyclopedia of Poetry and Poetics.*

Brendan Prawdzik has taught at the University of California-Berkeley, The University of the Pacific, and Christian Brothers University, and is currently at The Pennsylvania State University. His book *Theatrical Milton: Politics and Poetics of the Staged Body* is forthcoming. He has published on Andrew Marvell and is developing a book project on Ecclesiastean poetics and alternative temporalities in the literatures of the English civil wars and Restoration.

James J. Rutherford completed his PhD in English literature at Princeton University in 2014. His essay "The Experimental Form of Lycidas" appeared in *Milton Studies* in 2012. His current work focuses on the histories of logic, pedagogy, and literary formalism.

Louis Schwartz is professor of English and chair of the English Department at the University of Richmond. His essays on Milton and early modern English literature and culture have appeared in such journals as *Milton Quarterly, Milton Studies,* the *Comparatist,* and the *Lancet.* His book *Milton and Maternal Mortality* was the winner of the Milton Society of America's James Holly Hanford award in 2009. He is also the editor of *The Cambridge Companion to "Paradise Lost,"* and, with Mary C. Fenton, the coeditor of *Their Maker's Image: New Essays on Milton* and *To Repair the Ruins: Reading Milton.*

Danielle A. St. Hilaire is associate professor of English at Duquesne University in Pittsburgh. Her first book, published by Duquesne University Press in 2012, is titled *Satan's Poetry: Fallenness and Poetic Tradition in "Paradise Lost."* She has also published on Shakespeare in *SEL* and *Modern Philology.* Her current work examines how seventeenth century poetry attempts to work through the debilities of fallenness.

Joshua Lee Wisebaker has done graduate work at Cambridge and Boston Universities. His current research focuses on the intersection between early modern temporalities and English imperial ambitions in the New World. He has presented on Milton, Edmund Spenser, and Aphra Behn, and recently took part in a seminar at the Folger Shakespeare Library entitled "Entangled Trajectories: Integrating European and Native American Histories."

INDEX

———— ✳ ————

Abrahamic covenant, 25–26

acclamation, 15–18, 33

Adam, 46: Eve's relation to, 98–99, 214n38; Michael showing the world to, 187–88; offer of self-sacrifice, 100, 215n10; reason of, 107–08, 112–14, 216n35; taking blame for original sin, 100, 112. *See also* Adam and Eve

Adam and Eve, 178, 183; compared to Dido and Aeneas, 94–95; effects of relationship of, 110–12, 114; fall of, 107, 110–11, 177; marriage of, 56–57, 59, 93–96; reason of, 101–03; regeneration of, 101, 105–06

Aeneid (Virgil), 76–78, 210n7; deaths in, 86–87; influence on *Paradise Lost*, 83, 93–96; as poem of maturation, 83–87; similarity of Milton's *A Mask* to, 90–92

agency, 24, 26, 44, 79

America, 158, 160, 165, 168; effects of discovery, 173–76; located in biblical history, 179–80, 233n14; in *Paradise Lost*, 176–77, 185–86

Ames, William, 6–7

angels: fallen, 110; God's oath and, 4–7, 33; Son's coronation and, 4–9, 27–28, 199n102

Animadversions, 56

anointing, in coronation ceremony, 15–18, 32

An Apology against a Pamphlet (Reisner), 47–48, 54, 121–22

archbishop, in coronation ceremony, 19–20, 32

Areopagitica, 36, 53–55, 58, 78

Arianism, Milton's, 24–25

Arminianism, of *Paradise Lost*, 97–98

Artis logicae plenior institutio (*A Fuller Institution of the Art of Logic*), 61–63, 68, 70, 73, 75–79

"At a Vacation Exercise in the College," 46–48, 203n28

authority, 50, 63, 126; embodied, 51–53; rhetorical, 38–40; satanic, 36, 41–42, 49, 60; spectators and, 43–44

Banerjee, Pompa, 162

Barroll, Leeds, 161

Bennett, Joan S., 58

Bernard, Richard, 41

Bible, 57, 79–80; allegorical vs. literal interpretations of, 144, 146, 225n15; applying logic to, 66–67; New World in history of, 179–80, 233n14

Biddle, John, 68, 208n18

Blome, Richard, 41

body, 35, 54, 152; in actor-spectator relationship, 48, 50; emotion and, 37, 46; mediating differences, 36–37; Milton grounding theatricality in, 37–38; "motions" of, 43, 45–46, 58; passion and, 41–42; rhetoric and, 36, 47; of Sin, 49–50

Bradshaw, John, 3, 22

Brady, Maura, 129, 222n51

A Brief History of Moscovia, 165

Brief Notes upon a Late Sermon, 10–11, 17, 23